My World of Islands

METHUEN LONDON EDITORIAL DEPARTMENT ARCHIVE COPY
NOT TO BE BORROWED WITHOUT PERMISSION
PLEASE SIGN FOR ALL BOOKS BORROWED.

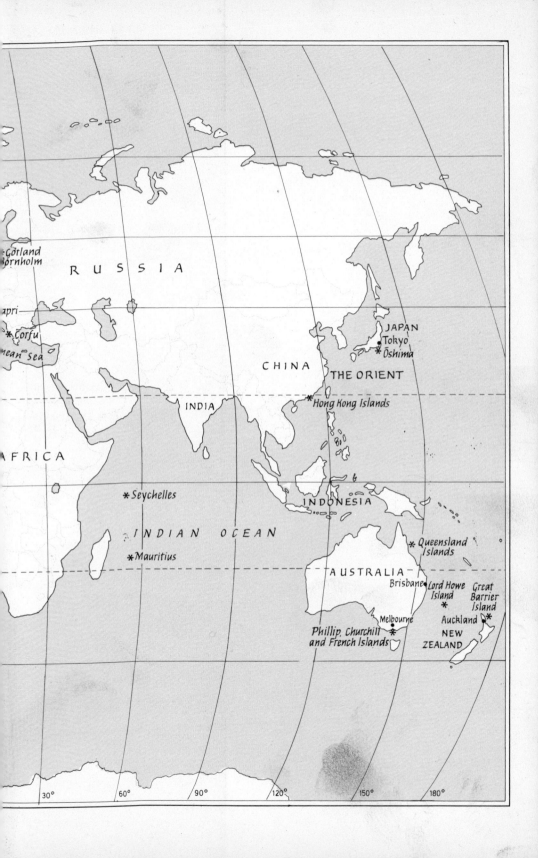

Götland
Bornholm

RUSSIA

apri
* Corfu
mean Sea

CHINA

THE ORIENT

JAPAN
Tokyo
* Ōshima

* Hong Kong Islands

INDIA

AFRICA

* Seychelles

INDONESIA

* Mauritius

INDIAN OCEAN

* Queensland
Islands

AUSTRALIA

Brisbane Lord Howe
Island

Great
Barrier
Island
*

*

Melbourne

Auckland
*

Phillip, Churchill
and French Islands
*

NEW
ZEALAND

30°   60°   90°   120°   150°   180°

MY WORLD OF ISLANDS

Leslie Thomas

with photographs by the author

Lord Howe Island rising straight from the Tasman Sea between Australia and New Zealand.

Methuen

First published in Great Britain in 1983
by Michael Joseph Ltd in association with Rainbird
This updated and expanded edition first published in 1993
by Methuen London
an imprint of Reed Consumer Books Ltd
Michelin House, 81 Fulham Road, London SW3 6RB
and Auckland, Melbourne, Singapore and Toronto

This edition copyright © 1993 by Leslie Thomas
Photographs copyright © 1993 Leslie Thomas
The author has asserted his moral rights

A CIP catalogue record for this book
is available at the British Library

ISBN 0 413 67660 9

Typeset by Deltatype Ltd, Ellesmere Port, Cheshire
Printed in Great Britain
by Clays Ltd, St Ives PLC

For my son Gareth

Author's Acknowledgements

At the conclusion of this long and, I believe,
unusual journey I wish to thank all those many
people who helped me to accomplish it;
too many to mention individually. Especially
I would like to thank those islanders who gave me
their knowledge, their friendship and
the comfort of their island homes.

L.T.

Contents

The Indian Ocean, The Orient and The Pacific Ocean

Illustrations

Introduction
One Man and Many Islands

Tales, marvelous tales
Of ships, and stars, and isles . . .
JAMES ELROY FLECKER

The world is strewn with islands. Clusters of islands, strings of islands, single lonely specks scattered through the oceans of the earth. Islands with their mountain-heads in the clouds; islands low against the sea; sunlit, windswept, populous, deserted. They mean different things to different beings – to one a paradise, to another a prison. But they have one common ingredient – romance. To people everywhere, and especially those who live in overcrowded cities, there are few more evocative words than 'island'.

Bouvet, in the South Atlantic, is the world's most isolated island. Beset by gales, ice and fogs, it is 1,500 miles from the nearest point of land. Few men have ever seen it and far fewer have set foot there. For years it was lost from the charts of mariners. There once was a story that it did not exist at all: that it was a legend, a dream, a mirage. Ross, the great explorer, reported that he could not locate Bouvet, 'that child of the mist'.

At the other extreme, the Scottish isle of Seil can be conveniently reached by a pretty stone bridge which arches across an ocean, or at least a small channel of it. It's called the Atlantic Bridge. On the island there is an inn where the men from the Hebrides used to change their kilts for trousers before venturing across the bridge to the mainland.

Between these two is a whole world of islands, each one different. It is many years since I first felt the fascination, the call to journey to them below their capes, in their achipelagos and bays or taking their solitary chances far out in the oceans.

It all began with the now-famous Falkland Islands. When I was a boy I spent a number of years in an orphanage where there was (I don't know why) a framed photograph taken long before at Port Stanley in the Falklands. I spent some time studying that worn old picture since wrongdoers were obliged, as a punishment, to stand facing the wall on which it hung. It showed a whalebone arch and some wild-looking buildings; it made me begin to wonder where the Falklands were and what people lived there. At the local library I found the information and there began an interest in islands which, over forty and more years, has grown into a fascination.

Synonymous with the word 'island' – and, for me, this has not diminished since boyhood – are 'treasure' and 'castaway'. *Treasure Island* must be the most evocative title ever penned by an author (who himself lies buried under 'the wide and starry sky' in Samoa in the Pacific).

Robert Louis Stevenson's epitaph is, curiously, a misquotation. The original version of his poem 'Requiem' has the line 'Home is the sailor, Home from sea' which on his grave has become 'the sea'.

Treasure islands have, more often than not, proved disappointments to the seekers. The stories of sea captains who buried valuables on islands after a shipwreck only to have mysteriously 'mislaid' the place when it came to recovering them, are repeated many times. Years have been spent on half a dozen islands from Anguilla, in the Caribbean, to Gardiners Island, New York, seeking the fabled treasure of Captain Kidd. On Oak Island, in Canada, a century and a half have been devoted to futile attempts to reach supposed billions lying at the bottom of a hole now called the Money Pit. No one has yet worked out a method to prevent the pit from flooding when it is excavated beyond a certain depth.

Treasure has been found on the sites of known wrecks, notably in the Dutch Frisian Islands, where the gold-loaded *La Lutine* sank, and among the Isles of Scilly in Britain, where the golden remnants of Sir Cloudsley Shovell's fated fleet are still occasionally brought from the bottom. Cocos Island in the Pacific has yielded much pirate treasure over the years, but so many people have tried their luck that Costa Rica, which owns the island, has forbidden further searches. In any case the treasure appears now to have vanished under a landslide.

Throughout this book I have related the fortunes – or more usually misfortunes – of many treasure hunters. It should not be forgotten, however, that even the thwarted hunter may have quite a comfortable, and certainly interesting, life if he is backed by a syndicate to provide him with funds, perhaps long after his own faith in the project has vanished.

Castaway stories are rarely as uplifting as *Robinson Crusoe* (Defoe's story is based on Alexander Selkirk, a Scottish sailor marooned on Más á Tierra in the Juan Fernández Islands for five years). Most are tales of dire privation, hardship and sometimes courage. I have always thought that the saddest of all is the story of the castaways of Clipperton Island in the Eastern Pacific – they were not shipwrecked but merely forgotten. Twenty people were sent to the island to work the guano deposits in 1913. Every four months a supply ship would arrive, for the island was too barren for self-sufficiency. It failed to appear in June 1914, and it was three years before another vessel visited the island. The company in Equador employing the workers had gone bankrupt and overlooked Clipperton and its castaways. Some of the men built a boat and died in an attempt to reach the mainland, and the rest succumbed to scurvy and starvation. A mad lighthouse keeper had to be killed by the women and when the USS *Yorktown* appeared in 1917, a sorry party of three women and eight children was left.

On 4 June 1963, exactly 334 years to the day after she sank, the wreck of the Dutch ship *Batavia* (from Texel, in the Frisian Islands) was found among the coral islands of the Abrolhos group off Western Australia. Its discovery set the seal on a terrible tale of shipwreck, followed by the callous murder of 125 castaway passengers by the deadly crew. Skulls were found with bullets wedged in them.

The survivors of another Dutchman, the *Zeewyde*, were luckier. They spent a year marooned on the Western Australian islands, living on seabirds, fish and seals and sitting on the treasure chests they had salved from the ship. From the wreck they resourcefully constructed a small vessel (the first built by white men in Australia) and sailed to the Dutch East Indies – taking the treasure chests with them.

It is now fourteen years since I set out on the singular travels recounted in the first edition of this book. I believed then that my journey and the book were unique, that no one had set out to visit such a wide range of islands in every part of the world and had set down their experiences in this way. I still believe that this is the case. In the ensuing time I have visited many other islands around the coasts of Britain and in other parts of the world. Accounts of three of them, Lord Howe, lying so beautifully, peacefully and spectacularly, far out in the Tasman Sea between Australia and New Zealand, Saint-Pierre et Miquelon off Newfoundland, the only remaining French possession in North America, and Sanibel and Captiva Islands, on the Gulf of Mexico, have been added to this new edition, which is also illustrated by photographs I took on my travels.

During the filming of the television series *Great British Isles* for Channel Four in 1988, I revisited some of the islands around Britain, which for me are as familiar as old friends. I also went to Barra, in the Hebrides, where I had never before landed. Barra is a great, spectacular island, the foreheads of its hills overlooking the flat of the coast. It was here, in the cossetted anchorage at Castlebay, that the MacNeil clan lived in their fortress, Kiessimul Castle, an island within an island, where the present chief of the clan, an American, now comes to spend vacations in a comfortable apartment within the old stone walls.

In former times, the chiefs lived more grandly; after supper each evening a herald was sent to the battlements to cry, 'The MacNeil of MacNeils has dined! The rest of the world may now eat!'

Here I followed in the footsteps of a great island man, Sir Compton Mackenzie (he also lived on Herm and Jethou in the Channel Islands) who had a house there, still to be seen. You can go in and have tea.

My abiding memory of Barra is of an old lady called Morag who lived in a cottage by the sea and still sang the old songs of the island, one of them called 'The Fair Maid of Barra' which was written for her. She knitted me a big pair of socks and sent them to me by post. The landing on the island itself was part of the adventure, as it so often is – this time by plane *on the beach*. It was an experience on a par with the journey I made years ago with the men of the Great Blasket, off the west coast of Ireland, who took me to their island in a curragh, the slimmest, flimsiest boat ever to cross a tortuous channel.

I also travelled to Bimini in the Bahamas by flying boat from Miami. It was there that Ernest Hemingway caught his first shark – by shooting it with a rifle (the next bullet went through his foot).

I sailed with an estate agent who was attempting to sell the pile of Drake's Island in Plymouth Sound; I returned to Guernsey to peer from the window from which Victor Hugo, exiled from France, looked out to the pencilled coast of his beloved country; and voyaged to Herm, my favourite of the English Channel Islands where Jenny Wood, who loved the island completely and had written about it in an evocative book, *Herm, Our Island Home*, had lived since the war with her husband Peter. Very sadly, she died just after my visit.

For me, one of the endearing things about islands is their names – the Desertas; Silhouette; Anonyme; Desolation; the Isles of the Bingo Sea; Nantucket; Anacapa; Murderer's Island; the Great Blasket; Turtle Key, Cat Cay and Dry Tortugas; the Hawaiian island of Kauai, which is anything but dry; the Grenadines and Ōshima. Sounds that made me want to set sail at once. Sometimes, now, in my house in inland England, especially in winter, I pause and wonder what people are doing at that moment in the Sulu Archipelago or the Lesser Antilles.

My choice of islands was eclectic. It was impractical to visit even all the most famous islands, including some of those which enticed me by their names. Easter Island and the Galapagos I did not attempt to visit because, although they are among the most isolated places on earth, they are also among the best known. Books, films and television have made them familiar, almost commonplace. I regretted being unable to visit the Diomedes in Bering Strait, one islet belonging to the United States and the other, only a channel away, part of Russia.

St Helena, Tristan da Cunha, the Maldives, the Gilbert and Ellice group, Yap, the Faroes, Ascension, Pitcairn . . . will all have to wait another time, as will the Falklands, my first magnet. I was all set to go when the Argentines got there ahead of me.

There have always been people like me, island-haunted. Joe Frahm, whom I met in New Zealand and who has lived on Great Barrier Island, coined the word *insulatilia* for the condition. Napoleon, the Corsican, exiled to Elba and buried on St Helena, was touched by islands; Mark Twain visited many and recorded the same comment about most of them – that when he died he would rather be transported there than go to Heaven.

Islandmen have constantly sought other islands. Joseph Banks, explorer of Tahiti and the islands of the Australian Barrier Reef, also explored Fingal's Cave in the Hebrides. A Nantucket whaler gave his name to Starbuck Island in the Pacific; and another Nantucket man, Foulger, found remnants of the *Bounty* mutineers on Pitcairn. It was men from the Shetlands, north of Scotland, who were the first real settlers on the tiny West Indian island of Saba. Among the Californian Channel Islands is remembered one William Henry Davies, a smuggler, who was the stepson of John Coffin Jones of Hawaii; and Coffin is also a Cape Cod island name. On Great Barrier I met a man from Lord Howe; in Mauritius one from the Whitsunday Islands. On Santa Catalina was a couple who loved Guernsey in the English Channel Islands and in Guernsey I was given names of people I would meet in Corfu.

I would like to think of myself as one of the company of islanders. I began the long journey in front of my own fireside, of a winter, reaching for every book I could find that had been written about islands. Then followed the joyful exploration of maps, discovering capes and coves, and learning the names of small places across the earth.

Then came the going – travelling (light with a single bag) from one island to another, those contours on the maps becoming real rocks and beaches, and those names transformed into towns and settlements, houses and people, who became my friends and whose lives and adventures I have recounted in this book. Every sort and facet of human life came my way on those islands. Show me an island and I will show you a world.

Given my fascination for islands, I have often reasonably been asked if I would ever live on one. I have to answer honestly that I do not believe I could. There are some, like the Isles of Scilly, or Lord Howe, where I could happily stay for an extended time. But in the end I know I would have to leave and return to my home in the middle of Southern England. Since writing the original chapters of this book I have moved house from rural Somerset to the cathedral city of Salisbury, a similar twenty miles or so from the sea.

But I continue to enjoy islands. The adventure of them, the maps, the approach, whether by boat or plane, the shape and size, the weather, the people, and above all, the stories. I always promise my hosts and myself that I will return. Sometimes I have. But there is always another island, a new place, beckoning somewhere.

I suppose I am one of those people who can be described as anecdote-prone and there were few places where some oddity did not occur. In addition I made it an object to reach as great a variety of islands as possible. Those I have written about in this book are in many different climes; some have an ancient civilization; some are still wild; some have the traditional beachcomber's palms waving about a lagoon; some are assaulted by regular storms; some creak with winter ice.

Men have seen islands in different ways – as a prison, as a paradise, as a penance. Islands have been sought as a refuge, although this motive can go awry as it did, so the story goes, for a wealthy American in 1939. He tried to find an island sanctuary for himself and his family – somewhere to hide throughout the oncoming war. He chose a spot far away in the wide Pacific ocean. It was called Guadalcanal, in the Solomon Islands, and it became one of the bloodiest battlegrounds of World War II.

For me the travelling to these small places of the world was both an adventure and a pleasure. I hope that you find you can share in the voyages and the feelings.

Salisbury
December 1992

NORTH AMERICA
AND THE CARIBBEAN

Everyday sunset in Antigua, West Indies.

Saint-Pierre et Miquelon
The Last Outpost

Look stranger on this island now . . .
W.H. AUDEN

The little isles of Saint-Pierre et Miquelon lie under the great bulk of Newfoundland. They are often foggy, often cold. They are all that remains of the once widespread possessions of France in North America, territories that included vast areas of Canada and the state of Louisiana.

It is not easy to reach them and the prospective traveller can count on little encouragement. At the Olympia Travel Exhibition in London, I went to the big and ambitious exhibit offered by the French and said to an official, 'I would like to visit Saint-Pierre et Miquelon.'

'Monsieur,' he replied dismissively blowing out his cheeks as they do. 'You are the only one.'

There is a story that gives more evidence of the French vagueness as to their outpost in the New World: in 1914 some of the North Atlantic fishermen from Saint-Pierre et Miquelon went to their mother country to become soldiers and found themselves in an 'acclimatisation' depot along with troops from Equitorial Africa. This is something on a par with the Mediterranean island of Corfu being placed under the authority of Japan because someone at the League of Nations thought it sounded Oriental. Diplomats often have only a tenuous grasp of geography.

I knew about Saint-Pierre et Miquelon when I was eleven years old because the islands issued one of the sets of beautiful stamps that came from all the colonies and territories of Free France, following the occupation of the home country by the Germans in 1940. This particular issue was a little delayed because, at the time of the surrender, the Governor decided he must obey orders and declared for the Vichy regime, under the thumb of the invaders. When America came into the war in 1941, it joined Canada in voicing disquiet about the presence of what was virtually an 'enemy' outpost, with a powerful radio transmitter, at the mouth of the Gulf of St Lawrence, broadcasting propaganda and noting shipping movements.

So the US and Canada decided to invade the nuisance islands. Before they could do so, however, four Free French warships sailed in and did the job first. Cordell Hull, the American Secretary of State, was furious and threatened to send in his forces anyway. It could have come to a battle between allies but the United States fortunately held off. Most people in the islands are convinced that if de Gaulle's ships had not arrived first, then today they would be a Canadian province or an American colony. As it is, they remain stubbornly and patriotically French; the tricolour flies over Place General de Gaulle, the language is as spoken in the home country – not to be confused with French Canadian – the cooking is French and you pay for it in francs.

Getting to Saint-Pierre et Miquelon is not, as I have said, easy. People travelling from France, who have the most reason for wanting to go there, must fly from Paris to Montreal, a seven-hour journey, and then retrace their flight for four hours on a slow and frequently bouncing propeller-driven aeroplane. From London (where the Air Canada check-in clerk admitted she had never booked anyone to Saint-Pierre) I went to Halifax, Nova Scotia, via St John's, Newfoundland, and then flew back one and three quarter hours in the same propeller plane. Since the islands are only fifteen kilometres off the south-western coast of Newfoundland, you might choose to fly to St John's and then taken a four-hour bus journey to the village of Fortune from which there is a ferry which takes an hour; but this route is available only in summer and at the discretion of the weather.

At Halifax Airport I checked in with a big, bald and beaming gentleman called Sam, who appears to *be* Air Saint-Pierre. He later turned up at the gate at the other extreme of the airport to collect the boarding pass he had previously given me and to usher passengers to the plane. One or two needed just that – ushering. I had noticed them staring with disquiet at the little aircraft with its twin motors standing not just alone but isolated, far out, rather forlorn, on the apron, while the big cossetted jetliners nuzzled against the terminal buildings.

We had to troop out towards it, thirty of us. On board we were given a paper bag with a bun in it. Sam appeared to be eyeing the propellers but, somewhat to my relief, he was not required to swing them. They each gave a cough, like a couple of old gentlemen clearing their throats, and then spun sturdily. They took a while to warm up. My fellow passengers kept looking out of the windows, as though to ensure they were still spinning. The only pair who seemed indifferent were a baby and a dog.

Eventually, Air Saint-Pierre strutted onto the runway and, with all the shining jets having their faces turned away, sprinted down it and up into the blue Nova Scotia sky as fine as any of them. All my fellow travellers seemed to be French-speaking. Some had that unmistakably glad, smug look of people going home.

One thing about our aeroplane – it did not fly so far aloft that you could not see anything. It pondered along the back of Nova Scotia (which was called Arcadia by the French; the people are still known as Arcadians). It was summer and the landscape below was full of glinting holes, big lakes, collared by pine trees. There were roads and lesser roads but few habitations. We crossed the narrow strait to Cape Breton Island, the coast indented, carved and curved, as though by someone gone mad with a fretsaw. It was one colour, a light fawn. In winter it is white from top to toe.

We droned across the Newfoundland Gulf, today purple and lightly furrowed, one of the world's most dangerous seas. You could tell when Miquelon Island was coming into view because the French people going home began to press breathlessly against the small windows, eager for the first sight of their home. We passed along the flanks of Langlade, the lower half of Miquelon, once a separate island now joined by a seven-mile dune. It looked, as it is, wild and unpeopled, moors and valleys rimmed by heavy cliffs.

At one time there were people living there, surviving by farming and wrecking. Sometimes they combined the agrarian and the aggressive by hanging lanterns on the horns of cows and luring captains to the rocks. There were so many disasters along this coast, accidental and by design, that the wreckage piled up in the narrow strait and, joined by sand and shingle, formed the seven-mile dune that today joins the island to Miquelon proper.

Air Saint-Pierre – the plane is its sole aircraft – banked in the summer sun and came in across its home island, the smaller of the two but the most populated and important. Now the passengers were almost squeaking in anticipation. The puzzled baby was held up so that it could get a good view.

It is a little hump of a place, dotted with bright houses at random across its terrain but built thickly around its fine harbour, for so long the reason for its prosperous existence; a virtually ice-free anchorage in the middle of a cold sea. But other factors have intervened; the great days of Saint-Pierre as a fishing port are gone, probably forever.

'Today,' said the taxi driver with a Gallic shrug, 'there is only a little fishing.

Seven boats. Three here, two at Miquelon, and two gone to Brittany for refit.' His arm swept the almost empty harbour. 'Once, monsieur, you would see fishing boats all across this water, French, Spanish, Portuguese, many, many. But now – look, what do you see?'

Two-hundred-mile limits and stringent fish quotas, after years of over-fishing on the once bountiful Newfoundland Banks, are to blame. The town appeared as vacant as the harbour, its tidy buildings, its vivid and variously coloured, wooden houses, like some film set when the actors have left. There were shops and French-looking cafés, and some cars, but emptiness echoed about the streets.

'Fishing, yes, this was a great place,' agreed Jean-Pierre Andrieux who, with his charming mother Mireille, runs the Hôtel Robert. 'But, monsieur, the heyday of Saint-Pierre was the time of Prohibition in the United States. The bootleggers stayed in this very hotel. Indeed, you will be staying in one of these rooms. We call it the Al Capone Suite.'

I stood at the window, as Al Capone must have done in the 1920s, although the rooms have been altered since his day (he did not have an ensuite bath). Smoking his gangster's cheroot he could survey the docks and the piers and witness all the prosperity he had brought to this small place.

Monsieur Andrieux has assembled a neat museum in the bar and it includes a wonderful photograph of a 1920s bootlegger, heavily cigared, surrounded by laughing gangsters' molls in bonnets and flappers' skirts. Another photograph is signed with a flourish, 'W. McCoy'. He was the man who guaranteed that his smuggled hooch was not watered down – and who, according to the islanders, gave the expression 'The Real McCoy' to the language.

It was McCoy who discovered Saint-Pierre for the bootleggers. A meeting with an islander in a hotel in Halifax gave birth to a scheme to counter the restraints that the Canadian government was putting on the export of spirits. The authorities naturally refused to countenance obvious smuggling across its border with the United States, but it was quite happy to export any amount of liquor to a Prohibition-free foreign territory – and Saint-Pierre et Miquelon were conveniently French!

Before long 350,000 cases of scotch, gin and other forbidden bottles, were being freighted every month to the harbour at Saint-Pierre. The town boomed, fishermen left their nets and helped to unload the cargoes and then to ferry them down by night to the creeks and harbours of New England. The wooden crates, however, were both heavy and noisy. Sometimes the Customs men lying in dark wait were alerted. So a new industry grew in Saint-Pierre – the bottles being wrapped in straw jackets and transferred to jute sacks. And yet *another* industry rose from that. Three hundred and fifty thousand crates is a lot of wood. At first it was used as fuel for the island's fires, but then someone realised it would make walls for houses. Even today, many of the island houses have some walls made from cases bearing the names of the great distilleries. One that is made entirely of whisky crates is called 'Cutty Sark Villa'.

Most of the inhabitants of Saint-Pierre et Miquelon originate from Brittany, Normandy and the French Basque region. There are some Arcadians, dispossessed by one of the frequent changes of ownership in Nova Scotia, settled in the one village of Miquelon, lying along a curved strand in the north-east corner of the larger and wilder island. In winter when the snow and ice and fog come upon the coasts it must be a very lonely place indeed. There is a boat which connects it to Saint-Pierre several times a week, an hour's voyage – weather permitting. There is also an occasional plane service. But, in winter, Miquelon must be one of the world's more solitary communities. Nevertheless, in true French fashion, there are several restaurants, a few thoughtful bars and a lonely café which advertises 'Dancings'.

This sense of isolation is not so much present in Saint-Pierre but that island also is often left to keep its own company in the six-month-long winter. The French Government has built an indoor sports complex, a community centre any urban place would enjoy, and a shopping complex, set between the sea and the cemetery. But the problems remain. There are half a dozen restaurants which try doggedly to keep up the French tradition, but almost every morsel of food has to be brought in. Fresh green vegetables are virtually a luxury. Almost the only reasonable growing-land in the island is soil brought from France as ballast in the ships of long ago.

One *crêperie*, making the traditional envelope-like *galette* of Brittany, attracts occasional tourist customers by offering 'Cheeseburger Galette'. But the wines are from France and sometimes someone will play the songs of the homeland on an accordian.

Every summer Monday afternoon a Canadian cruise liner anchors off the port for four hours. Two hundred people come ashore and look in the shops, take photographs, and go on a forty-minute bus tour, which is about as long as the driver can make it. Madame Andrieux is busy in the wooden hotel's shop, then the cruise passengers, mostly middle-aged, get around the tables of the bar, someone plays the piano and they sing and drink. 'But,' shrugs Madame Andrieux expressively, 'at the end of the afternoon – poof! They are gone. And here we still are.'

Difficult though it is to reach, some people do go to Saint-Pierre simply because it is a piece of true France. There is a college on the island for students from Canada and the United States who want to learn to speak the French they speak in France without actually going there. The tricolour flies over the prefecture in the Place General de Gaulle, as it does from many outlying cottages, which also display the flags of the islands, stretched out in the brisk wind. This incorporates the strange red, green and blue 'Union Jack' of the Basques. The Governor of the islands is sent from France and serves a term of two years, as do the Prefect of Police and his thirty-six gendarmes, the hospital doctors and the schoolteachers. Most bring their families. Teenage children (thirty-seven per cent of the population is under twenty) are entitled to complete their education in France, at the government's expense, and most do. Many never return.

In the Hôtel Robert is a remarkable photograph taken a century ago of a sailing ship wrecked against the graveyard on the Ile aux Marins, just outside the Saint-Pierre harbour. It is a scene, frozen like a still from an early film melodrama, stark and eerie. The stricken vessel sags against the rocks, its masts and torn sails hang above the tombstones. Figures stand helplessly in the wind, the beach is covered with snow.

'It was Christmas Eve and her captain believed the light in the church tower, calling people to midnight mass, was the lighthouse,' said Jean-Pierre Andrieux. 'It was just one wreck of many. There have been 600 around these islands.'

He keeps mementoes of such things and among the more curious items in the room were two Wurlitzer jukeboxes, circa 1970, and a small, motorised lawnmower. 'Another wreck,' he said patting the chrome of the jukeboxes. 'She was called the *Transpacific*, her radar had failed and the fog came down. Her master decided to make for the harbour here, but he missed it by a long way and the ship went onto the rocks, again on the Ile aux Marins, the Isle of Sailors. They tried to pull her off with tugs but it was no good. When she was declared a total loss, more than sixty local boats went out to claim the cargo.'

He laughed wanly. 'Not much of a cargo for them, 350 jukeboxes.' He gave the lawnmower a touch. 'And 250 of these – in a place with scarcely a few blades of grass to its name.'

There are still useless jukeboxes in the corners of some living-rooms in Saint-Pierre. I asked Jean-Pierre what had happened to the motor mowers. 'They were adapted,' he smiled. 'The children used them as beach buggies.'

On the following day I went out to the Ile aux Marins. The small isle lies low against the near horizon, its roofs and the sturdy tower of its church standing like cut-outs against the sky. The rubber boat (the normal ferry was 'broken') passed below the muzzles of the four ponderous guns placed at the port entrance by the French many years ago to ward off the British, who never arrived. The channel was brief and flat on a summer afternoon of breezy sunlight. On the isle the houses, wooden and in many colours, glowed, the shingle sounded under my feet.

But now there are no people permanently living there. Many of the houses have been restored by people from Saint-Pierre as holiday and weekend homes. (Some families have taken over former fishermen's cottages on the main island itself, moving only a matter of a mile or so from their homes for vacations.) The Ile aux Marins was alive with wild flowers, there were mosses and marigolds beside little streams, the compensations of a short summer. I walked across the hummocky grass and down to the rocks, shells and sand on the far side of the island. Out there, lying like a big rusty axehead on the beach, was the stern of the jukebox-and-lawnmower-carrying *Transpacific*.

While I was on the island I heard another story about her. Apparently when the tug boats had failed to pull her off the rocks and the insurance men had done their sums, the sad skipper decided to invite the captains and the accountants, together with the leaders of the Saint-Pierre community and his own officers, to a final meal on board. The best silver and napery was brought out, the good glasses polished, and the table set. The choicest wines and the best food was served and the last dinner went on long into the night before the sorrowful skipper and his guests went ashore for the last time.

In these latitudes, in summer, they have long evenings, often grey and rather eerie, which the Scots of the Shetlands and Orkneys call the 'simmer dim'. It was almost uncanny walking along the harbour at that time, a lovely melancholy feeling, scarcely another soul about; the water creaked, the boats stood dumb, and there are few gulls in Saint-Pierre now that the fishing is virtually finished.

I felt sad for the staunch little place. Lights shone from the new sports hall and there was muffled chatter from the windows of the tabled bar of the

Hôtel Robert. In the last of the light three boys kicked a ball across the longest and widest stretch of grass for many miles – the Saint-Pierre football pitch.

That day there had been talks in Quebec between France and Canada about increasing the fish quotas for the islands, but the inhabitants knew that it would not be enough. The fish are as likely to come back as Prohibition. With the short summer and the difficult journeys tourism is scarcely going to boom. France has made it staunchly plain that she intends to retain this, her last toe-hold in North America, and is willing to pay for it. Many of the islanders, fishermen, sailors, and their sons, believe that their future may be in the hands of the bankers, that they may become an offshore tax-haven and financial centre. The Grand Banks would take on a new meaning.

The evening gathered late and by morning the fog had come down. From the window of the Hôtel Robert I could not see across the harbour to where the solitary aeroplane sat on the apron of the airport. She had flown in late the previous day. My taxi arrived. Madame Andrieux assured me that if the plane could not leave then the Al Capone suite would be mine for another night. The journey around the port was not encouraging. The driver shrugged and said 'le brouillard' might lift but then it might not. When we got to the airport, it was shut.

Never before had I been confronted with a shut airport. But the door was firmly locked and there was no sign of anyone. The plane sat like a large, sad, wet bird. The taxi went and I stood in the airport doorway watching the fog drip from the aircraft's wings. A man appeared on the other side of the glass door; he held up eight fingers and mouthed the word 'huit'. It was five to eight anyway so he opened the door. Where was I going?

'Halifax,' I told him. 'No 'alifax, aujourdhui,' he shrugged. He pointed to the plane. ''Im . . . 'im go Montreal aujourdhui midi.'

I looked at my ticket. Not for the first time this intrepid island traveller had mistaken the day. I shrugged like everyone else did and waited for the taxi to take me back. The next day I was at the airport at eight and this time ''im' was going to Halifax. It was still misty but the pilot was used to that. We shook the town with our roar down the runway. I looked from the window but the islands were quickly vanished below the clouds. I wondered what will happen to them.

SAINT-PIERRE ET MIQUELON situated latitude 47°N and longitude 56° 50′W; area 93 sq. m (242 sq. km); population approx. 6,500

Nantucket
The Far-Away Land

. . . these naked Nantucketers, these sea-hermits, issuing from their
anthill in the sea . . .
HERMAN MELVILLE, *Moby Dick*

The traveller arriving on Nantucket from the sea on a day of calm and fog
experiences something that is almost mystic. The small steamer from
Hyannis on the Massachusetts mainland had sailed in July afternoon sunshine
but as soon as we were beyond the harbour bar the fog lay like a cloth over
the ocean. It was as if it had been awaiting us.

For more than two hours the ship travelled blind on water as flat as tin,
sending out baleful little grunts from its fog horn. Misty seagulls followed for
a time, like hovering ghosts. We had nothing of the special joy that comes on
approaching an island; to see it grow from the sea, take shape and colour and
size. Instead there was a different joy: Nantucket crept towards us from the
fog. First a swaying buoy, like a surprised man attempting, and just
succeeding, to walk on water, then another, and then the dark low shoulder
of land. It drifted towards the boat, rather than the boat towards it. There
were two long green stony breakwaters, an opening channel, a pepperpot
lighthouse on a sandspit. And then the houses of the town, the sea on their
doorsteps, moving mistily, dove-coloured, old and dreamy. No wonder the
sailors called Nantucket the Little Grey Lady of the Sea.

As soon as we had rounded the point into the arms of the harbour, a
surprise to the voyager, the sun emerged and within moments the mist had
gone about its business, out to sea. It had done with us.

As always on islands the arrival of the ship, whether it comes once a month
or half a dozen times a day, is a matter of excitement and importance. For
different people each docking is different. Now there were shouts from ship
to shore, waving and anticipation. An apparently eccentric lady trotted a
black horse in circles on the beach while three youngsters held a banner
proclaiming, 'Crazy Aunt Rides Again'. The performance caused a family
standing at my elbow to almost weep with joy and surprise.

To be alone, as I was, on such occasions as a landing is a strange thing.

Families disembark, piled and hung with luggage and paraphernalia, children shout, people embrace and kiss and sometimes burst into tears on the quay. The solitary explorer can only creep through it all, rather guiltily, and look around for a taxi.

My taxi, quickly discovered while everyone else was occupied with their gregarious business, carried me only half a mile to an elegant wooden house, set on a knoll at the centre of the exquisite town of Nantucket. Appropriately called the Overlook it has long balconies like the deck of an old-time paddle-boat and from one of these it is possible to look out over the maritime streets, over the shingled walls, white windows, the roofs with their walks, over the summer elms and far out onto the evening sea. I smiled to myself, the grin of an explorer who knows he has not made a mistake. He has come to the right place.

Ever since I first saw the Nantucket lightship, the first eye of the New World, on a ship voyage to America, I had wanted to be on the island. Now, here I was. And in the quietness of the evening I heard the town clock strike fifty-two.

The clock struck fifty-two again at seven the next morning, as it has been doing for generations. It used to be (and probably still is) to ensure that people woke up to the day's work. It calls the curfew at night and sounds another fifty-two strokes at noon to remind everyone it is time to go to lunch.

Walking about that place in the sunlit morning I was entranced. Here, thirty miles out in the ocean from the heat and business of an American July, was an island and a town that its inhabitants from two centuries ago would have no difficulty in recognizing. Trees spread like clouds over the streets, their ancient roots pushing the brick pavements into hills and furrows. The main streets are cobbled, laid down in Nantucket's whaling days to prevent the horse-drawn drays, used to drag the casks of blubber from the quayside, from sinking into the mud of unpaved streets. Some say the cobbles were brought from Gloucester, Massachusetts, others from Gloucester, England, taken across the Atlantic as ballast in ships come to fetch the whale oil.

For this small town on an oddment of land fourteen miles long and five miles at its widest, was, in the last half of the eighteenth century and the first of the nineteenth, the greatest whaling port in the world. Silver door knockers and letter-boxes on the elegant doors of the rich houses built in those times are testimony to its wealth; those houses were later to see ruin and poverty and grass growing in the streets.

Nantucket has kept its name from the earliest Indian inhabitants, the Wampanoags (part of the Algonquin tribe) who called it the Faraway Land. Explorers busily charting the eastern seaboard of the New World in the 1600s, noted its presence; among them Bartholomew Gosnold who sailed by, however, and landed on the Elizabeth Islands (named after his sovereign) and later on Martha's Vineyard (named after his daughter), which was another day's sailing. Even now the Nantucket people find it hard to understand or forgive Gosnold for sailing by. What sort of explorer, they ask, could leave Nantucket aside and discover Martha's Vineyard?

Later men came ashore, found the Indians anxious but equable, and made the customary sly deals involving pretty beads for landrights. An Englishman called Thomas Mayhew was the island's first white owner and he sold it to a group of nine compatriots who had grown tired of the religious intolerance in the new settlements of Massachusetts. It is strange to think that the near-descendants of those who had first gone to America to escape persecution were themselves made to flee it. They knew they could live unmolested on the island far out in the uncertain sea and they bought it from Mayhew by deed dated 2 July 1659 in a poetic contract involving 'Thirty Pounds in good Merchantable Pay and Two Beaver Hats, one for myself and one for my wife.'

The names of the signatories still ring familiar in Nantucket, in mainland Cape Cod, and in the West Country of England from whence they originally came. One of them, Tristram Coffin, a Devon man, was the sire of a family that reached a thousand names within a few generations.

Tristram died in 1681. Not much later his grandson, Jethro Coffin, married Mary Gardner, a union that healed a breach between the two pioneer families dating from their earliest days on the island, the settlers having brought their politics with them. The couple lived in a house which can still be seen in Nantucket today. Walking on its bent floors, climbing its tight stairs, seeing the furniture and implements, the guns, the cooking pots and the farm implements of those shadowy times brings a feeling of great poignancy. In that house you can smell the dust of history; to stumble around it is to touch the life of those far days. There is one legend about the little closet by the bedroom where Mary and her baby are said to have been sleeping one night while Jethro was away. In the early, dark hours a drunken Indian, hiding in the loft, fell through the ceiling into the closet. Mary, a capable lady, chased him out but never again slept in the house without her husband. Who can blame her?

*

It was accidental, but appropriate, that I should be in Nantucket on the Fourth of July, for the very roots of the rebellion that gave America its independence are right there among the cobbles in Main Street Square.

As one of the vanquished British I found it politic to remain under the shade of a large hanging bough while the touching little parade that marked the day for the island went by. It was led by a portly but stern-faced contingent of National Guardsmen, veterans sloping veteran carbines, but bearing the Stars and Stripes with all the uprightness they had in youth. Behind them came a band, playing its best, and then children, all gloriously out of step as only children can be. It was not that some left legs went forward at the same time as some right legs; that would have been too simple. No, by some miracle of timing *each* boy and girl marched somehow one out of step with *all* the others. Several trucks bearing old people came next, waving vigorously to bystanders and appearing in danger of plunging from the vehicles by reason of sheer enthusiasm. Then a pair of clanging old fire engines. In the middle of it all, incongruously, considering the day and its history, was a vintage British sports car, an ancient MG.

Short and nondescript though it was, the procession entirely matched the smallness and sincerity of Nantucket. As it marched by the fine brick building called the Pacific Club, the Stars and Stripes wafted across the names of three ships engraved above the old windows – *Dartmouth, Beaver, Eleanor*. In 1773 the three vessels, owned by William Rotch, whose Counting House was in the building, sailed for London with cargoes of whale oil. Upon their return, loaded with taxed tea, they put into Boston, and it was on these vessels that the Boston Tea Party, the first rebellious act that led to war, took place.

Nantucket, with strong ties, both emotional and, perhaps more important, commercial, with London, made some forlorn attempt to remain neutral, with the result that her whaling vessels were fired on by *both* sides; it was a lesson that, even then, went unlearned for the warring British, French and Americans all sank Nantucket ships during the war of 1812, two generations later.

But small islands are good at survival and at the end of the Revolution another ship made sail with her orders from the Rotch Counting House in Nantucket. She was called *Bedford* and was the first vessel to fly the Stars and Stripes in a British port. Londoners flocked to the banks of the Thames as she sailed in with a cargo of whale oil.

The whaling days were as unpredictable as the Atlantic weather. Fair times were followed by foul. Nantucket men had first seen Indians taking oil from beached whales while they themselves were tilling the traditional farms and trying to raise sheep. It was not long before they were out in the seas with the Indians catching the great creatures and dragging them into the port. They invented the dangerous art of deep-sea whaling and their adventures knew no bounds. Before the start of the nineteenth century the *Beaver* ventured far down the ocean, rounded Cape Horn, and sailed triumphantly into the widespread Pacific to hunt the great whales there.

A visit to the wonderful Whaling Museum in Nantucket Town today makes you realize the thrill of those amazing days. Men would go away for five years at a stretch, sailing home one day with a full cargo of oil that made the owners, at least, rich men. Sometimes they voyaged from the harbour never to return. The 'walks' on the tops of many houses, the white balconies on the very pitch of the roofs, were places where those left behind waited and stared out to the blank ocean for the ship and the loved one who never returned. Some call them 'widows' walks'.

A cargo worth $50,000 was not uncommon. Guns were fired and bells would ring as the whaler came home. But the risks were huge and the price in human life high. One of the Coffin family, a captain, lying bleeding on his deck in a terrible sea, ordered his servant to amputate his leg and 'not to hesitate'. The man did as instructed, using a whaling knife. He cauterized and sewed the stump – then both captain and servant fainted.

In the museum is a print showing how the crews of seven ships escaped across the Arctic ice when the winter closed in on them. In the background are the islands of Great and Little Diomede, at the top of the Bering Strait. Stories of Nantucket men travelling across the ice-cap for hundreds of miles are not uncommon. Boats overturned in awesome storms, men drowned as the angry harpooned whales towed them through the sea on what became known as the Nantucket Sleigh Ride. Disease, mutiny, great privation, took toll. The man who came home was lucky as well as wealthy.

Today in a safe in the town archive is an account of an adventure without parallel, written in the hand of Owen Chase, mate of a Nantucket whaler. It begins:

Narrative of the Most Extraordinary and Distressing Shipwreck of the Whale Ship Essex of Nantucket; Which was attacked and Finally destroyed by a Large Spermaceti Whale in the Pacific Ocean; with an Account of the Unparallelled Suffering of the Captain and Crew during a Space of Ninety-three Days at Sea in Open Boats in the Years 1819

and 1820. By Owen Chase of Nantucket, First Mate of the Said
Vessel.

Even today people on the island do not like to be reminded of the story
because the starving men resorted to cannibalism, eating their dead
shipmates. One of the first to read Chase's account, however, was Herman
Melville. The destruction of the *Essex* by the great whale later became the
epic *Moby Dick*.

Ashore, the leading whaling families lived with tremendous riches. No
commodity in the world, whether silk from China or perfume from Paris, was
too fine for Nantucket. Opulent houses were built, materials being brought
across the sea at much cost. Social life flourished.

But there was in the island a strong Quaker conscience, harking back to its
early days, and with that came the inherent feeling that at some time things
would go wrong; all was vanity and the piper would have to be paid. The
feeling became reality. First the sand bar of the harbour became a barrier for
heavier ships and they went instead to New Bedford on the mainland. An
ingenious pontoon called a Camel was devised which lifted the vessels over
the bar and into the deeper harbour. Then, in the true tradition of American
stories, an epic fire burned through the wooden streets in the town,
destroying the warehouses and raging among the ships in the harbour. Then
kerosene was discovered in Pennsylvania. It was cheaper, far cheaper, than
whale oil.

Depression closed over Nantucket. Men went off to the Californian gold
rush, never to return; the harbour clogged, houses were deserted and fell
down. The blackened ruins of the fired buildings were left like some dire
Biblical warning; weeds sprouted between the cobbles. The island which had
known the best of everything sank into poverty, its trade vanished. It
required a miracle to restore it to life. In due time the miracle occurred.

With the coming of night the island – as all islands do – became a different
place. It was as though the sea and its cousins, the wind and the rain, took
advantage of the darkness to make their raids; on other nights the dumb fog
patrolled the coast. One night, in my bed in the old wooden room at the
Overlook, I lay through the early hours and enjoyed the racket of a hooligan
storm charging in from the ocean, banging its way through the hollow
streets, clattering the wooden roofs with rain. On another, the fog came

slyly back, moving across the low island. All night the foghorn sounded, like a single morose note on an organ played again and again.

But the mornings were washed clean. The sun shone on the unending sea and the town was bright. In Main Street the Nantucket farmers and gardeners sold gleaming vegetables and fruit from carts. The cobbles were thronged with visitors and from the harbour came the happy hoot of the steamer as it approached from Cape Cod.

It was the ubiquitous Coffin family who once again began it all – the return to the good days. Unwittingly perhaps but with that strange serendipity that is the gift of some. It was in the 1880s when the island was at its lowest fortune, the whaling days gone forever and the people living an almost castaway existence in the Atlantic, that someone had the notion to have a family gathering of Coffins at the place where they had first landed as pioneers.

Five hundred assorted Coffins from the New England states arrived in Nantucket, crowding the decks of paddle steamers, and toured the quaint place that was the primitive home of their sturdy ancestor Tristram. Accommodation had to be found for them. Houses were quickly converted and there is an evocative photograph of the balconies of the Overlook (then Veranda House) lined with Coffins. It was the beginning of a new life for Nantucket.

Today the summer visitors outnumber the inhabitants by five to one, but Nantucket keeps its head and its appearance. The natives have a shrewd eye and a hospitable nature, a difficult combination. But, for all their friendship and optimism, they keep something of themselves to themselves. Although Carol Nickerson has lived in the island since 1945, after her husband died in France, she is still regarded as an off-islander. 'There's a story,' she smiled, 'of a man who came here as a small child and died at the age of ninety-one. On his tombstone they wrote "Farewell Stranger".'

She was a busy lady, born in 1911, whose mother still swam every day. She was married now to Gibby Nickerson, a Nantucketer and a fisherman. Once he was asked to take a funeral party out to sea and to scatter the cremated ashes on the waves. This accomplished, he suggested that they might like to do a little fishng. They declined.

In the summer Carol took visitors around and in the winter she helped with the scallop harvest. 'That starts about November,' she said, 'and it sees us through the winter. All the people are gone then and the permanent residents have the place to ourselves. Most of the shops shut and the shutters go over the windows of a lot of the houses. We go around and cut a few blooms from the gardens. It's called pruning.'

She recited the names of the Nantucket streets like a little poem. 'Easy Street, Candle Street, Whale Street.' She said, 'You'll notice that the bank here is the Pacific Bank; that's from the whaling days when the men used to go around Cape Horn. The place was virtually run by women then.' She pointed to yet another line of sweet houses along a bricked pavement. 'They used to operate the business side of the community from here,' she said. 'They called it Petticoat Row.'

You could see that she loved the island. 'Take a look at those railings,' she suggested. 'And those balconies. Just like ships' rails. That's because they were made by ships' carpenters.' We were wandering about the town now, under the fine trees. Every house had its own beauty; some were magnificent. 'Those three,' she said, pointing to a line of big, fine, brick houses, 'they are called the Three Bricks. Joseph Starbuck, a wealthy whaling man, built them for his three sons. Each is identical. So they wouldn't quarrel.'

If the houses were splendid, their porches and doorways were delicately elegant. The richest families, descendants of those first tough settlers, of Jethro Coffin, lived here, silver knockers and letter-boxes on their doors. The Coffins, the Foulgers, the Macys, names that went from the island to make their marks on American history. Here too were born Benjamin Franklin's mother, and Maria Mitchell who, one night looking at the heavens through a telescope, discovered a new comet. It was not an important comet, but a comet it was. She was the first woman to be inducted into the American Academy of Arts and Sciences.

For once, and for me it is a rarity, I found the town more fascinating than the island. The hinterland is pleasantly moored and wooded, wild cranberries flourish and there are deer (hunted two weeks in the year, one week with guns, one week with bows and arrows). There are widespread beaches, some modest cliffs; and a quaint wooden fishermen's village called Siasconset, known as Sconset, is hung with roses and heavy with sea scents. A clanking railway once ran the seven miles to Sconset and back. Its headlamp, the size of an icebox, is displayed in the Peter Foulger Museum in Nantucket town, another wonderful exhibition of the island's past. It is next door to the Whaling Museum, formerly the Candle House where spermaceti candles were produced. Rarely has the history of a small place been so splendidly preserved.

On the fringe of the town, on the forehead of what passes for a hill in Nantucket, stands a windmill waving its arms like a bonneted woman in a mild panic. Carol Nickerson said, 'It still grinds corn every day and it's been there for 235 years. Not bad considering it was built of driftwood picked up from the beaches.'

There were four windmills once. The others have all ended up as firewood. 'That's the greatest problem on this island – always has been,' said Carol. 'Fuel. Once the sailing ships were finished, so was the driftwood. The Quakers never had a fire lit in a bedroom, it was considered a terrible extravagance. Even today wood is very expensive. When the harbour froze last winter and the weekly oil tanker couldn't get in we began to shiver. For some it was almost as bad as the beer not arriving.'

Once more I returned to the cobbled town, wandering down by the quay. Now the yachts and businesslike fishing cruisers are at the berths where once lay the brave whalers. But sitting among them is another piece of Nantucket's history – its famous lightship. Once it was the first light of the New World, signalling landfall to ships crossing the Atlantic. I remember the thrill when I first saw it many years ago from the deck of the *Queen Mary*.

Now it sits like a large, red, friendly dragon; its huge anchors like protruding teeth. Its mast-top lanterns in their cages rival the domes and cupolas of the white churches and civic buildings behind it. Once its marooned crew used to occupy their lone hours by making exquisite lidded baskets which are still made on the island today, often ornamented with scrimshaw work, the carving on tusks and teeth of whale and walrus, which the whaling men perfected in their years of voyaging.

Turning from the waterside I paused at the door of the Pacific Club, on Main Street Square, formed by the famous whaling captains. The old Nantucketers still sit in there, winter and summer their feet on the rail of the stove, around them on the walls more pictures, models and mementoes of momentous voyages to a distant ocean. One of the members told me that, generations back, his family had come from 'the Western Island of Portugal'. He meant Madeira. His name is Herbert Wood and it was not until the next day that I realized the probability of why his family had adopted their surname. In Portuguese the word *madeira* means 'wood'.

It was a hot, late afternoon when I reluctantly left Nantucket Island. I walked on the bumpy brick pavements beneath the dusky shadows of the elms. Close, all around, was the feel and the smell of deep summer. A window was open facing out onto the lawn of a shingled house. Someone was playing a piano and the gentle notes drifted out into the sunlit air.

The steamer was calling from the harbour and I just reached it before the gangway was pulled away. People waved and, again, some cried. As we left, the houses lining the town and the bay seemed to be watching, quiet but intent, as they have done for many a thousand ships before.

Rounding Brant Point, by the pepperpot lighthouse, I saw that many people were each throwing two coins over the side, a tradition which, they say, ensures the traveller will return to Nantucket, the Little Grey Lady of the Sea.

I threw my coins also. For I want to return some day. It is a delectable place.

NANTUCKET situated latitude 41°17′ N and longitude 70°10′ W; area 56 sq. m (128 sq. km); population approx. 7,200; USA

The Californian Channel Islands
California Dreaming

. . . the island-valley of Avalon
Where falls not hail, or any snow.
TENNYSON, *Idylls of the King*

Spring comes to the Californian Channel Islands in a flush of fresh flowers; the seas are quieted, the seals are breeding and the winter storms are past. Great, conscientious whales make their annual voyage to southern calving grounds, cruising off the untouched and deserted islands. Los Angeles, one of the world's most popular, peopled and polluted cities, with its unending environs, sits under a shelf of smog on the adjacent coast.

Spaniards, nosing up from Mexico in the sixteenth century, found the islands – inhabited by harmless Indians – and gave to some of them names from their ever-ready reckoner of saints, San Miguel, Santa Rosa, and Santa Cruz, with Anacapa keeping close company in the Santa Barbara Channel; further south and more apart, like distant relatives, are Santa Barbara, San Nicolas, San Clemente and Santa Catalina. Santa Barbara, Anacapa and San

Miguel are reserved for nature and San Nicolas and San Clemente are reserved by the US Navy. Only Santa Catalina has a settlement of any consequence, the mild little town of Avalon.

The islands are places of sun and seafrets, storms and stories. San Nicolas, the most isolated, is haunted by the shade of a pathetic Indian woman who lived there alone for eighteen years.

It was in 1835 that the Mexican government, for reasons unknown, sent the ship *Peor es Nade* to remove the Indians from the island to the mainland. The captain, primarily interested in otter-hunting, chafed at the chore. The weather was souring. There was distress and confusion among the simple Indians and one woman realized her baby had been left in the hills. Frantically she returned for the child and the ship sailed without her. Until 1853 she remained wild and marooned on San Nicolas, occasionally sighted by hunters and sailors, but always vanishing. Eventually sealers George Nidever and Carl Dittman (a German, known as 'Charlie Brown') found her dressed in feathers and crouching in a hut made of whalebones. They took her to the mission at Santa Barbara. She spoke a language none could understand and no one discovered what had happened to her child. She was baptized Juana Maria Peor es Nade, but the woman who had survived eighteen years in the wild died within a few days. It was probably the change of diet. *Peor es Nade* means 'Better than Nothing'. Ironically it was not.

Hardly had the small plane, flying me across the channel, taken off from Santa Monica and turned from the land to the sea when the pilot, Bruce Hanson, grimaced and banked the aircraft away. 'The Navy have just warned us off,' he sighed. 'They're having practice bombing runs from the air station at Point Mugu. We can go back at noon when they quit for lunch.'

Mugu, the way he said it, sounded enough like Magoo, the cartoon character who doesn't see very well, to make me more than willing to wait a couple of hours until they had stopped their war for lunch. We returned to Santa Monica but, as it happened, the time was not wasted. Santa Monica airport has a huge runway built in World War II, now used exclusively by light aircraft, so that the Cessnas and Pipers take off from its vastness like sparrows flying from a freeway. It also has the singular sight of aircraft driving along streets in the company of automobiles and halting, like them, obediently at traffic lights. There are, in addition, a small museum and library, mostly concerned with aviation but in which I unearthed records of the strange happenings among the Californian Islands on the night of 23 February 1942.

At seven o'clock that evening there took place the only enemy action directed against mainland America in World War II. A Japanese submarine surfaced among the concealing Channel Islands and fired thirteen shells into the coastal oil refinery at Tidewater near the town of Santa Barbara. President Roosevelt was broadcasting one of his famous radio fireside chats at the time. Few of the population listened to the end. For twenty minutes the submarine fired shells from her 5½-inch guns causing unimportant damage and no casualties. Later a rumour circulated that the Japanese commander knew the Tidewater Refinery well and this was an act of personal pique since he had once been refused a job there!

At noon Bruce Hanson wheeled out the Cessna again and we trundled along the Santa Monica roads, crossing to the runway while cars waited at the stop signal. He was a young man; made redundant as a commercial airline pilot, he was filling in time piloting charter flights. 'It's usually to Las Vegas, Palm Springs or Reno, some place like that,' he said. 'This is more interesting. I've never been out to the Channel Islands. I'd like to take a look.'

In the event the delay had worked in our favour because early mist that had cobwebbed the channel had now dispersed and it was a spring day, sharp and sunny. We set out over the bright sea and headed for Anacapa.

Anacapa was the only island in the archipelago to escape being canonized by the Spaniards. Its name means a mirage or a dream, a word used by placid Chumash Indians who had made their homes in the islands, later to be wiped out by the savage men from the Aleutian Islands, off Alaska, recruited by the Russian-American Fur Company to hunt seals and sea-otters.

From the sky, as from the ocean, it is easy to see how appropriate were the poetic Indians, for the island changes shape and form with distance, weather and season. Sometimes it lurks in fog, at others it appears to be progressing through the waves, wagging a tail; in the damp winter it is the colour of a greengage, in spring spread with bright flowers, and in summer heat as brown as a loaf of rye bread.

Now it was spring with the flanks of the isle vivid yellow with the flowers of the giant coreopsis. Their glow in the sunshine can be seen on the mainland twelve miles away. We lost height as a Navy jet, late for lunch, streaked homewards just above. Now I could see that Anacapa was divided into three sections: a big one towing a medium-sized one and that in turn towing a small island. It looked like one of those disjointed toy snakes derived from Professor Rubik's renowned cube.

At the most easterly tail of the smallest isle, which we came to first, is one of those wonderful pieces of accidental architecture, an arch rock, sculptured over the sea, waves rushing through, iced with the deposits of generations of seabirds and, today, patrolled by a thoughtful squadron of brown pelicans.

There is a lighthouse on the East Island, keeping its eye on Arch Rock. In 1853 the paddle-steamer *Winfield Scott* clattered ashore on Middle Anacapa in fog. She was carrying 250 passengers from the California claims, all clutching their gold. They managed to reach the shore but it was eight days before they were rescued, cold, wet, miserable, and having spent a worrying and sleepless time sitting jealously on their bags of gold dust.

People who travel across to Anacapa, to watch its migrations, marine life and to marvel at its million flowers, are warned by the US Coast Guard Service to stay clear of the lighthouse and its foghorn. The foghorn, say the serious authorities, is loud enough to damage your ears permanently. Perhaps the pelicans are stone deaf.

After the wreck of the *Winfield Scott* the US Coastal Survey commissioned a series of drawings of Anacapa's varied shapes and forms to determine whether a lighthouse could be built. A coastguard named James Abbot McNeil Whistler added sketches of seagulls drifting across the cliffs to the drawings. That was eighteen years before he left the service (under a cloud), went to Paris, painted his mother, and won fame.

From the Cessna the basic human additions to the offhand brilliance of nature were easily apparent. A spidery path, the lighthouse itself, random red-roofed buildings like Monopoly houses set on the swaying back of the island. The authorities used to have trouble with the water-tower because men in passing boats, with nothing better to do, would shoot at it with rifles. The tank began to leak like a sieve, so the target was rebuilt disguised as a church. As a warden of the US National Parks Service put it, 'Only a few people shoot at it now.'

We traced the steep red coast, its indentations pushed inland and becoming shadowed valleys. No people were visible, only the birds cruising against the green, or the seals and sea-elephants lounging like holiday-makers on some of America's most private beaches.

Anacapa's Middle Island is separated from the eastern segment by a gulf 200 yards in breadth, which, even on our fine day, frothed and gurgled below us, the southern oceanic waves meeting the seas of the Santa Barbara Channel with great conflict.

In sunlit clearings of the kelp forests below the sea on the eastern end of the island you can still see the shadowed skeleton of the paddler *Winfield Scott.* Unlikely as it is that any of the goldminers left their gains behind, a Captain Martin Kimberley of Santa Cruz Island came upon the wreck a few days after the disaster, 'filled with the choicest sort of food and wines, and a great many other things' – and this when the survivors had been shivering and starving on the shore. A fine mirror and a large carved eagle were also rescued by the lucky captain and hung thereafter in his island home.

Bruce Hanson was examining the land with as much intensity as I was. 'Gee, I never realized it was like this,' he muttered. 'See what you miss when you just fly to Vegas.'

While the gulf between the first two of Anacapa's three islands is considerable and turbulent, that between Middle and West isles is a gully barely wide enough to thread a rowing boat.

West Anacapa, burly, razor-backed and crimson-cliffed, rises to nearly 1,000 feet. This is the place where pelicans nest, flying about with their charming ungainliness, as if their minds were elsewhere. We could view them ambling below as we flew at not much more than a pelican's pace around the flank of the all-but-inaccessible island.

Few people have ever tried to survive on West Anacapa, although the Chumash Indians managed it, and their middens and the remains of their camps are traceable. Archaeologists have disinterred them and have found also, with wild delight, the bones of the extinct white-footed mouse.

This is a place of caves, some of which have only ever been seen through binoculars. Coves and rockpools are thick with sea anemones; limpets, crabs, lobsters, crayfish and abalones are piled high. Chinese and Japanese fishermen used to make a harvest here but they don't any longer although it is still a popular fishing ground. Otherwise it is a place left to nature. On a good day, from the highest peak, Vela, a peaceful man with a spy-glass could probably see the traffic on the Ventura Freeway on mainland California.

Across a channel from Anacapa the misty hills of Santa Cruz Island climb to 2,500 feet. It is riven with sharp valleys as though it had at some legendary time been attacked by a giant wielding an axe. Through many of the valleys springtime streams were tumbling and spilling out into the blue Pacific. When fog gathers on the peaks it splits and crawls separately through the divided valleys like slowly unrolling muslin. The Chumash used to think these were the fingers of God.

Once there were many Indian villages on the island; there may have been a population of several thousand. Their bones and belongings have been found in caverns and tunnels that emerge along the coast. From the aircraft there seemed to be hundreds of caves, row upon row, and up and down the cliffs at all levels, like the open mouths of a singing choir. In these dark places also have been unearthed the teeth and bones of even earlier inhabitants – dwarf elephants.

When Spanish explorers first made a landfall on the island they found the natives pleasant and honest. So honest, in fact, that a metal crucifix, carelessly left behind by one of the Fathers, was returned the next day. One priest recorded, 'At daybreak it was discovered that one of the little canoes of the island was coming to the ship, and that one of the heathen was carrying in his hand the staff with the holy cross.' So they called the island Holy Cross – Santa Cruz.

For their pains the Chumash were eventually reduced to serfdom and penury before final elimination. The Mexicans chose Santa Cruz as a penal colony. In 1830 cargoes of malefactors were shipped across to what is now known as Prisoners Harbour. A contemporary account describes the convicts as 'naked and in a filthy condition' as they stood and listened to the commandant telling them that they had been sent to 'improve their morals and for colonizing California'. The second condition they fulfilled quickly and exactly. They built quiet rafts and boats and slipped across to the mainland where they dispersed and mixed with the population and where their descendants live today.

Ownership of Santa Cruz has passed through many hands including that of a Scotsman, Dr Barron Shaw, who married a London girl called Helen Greene in San Francisco in 1861 and settled with her on the island. A Frenchman called Justinian Caire used the place for farming and ranching, employing French and Italians, and harbouring some scheme for starting a Little Europe there. He also established vineyards which produced, among their wines, something ominously called Dago Red.

Today the verdant flanks of Santa Cruz are still grazed. From the aircraft we could see dirt roads winding up the sides of the incisive valleys, random roofs and, on the floor of one gully, an airstrip with a plane sitting still as a butterfly. 'Didn't know that was there,' commented my pilot. 'Might turn out to be useful sometime.'

We flew away, now for Santa Rosa. The dividing channel is five miles wide, green choppy sea, crusty with white, punching against rocks, surging up beaches where hundreds of seals congregated in the April sunshine. This is the haunt of the sea-elephant also, a giant, bemused, creature with a comic proboscis and entreating eyes, and the sea-otter, once thought to have been made extinct by the ravages of hunters but now, protected by more enlightened men, making an infrequent return to the local seas. With the sharp eyes and whiskers of its countryside cousin, it is much bulkier and has a luxurious coat. It performs the same endearing family antics. Much of its time is spent swimming on its back, its portly belly protruding, its legs languidly paddling, a relaxed, vacant sort of smugness around its whiskers.

Santa Rosa is also high and riven with deep clefts, the schisms of a volcanic age. Red earth and vivid green scrub fall into a disturbed blue sea. Elk, deer and feral pigs inhabit the winding and windy hills of Santa Rosa, but the mid-nineteenth-century hunters, the fierce Aleuts from Alaska, came for the seal and the sea-otter. There were fights, murders and desertions. A giant and gentlemanly Black man called Allen Light lived on the island for years, having deserted from a ship called *Pilgrim* – the same vessel in which Richard Dana sailed before writing his epic *Two Years Before the Mast*.

Later days were more pastoral. Sheep were farmed extensively and, according to an account in the San Francisco newspaper *Morning Call*, were rounded up not by dogs but by two hundred trained goats.

As our aircraft followed the coastline, I saw below something for which I had been specially looking – the wreck of the cargo ship *Chickasaw* which ran into Santa Rosa in a howling rainstorm one February night some twenty years ago. She was homeward bound from Yokohama to Wilmington, California. There was no loss of life but passengers and crew had the unnerving experience of being trapped aboard for two days while the vessel broke up around them. Now I could see that she remains in separated pieces, like a wrecked toast rack – the bridge and the sagging funnel on the final section, the bow thrust in hopeless belligerence against the rocks ahead. Waves lick around her corroding walls. Within a few years she will be worn away, exhausted, and will quietly collapse into the ocean like the SS *Crown of England* which met a similar misfortune at the south of the island half a century before. She does not look like the crown of anywhere now. All that remains is a sad mast and some rusty remnants of machinery from her deck, which the seals gratefully use for scratching their backs.

*

Of all the islands of the Santa Barbara Channel, San Miguel is the most solitary and mysterious. It is haunted by fogs, beaten by winds, exposed to all the ferocity of the ocean, for it lies at the extremity of the archipelago. As we flew the pyramid sand dunes below seemed to be moving in a solemn dance. Gales have whittled away at the hard sand making an eerie petrified forest of spectral sand-trunks, themselves ever-changing and, in turn, changing the notes of the wind itself.

There is an islet, Prince Island, where a stone cross is said to mark the aloof grave of Cabrillo, the Portuguese discoverer of the Californian Channel Islands, but no one knows if he really lies beneath it. There are other suggested places on Santa Rosa and Santa Cruz. The man who spent his exiled life charting the Pacific coast has had his own resting place mislaid.

Now there is no one living on San Miguel – except for the park ranger. It is left to the pelicans, the abundant seals and the little island fox. ('So tame,' reported one chilling scientific explorer, 'it was easily caught and killed.') Only a few people have lived on San Miguel's frequently wild and cheerless shore and one family did so for twelve years in the 1930s to the early 1940s. Herbert Lester, an adventurer out of his time, married a sedate girl called Elizabeth Sherman who worked in a New York library, and carried her off to San Miguel to begin life all over again. They lived in a house built from the wreckage of ships, farmed and fished, opened a school (with a bell) for their two children, raised the Stars and Stripes and beachcombed, furnishing their home with the rich debris of the sea, including a fine safe from a ship called *Cuba* which came to grief off the shore. Herbie had a Model T Ford which he drove roughshod across the island. Much of his time was spent pursuing an unquenchable curiosity about his island and one day he came home with two tusks, each measuring six feet, from the skeleton of a prehistoric mammoth. He was altogether a remarkable man. He is buried on the island, at Harris Point, in a homemade coffin. In 1942, handicapped and ill, he killed himself having first asked his wife for some paper to write a note. She found the suicide note in the place where they kept all their private documents – the safe from the wreck of the *Cuba*.

Sailing to Avalon on a shining spring morning would seem to be a suitable beginning for an idyll. It was strange for me to be doing so, because the Avalon of Tennyson's *Idylls of the King* is said to be Glastonbury, still a spellbound place, near the village in England where I once lived. This was

Avalon, Santa Catalina – although named from the same source – the place of the 1940s songwriter who left his love there beside the sea.

From the San Pedro pier in Los Angeles harbour the chirpy two-funnelled ferry takes two hours. The sea on this April day was green and bumpy, but the sky was clear and whirling with gulls. Santa Catalina poses on the horizon throughout the voyage, a grey double-peaked mountain that gradually softens into green-flanked valleys descending to a white town by a bay. A committee of seals, with heads protruding from the water, met us outside the harbour, staring in comic disbelief as if they had never before seen a boat.

For most Europeans the immediate recognition of Avalon is that it has more than a touch of the Mediterranean, and so it has: white, red-roofed houses rising up from the streets and alleys to the close hills; flowers flowing over walls and bursting from urns; restaurants and cafés by the pavements and the shore. But for me, also, it had that happy niffy smell of the English seaside: an aroma of breeze, and fish, and salt. And the pale sea, not blatantly blue, was gurgling over rocks and into pools where children searched for crabs and other culvert creatures. If there is one thing missing in the Pacific and the exotic islands of the world it is that smell, that feeling.

After the heavy breathing of Los Angeles, its gritty light, its packing-case buildings, Avalon affords a sweet surprise. It has more than a hint of recent yesterdays about it. On one reach of the bay is a great round building, like a Spanish bullring, quite out of proportion to the modest town. This was, and occasionally still is, one of the most famous ballrooms in the world. In the days when people danced to the big-sounding bands this was the place they came, crossing the channel in order to quickstep, tango and jitterbug on the immense circular floor to music played by men with legendary names. On special days they still arrive by excursion boats to relive the past. Now, appropriately, the ballroom also houses a museum.

The earliest half-day excursion to Santa Catalina was made by its discoverer, Juan Rodriguez Cabrillo, who was Portuguese, although in the service of the Spanish government. He sailed out at dawn from San Pedro (just as I had), pacified the natives, claimed it for Spain, and departed by noon. It was named Santa Catalina after the patron saint of spinsters, and has since become a haven for honeymooners. The Chumash were quickly converted to the Spanish God and this intelligent, handsome and peaceful people, who lived on an island of quiet beauty and who called their seashore the Bay of the Seven Moons, were 'Told about Heaven'.

Since that time Santa Catalina's strategic position has made it an attractive proposition for Chinese pirates, Californian smugglers, fugitives, hunters,

hopeful goldminers, garrisoned soldiers and the bootleggers of the Prohibition. It was once mooted as a prison camp for troublesome Apaches but
the plan was dropped after protests. The *Los Angeles Herald* in 1886 grunted
that it was 'too good for the proposed occupants'.

I found it soberly settled into the late twentieth century with the local cop
eating an ice-cream on the corner, teenagers on motor-scooters and a lone
ranger looking for a herd of buffalo who roam about the bumpy little interior.
The buffalo are not indigenous. They were imported in the 1920s by Cecil B.
de Mille who needed them for a film. He left them behind and the herd has
remained there ever since.

Walking the promenade of the town on this day in springtime was a slow
pleasure. Palm trees and banks of bright button flowers. The Mediterranean
feeling was once more, however, offset by a jaunty English pier with a fish-
and-chip shop at its end. People queued for bus excursions to the few miles
of interior on the route once run by stagecoach. The island was once the
domain of the Wrigley family and was consequently unhappily known as
Chewing Gum Island.

I had lunch and a bottle of cold wine, went into the museum, talked to the
policeman and then went by taxi up into the gentle, enfolding hills. I found the
buffalo roaming a couple of miles from town.

On Santa Catalina there is a story about a man called Prentiss, a Rhode
Islander, who received from a dying Indian chief a map showing the
concealment of a fantastic treasure on the island. He built a boat (from the
pieces of a vessel in which he had himself been shipwrecked) and sailed from
California for Santa Catalina. A storm swamped his boat and washed
everything overboard – including the Indian's map.

Prentiss spent the next thirty years looking for the treasure which he
never found. The headstone of his grave is still to be seen overlooking
Emerald Bay at the remote northwest of the island.

I stayed longer than Cabrillo but less time than Prentiss. In the evening
the red-funnelled steamer took me back to mainland America. Santa Catalina
merged with the sky of the gathering evening, taking itself away,
somewhere apart. Such as it has always been.

CALIFORNIAN CHANNEL ISLANDS situated between latitudes 33°20′–34°8′ N
and longitudes 118°20′–120°30′ W; Channel Islands National Park – land area 194 sq.
m (502 sq. km); population approx. 100. Santa Catalina – area 70 sq. m (181 sq. km);
resort island (USA private ownership)

Bermuda
An Accidental Place

We saw the island of Bermuda, where our ship lieth upon the rock, a
quarter of a mile distant from the shore where we saved all our lives
and afterwards saved much of our goods, but all our bread was wet
and lost.
SIR GEORGE SOMERS to the Earl of Salisbury, 1610

Viewed in ocean sunshine the many islands of Bermuda present a pastel
scene. On a cloth of turquoise water and pale blue sky they appear green and
bright white: white beaches, white roofs, white hulls. The buildings glow
pink, apricot, coral, blue, orange and yellow. When the Atlantic weather
closes in they become the 'remote Bermudas', once the terror of sailors, the
scourge of ships. Looking out across Hamilton Sound on a stormy day is to
see everywhere white limestone roofs against grey, casuarina trees
shivering like northern pines on a landscape cold and grim. It is just as if the
sunny islands had been somehow transported to winter Canada.

When seventeenth-century adventurers sailed the new voyages to the
Americas, they came across the archipelago three quarters of the way over
the ocean but avoided its frayed edges because it had taken on a perilous
reputation. The disasters of Bermuda's fabled Triangle have been nothing
compared to the wholesale wrecks that occurred on the reefs and shoals of
the islands themselves. In 1609 seven ships set out from Plymouth with
supplies and new settlers for the infant colony in Virginia. The little fleet was
commanded by Sir George Somers in the 300-ton *Sea Venture*. In his
company were Sir Thomas Gates, the deputy governor of Jamestown,
Virginia; John Rolphe, destined to marry the Indian princess Pocahontas; a
priest, Richard Buckle; and various gentlemen and gentlewoman and two
Red Indians who had been on display in England, Namuntuck and
Marchumps.

It was summer and they sailed the unfamiliar direct route across the
Atlantic instead of the charted trade-way to the Caribbean and then north to
Virginia. On the night of Tuesday 25 June, they knew they had made a
mistake. A storm gathered like an army on the skyline and then advanced on

the exposed fleet. For four days it ranted, scattering the small vessels through ugly seas. Personal belongings, cargo, even guns were thrown overboard to lighten the load of the *Sea Venture*.

Then, with the crew and passengers spent, sprawling on the rolling decks, the other ships lost, Sir George Somers sighted a windswept land – the Bermudas. The vessel was coaxed around a headland and into a bay. Leaking through every rib it ran towards the shore, tore its keel on a shoal and settled with, no doubt, a grateful sigh into the shallow water. Its stumps remain to this day.

It was thus by accident that the first English came to Bermuda. They survived on hogs and seabirds. There were no other people there. Henry Ravens, the master's mate of the *Sea Venture*, set out in the ship's longboat with a crew of eight, to sail for America. After a certain time a bonfire was built on what is now St David's Head to guide the hoped-for returning boats to the anchorage. It burned blindly for two months. Ravens and his longboat men were never heard of again.

Today, in the neat, showpiece town of St George's, against the harbour, is a replica of the ship the wrecked English managed to construct from the debris of their original vessel.

It is called the *Deliverance*, and is a stout vessel, today's reproduction looking quite capable of making the same successful voyage as the original almost three centuries ago. While she was being constructed Sir George Somers explored the islands and realized how unjustified was their reputation, for he saw that within the rocks and reefs lay a huge and wonderful anchorage. He made an excellently accurate map which is kept today in the Hamilton town archives. The archipelago was called the Somers Islands, an unintentional, but appropriate, pun.

Two of the marooned migrants, glancing about them in the sunshine, also perceived that the reputation of this place was far from the reality. They decided to stay and found a settlement, St George's, which, after Jamestown, Virginia, became the second town to be established in the New World in 1612. One of the settlers, Christopher Carter, never again left the island and his descendants still live in Bermuda today.

Sir George Somers returned to Bermuda from the American colonies and died on the island. His nephew took his body back to his native Dorset, but buried his heart in the place he had discovered. It lies now beneath the flowers of a garden in the centre of St George's.

St George's town is perhaps a little too well preserved, the buildings, the harbour, the reconstructed oddities of the stocks and pillory, the old scold's ducking stool, every wall a different pretty colour from its neighbour, flowers dripping over steps and doors and trees gathered in colonies of shade. But any suspicion that it is merely a tourist exhibit is dispelled by simply going into the church of St Peter's, the root of the earliest colony and as full of memories as any museum.

If you walk into the nave from the sunshine of the welcoming-arms steps outside you are at once cloaked with coolness and peace. It is a wide, white-walled church, raftered like a barn, the timbers amply provided from the cedars of the island and from the wrecks of its coasts. Memorial tablets to the forebears of the town patch the walls like pictures at an exhibition. There is one recalling Bridger Goodrich, one of an American family who, well-named, engaged in privateering. Wealth and craft got Goodrich into the Bermuda Governor's Council, with the right to the word 'Honourable' before his name. The title is engraved on the tablet but, looking carefully, it is clear that someone at some time has attempted to deface the word 'Honourable'. Why they did this, or who it was, is one of Bermuda's untold stories.

Another tablet records happier relationships. 'To the memory of Mary . . . wife of Commodore Sir John Poo Beresford . . . An attractive person . . . with gentle manners and captivating mirth.' She died aged twenty-three.

Every niche and corner of the church has something to interest the visitor. There are pictures and wise sayings; a delightful railed gallery at one side; a model of a ship against one wall; brass tablets commemorate long-gone corporals and gunners. The church silver is touched with the London hallmarks of 1625. On the communion paten, however, are distinct knife marks, it having been used as a dinner plate by a rascal governor, Samuel Day.

There is an extraordinary three-decker pulpit dating from the seventeenth century, the clerk occupying the bottom shelf (St Peter's has a tradition of singing clerks), the middle section – the prayer-book deck from which the minister conducted the service – and the top deck from which he delivered his sermon. A turkey hen once got into the church and nested in the top deck. The minister was obliged to preach from the middle level until Easter when the bird emerged with a brood of thirteen.

The churchyard of St Peter's is like a stone furniture shop. Tombs and slabs stand haphazardly about like tables, beds and benches among the palms and cedars. Here are buried the slaves from the early days, the pioneers, the sailors and soldiers and the families who fell to yellow fever. A sad little rank of small stones marks the graves of all the children of one house.

By the back door of St Peter's is a Bermuda cedar, now reduced to a frail stump, which was there when Sir George Somers and his people were shipwrecked in the bay. It had probably been there two further centuries beyond that. It is still called the Belfry Tree for the church bell was once suspended from its branches; it has been taken down now for the ancient arm could hold it no longer.

For a century until 1973 there were no burials in the churchyard. It was full. Then on 10 March that year Sir Richard Sharples, the Governor of Bermuda, and his aide Captain Hugh Sayers, were assassinated in the grounds of Government House. Because of the Governor's affection for the slow town of St George's and its peaceful church he and Captain Sayers were buried among the first settlers of the old colony.

St George's is carved with odd corners, squares and tree-roofed courtyards, most of them so unattended that you can hear your footsteps on the stones. The place names are evocative – Barber's Alley, Old Maid's Lane, Blockade Alley and Featherbed Alley. In Barber's Alley lived Joseph Hayne Rainey, a freed slave from South Carolina who, with his wife, reached Bermuda on a blockade runner. He set up as a barber in St George's, educated himself by reading between customers and eventually returned to America to become the first black man to be a member of the House of Representatives.

The old houses of St George's could tell a good many stories. At the top of King Street is the State House, built in 1620, the oldest building in Bermuda. Its annual rent is still one peppercorn. The rectory, a welcoming little place with a cat asleep on the windowsill and the sunshine streaming down the chimney, was built by a penitent pirate. In King's Square, just across from the pillory, the stocks and the cheerful local inn, is a house built in 1700 by Governor Day who used the communion plate at dinner and who died in prison. Years later, during the American Civil War, it was used by Major Norman Walker, the Confederate agent, who stage-managed Bermuda's not-altogether-neutral part in that conflict.

The blockade of the Confederacy ports by the Northern navy resulted in St George's becoming a transhipment harbour where cargoes were unloaded from heavy vessels onto lighter craft which would scurry across the stretch of water to the South undetected by the Union guns. The little town had never known such activity or prosperity. Ships crammed the harbour, money rattled, gracious living arrived as it so often does with the misadventures of others. Today Major Walker's house is a museum with flags, misty photographs of posed generals and captains and other relics of those heady times.

More than a century earlier, during the American Revolution against the British, St George's was the setting of another drama. A raiding party from three American ships slid ashore on the night of 14 August 1775. From the armoury they calmly rolled barrels of His Majesty's gunpowder down to their whaleboats for transportation to the war against the British. They were disturbed by only one man, an ally as it happened, a captured French officer on parole. Not recognizing his uniform the raiders killed and buried him. His body was not found for more than a hundred years. It was discovered when the foundations of a new church for the town were being dug on the ground behind St Peter's. The front of this church was raised but it was never completed and its stands hollowly today, a huge and chance memorial for a French prisoner who disappeared without trace one summer night.

Bermuda is formed like a lobster's claw (a similar shape to Nantucket) with St George's at the blunt end and the homely-named parishes, Pembroke, Devonshire, Warwick, Southampton, Smiths and Paget, extending to the extreme of the hook at Ireland Island, with the village of Somerset located just below it. Castle harbour is in the northeast, lapping alongside the civil airport, and the promontory of St David's where the people are acknowledged by everyone (including themselves) to be 'different'. They have their own ways and their own lives, cut off from the rest of the islands. The texture of their skin is different for they are a mixture of Negro slave, Irish immigrant and American Indian. To the other people they are known as Mohawks. During World War II they were assembled and told that three-quarters of their land was to be taken over as a United States Air Base (one of those leased in 1940 in trade for fifty old warships). Silently they went away and removed their belongings to the remaining quarter of land. The air base was still there – and so were the Mohawks. Harrington Harbour, a marvellously enclosed anchorage, touches Front Street in Hamilton, the island capital, whose shops and houses line it in vivid and varied colours like laundry hanging on a line. The curled claw itself hooks around the Great Sound gathering in its shelter a whole bevy of small and pretty islets.

Hamilton looks almost too good to be true; a confection of pastel buildings like a film set which might be dismantled and carried elsewhere by tomorrow. At the town's junction is a little dais, like a miniature bandstand and it is here that the policeman, uniformed like a London 'bobby', conducts the sedate traffic wearing a serious expression and white gloves, much to the satisfaction of American visitors who feel that they must be at least halfway to Europe. There are some good inns, one called the Forty Thieves, the nickname given to the original landowners and another the Hog Penny from the first coins issued there, depicting a hog, the most widespread land inhabitant before man.

There are shaded wooden walkways at the front of the shops and outside Trimmingham's Department Store comfortable canvas chairs and settees placed with consideration for the warm and weary shoppers. At one time Bermuda's railway chuffed right along the middle of the street on its journey from one end of the island to the other. That was in the days before the introduction of cars to the island in 1946. Bermuda entered the motor age late and with trepidation. A speed limit of twenty miles per hour was voted when the first vehicles appeared and it remains so to this day. Many visitors, particularly the young, take to small unaccustomed motor bicycles. On my first morning, as I walked along Front Street, a youthful American dived into the harbour without getting off his scooter. He was pulled out by a Bermudan who then hurried off. He was, he explained later to the newspaper, already late for work.

A few yards uphill from the traffic policeman's stand is a delightful white building, flat at its front, balconied and tree-shaded behind. It is the Perot Post Office, restored to its original quaintness, still in business with its polished lamps and grilles, its high writing desks and lofty stools. Venerable candlesticks are placed on the desks and above there are loyal pictures of Queen Victoria and postmaster Sir Rowland Hill. Customers come and go, the staff perch behind the solid wooden counter that was in use in 1849 when William B. Perot, the Hamilton postmaster, produced his own stamps and appended his signature – stamps which are now highly prized and priced.

From the Hamilton waterfront the many isles of the Great Sound merge and mingle. Some, hardly humps in the sea, are simply named Alpha Island, Beta Island, Delta Island, which sounds better than ABC; others have names and stories like Murderer's Island.

This island is also called Burt's Island and Skeeter's Island, a few acres of scrub and rock with some windy trees at its centre and a gaunt crucifix raised above its landing place. The Cross represents a late attempt to consecrate the place after Skeeter, a murderer whose case touched even the corridors of law in far London, was interred here along with a sorry company.

Richard Cox, the young man who took me across to Murderer's Island in his dory, had never been there before, although he had lived all his life in Bermuda and his family have been settled in the island since the arrival of the ship *Golden Rule* from Brixham in 1620.

Skeeter was a man living at Somerset at the end of the nineteenth century. The previous day I had gone there and found his fishpond, still carved out by the shore at the spot where his now-vanished cottage stood. The story is that his wife, after going to a wedding party, disappeared, and Skeeter gathered his neighbours to search for her. But they did not find her and it was even supposed that she might have left the island for America.

Weeks later, the missing woman's brother was sitting on a rock when he saw something odd off the shore. He took a boat out and there saw his sister's body beneath the waves. She was tied to a large boulder. Skeeter was arrested, convicted and executed. The most amazing thing, however, was that Skeeter's body was taken to Murderer's Island and buried – and the stone which he had tied to his hapless wife was used as the headstone above his grave.

Skeeter's grave with its gruesome and apposite reminder has been long lost among the rubble and rocks of Murderer's Island, but there are remnants of history on many of the other midget islands in the Great Sound. During the Boer War a contingent of prisoners was taken to Bermuda (deemed to be a place from where they were unlikely to run back to South Africa) and was distributed among the smaller isles where they made the best of the monotony by whittling wood carvings which were advertised for sale in the local newspaper and some of which can be seen today.

Darrell's Island, just across an elbow of water from Murderer's Island, became the prison of more than a thousand Boers who also whittled and whiled away their time. Apart from their carving activities, they laid out a tennis court and a croquet lawn. In 1902 when the war ended some of the Boers refused to be repatriated and had to be forcibly removed.

Thirty years later Darrell's Island had another role. The ladylike flying boats of Imperial Airways and Pan American Airways began flights from London and New York to Bermuda. They came down in the cosseted waters of the sound and taxied to Darrell's Island where they disembarked their passengers who were taken the final mile to Hamilton by boat. The great aircraft were housed in hangars, the foundations of which still jut from the land near the water's edge, the last remnants of an elegant age.

The now sadly-gone flying boat had a notable part in linking many islands of the world. Pan American pioneered the trans-Pacific route to China, using

Honolulu, Midway, Wake and the Philippines as 'stepping stones'. Midway and Wake were arid atolls until the arrival of the Americans who had to swim ashore from freighters carrying the first materials that went into the building of the important air bases.

Richard Cox, who took me across to Murderer's Island, had been at college in the United States and was filling in time working in Douglas Fetigan's boatyard in Pitts Bay, Hamilton. Richard and his father Harry spend much of their time diving along the fruitful reefs of Bermuda, rummaging through the debris of the many ships that came to grief there. Their home is a treasure chest in itself; bottles, bells, binnacles recovered from the cellars of the sea stand around like ornaments might in another home. Their pride is a brass musketoon, a gun like a polished telescope, and Richard's mother has built two fine fireplaces from bricks that came from the kiln centuries ago and were doubtless destined for some settler's house in the New World.

Richard tapped the ship's bell which hangs outside their door. 'Our family records show that we lost three ships on journeys from England and they lie somewhere around these coasts,' he smiled. 'Wouldn't it be strange to be down there one day and realize that we were looking through cargo that was loaded by our ancestors, or that the bones lying there could be my great, great, great, great-grandfather?'

Across the anchorage from Hamilton the land elevates a little, not much, in the parishes of Warwick, Paget and Southampton. It is the white roofs that fill the scene, like squares of paper. With few exceptions Bermuda roofs are white, constructed to catch every speck of rainwater and to carry it to the householder's personal barrel or tank. Shortage of water has been one of the island's problems; it is hoarded and never wasted.

Over there Gibbs Hill lighthouse, built by the Royal Engineers in the 1840s, bleeps through the night. I climbed its 185 steps and went out onto the lantern-gallery into a gale that would have been at home in Cornwall. It chopped the sea and shredded through the palms. Up there it was necessary to press back against the lighthouse wall, like a child pressing against the leg of a parent. Even so it was worth it for from that elevation you can see the whole scope of Bermuda's Great Sound, its fragments, coves, settlements and seas spread out conveniently beneath your nose.

Within the lantern-house I found Maurice Nearon, the keeper, in his seventies and then still clambering up the stairs several times a day. He has that cheerful calmness that is the demeanour of lighthousemen everywhere from Scandinavia to the Southern Ocean. 'My grandfather came here from Wales,' he said squatting in a well-used chair and tuning a radio. 'He met my grandmother who was a Bermudan lady. And here I am.' He listened intently to the radio. Was it the weather forcast, I asked.

'No, no,' he replied. 'I'm not worried about the weather up here. That's for others to think about.' He detected something on the radio. 'Ah . . . that's it,' he smiled settling back.

The sound of melodious, hymn-singing voices came over the air. 'My own church,' said Maurice nodding towards the set. 'St Paul's, Hamilton.' It was said with pride as if the broadcast was coming from the other side of the world. He began to mumble the tune and so I left him, clanking down the curling stairs, leaving a happy man humming the Lord's praises 130 odd feet in the air.

The road from the lighthouse out towards Ireland Island, at the end of the lobster's claw, is enclosed with extravagantly flowering shrubs intersected by what have been known from the times of the first maps as tribe roads. These cut across the short width of the islands from shore to shore – always just wide enough to roll a barrel, which shows that the early settlers had their priorities in order.

The land narrows quickly as you enter Sandys Parish, a crossing accomplished on an odd little wooden structure, which is the smallest drawbridge in the world. The drawbridge is, in effect, a hinged groove about twelve inches wide which opens up to allow the masts of small vessels to go through. The bridge even has traffic lights at each end.

Bermuda's great naval base was at Ireland Island, now disused, its rusty guns pointless but still directed out to sea from their stone and concrete bastions. On the extreme cape is one of the most singular buildings I have ever encountered: the Commissioner's House, a former elegance, with cast-iron balconies and balustrades, now fallen to ruin (but happily being restored). It creaks and echoes as you walk through it like the house in *Gone With the Wind*. When it was almost finished in the early part of the nineteenth century, there was an outcry in Britain over its cost of £42,511, after an estimate of £12,400. 'The extraordinary, and to all appearances improvident expenditure on this house must stop all proceedings concerning it until the subject has received all and every explanation of which it is capable,' bellowed a memorandum from the far-off Navy Board in London. In 1832 it was considered to be too big for any one family and was relegated to the role of 'billets' which it fulfilled until 1951 when the British Navy sailed away for the last time.

Nearby within the hefty walls of the former dockyard a Maritime Museum has been established, arrayed with boats and interesting oddments. Outside is a superb ship's figurehead of Neptune which was lowered into place by helicopter. The most intriguing exhibit here is still the subject of a great mystery in the Bermuda islands. The museum houses Tucker's treasure, a collection of gold bars and jewelled ornaments brought to the surface from a wreck in 1955 by Teddy Tucker, a local diver. It was purchased by the Bermuda Government and sent to the Maritime Museum in time for the museum's opening by the Queen in 1975. As the fabulous treasure was being laid out on exhibition it was found that the centrepiece of the display, a rich cross in which were mounted seven emeralds, had vanished. It had been replaced by a plastic substitute. The real cross – called Tucker's Cross – has never been found.

The most eyecatching exhibit there, however, is the gate attendant Douglas Little who wears a nautical cap and jersey. He has a beard sad enough to impress the Ancient Mariner and, to boot, a wooden stump. Every inch the part; he confesses, however, that his lost leg was the result of neither shark nor storm. 'Lost it when I was a boy in Nova Scotia,' he said. 'Wheel of a cart ran over it.'

BERMUDA situated between latitudes 32°15'–32°23'N and longitudes 64°38'–64°53'W; area 22.5 sq. m (58 sq. km); population approx. 61,000; associated British colony

Sanibel and Captiva
A Hurricane is Coming

I have been here before
But when or how I cannot tell:
I know the grass beyond the door,
The sweet keen smell,
The sighing sound, the lights around the shore
CHRISTINA ROSSETTI

I never saw better storms, skies and sunsets than those you get on the Gulf of Mexico. The August morning would begin untouched blue, the sea sage to bottle green, a breeze nudging from the south. Shell-seekers would be out early peering into the shingle and then, oddly, looking up to see if a storm might be lining the horizon, knowing that if one came up then the turbulence of the sea would throw up more of their particular small treasures.

Quite often they were not disappointed. By mid-afternoon it would become deep and sultry and there would be rumbles from a distance as though someone big was grumbling about the heat. Then the clouds would sail in, the ocean would frown, and there would be thunder, lightning and violent and impenetrable rain.

But it would all be gone in an hour; gone towards Louisiana or Texas or Mexico itself. The rattling on the roof would be reduced to taps and then stop altogether; the trees would calm, the sky would move over like stage scenery, and the late sun would flood the gulf. Sometimes events overtook each other. One evening there was a vivid sunset, forked lightning and a rainbow, all in the sky at the same time. Then the moon appeared.

Captiva is one of the narrow Florida Barrier Islands, joined to its longer neighbour Sanibel by a bridge; and Sanibel is joined to the mainland by a low causeway. North Captiva, a separate island, can only be reached by boat or by seaplane (some residents are wealthy enough to have their own seaplane) and beyond that are Useppa Island, which is very select indeed, and Cabbage Key, upon which is a wooden pub with 30,000 dollars pinned to the walls.

During my wanderings around the islands of the world, I have usually been alone but this time I had a family with me, Diana my wife, my son Matthew and his pretty girlfriend Sophie, and seven-year-old identical twins, Charlie and Joe, the children of my daughter Lois. We stayed for a month in a large and airy wooden house divided from the beach only by a line of trees. It was often quite solitary. We were like castaways.

Seeing what Florida is like today, it is difficult to imagine that well into this century most of it was swamp and jungle. In the 1920s, they used to have a car rally from Tampa, halfway up the state on the Gulf Coast, to Miami. The vehicles had to navigate old Indian trails, be ferried across rivers and swamps on rafts, and generally hope for the best. The journey, which today (along a route still today called the Tamiami Trail) you could accomplish in five or six hours, took eleven days.

The string of barrier islands were naturally isolated. There were towns along the coast and Fort Myers was a growing city. Edison had his winter estate there; you can visit it today and see the things he left behind. (It is interesting to know that, having been involved in the development of the telephone, he recommended that it should be answered with the word, 'Ahoy', a suggestion soon fortunately dropped in favour of 'Hello'.)

In those days a ferry would carry passengers across the brackish waters of the San Carlos Sound and the communities which grew up on Sanibel and Captiva were very tight indeed. They were really the first white settlers (any business on the islands established before 1930 proudly advertises the fact). There had once been Indian tribes but they had gone. The most notable building on Sanibel, and the highest, was the iron lighthouse. It still is.

Sanibel may be an abbreviation of Saint Isabel, while the story of Captiva is that it was once used to confine women captured by the pirate Gaprilla. How anyone knows that the detainees were female is hard to understand since the only tentative evidence is said to be the stumps of a stockade. No bangles, rings or beads.

In pre-war days the inhabitants saw themselves as people apart and there was outrage when it was proposed to construct a causeway joining Sanibel to the urban fringe of Lee County on the mainland and a bridge between the two islands. But built it was and today they present a curiosity – two American suburban islands, with streets and homes and shops, supermarkets, gas stations, two golf courses, a theatre and a cinema, combined with the most extraordinary wild beaches, swamps, bayous, lagoons, and inlets, and an amazing diversity of wildlife including the sea-otter, the manatee and the American alligator. A Sanibel housewife, fetching her children from school, is likely to have to stop her car to allow a female alligator and *her* offspring to cross the highway. As the roadside signs indicate, the alligator has right of way.

The American alligator is a protected species and it knows it. They lounge in waterways, mangrove swamps and other backwaters, lifting an eye at any human legs that appear in view but, whatever their thoughts, doing nothing more. One lived until it was seventy and was seventeen feet long. It had always distrusted people since someone once hit it with an axe.

Each of the several local newspapers and island guides carries a stern warning about alligators. Do not feed them or they will lose their inborn fear of man. Do not annoy them. Do NOT prod them with your feet. Keep your dogs on a lead and make sure your cat does not wander too far.

'A 'gator had my Dobermann,' an islander told me. 'It never had a chance.' People also have cages around their swimming pools. Otherwise an early morning dip could bring an unpleasant surprise.

There are warnings by bridges and streams. 'Five hundred dollar fine for feeding alligators – and possible INCARCERATION!'

'They can be a traffic problem,' admitted an officer leaning from a car marked Sheriff. 'They have the right of way but if you hit one in the dark it can do a lot of damage – to the 'gator and to the car, fenders, ripped tyres, that sort of thing.'

An alligator accident makes occasional vivid reading in the homely Police Report columns of the newspapers, which otherwise list such incidents as, 'A European lady who spoke little English called the police after seeing what she thought was smoke coming from her car engine but it was only condensation.' . . . 'A stranger was seen hanging about outside the Bailey Supermarket after closing on Monday. Police investigated but no trace was found.'

It could have been the great white egret which *does* loiter outside the supermarket liquor department because the manager there feeds it. 'Hot dog,' the manager said when I asked what the attraction was. 'Small pieces of hot dog. He's been coming every day for a year now.'

It is curious and pleasant that wild animals and birds fit so well into the social framework of both Sanibel and Captiva. Ring-tailed racoons sit by the side of the road washing the faces of their cubs, sea-otters and manatees, two species almost extinct, come close to the shore at Blind Pass on Captiva at sunset; there's an armadillo trudging along a lane; we all run shouting and clapping to encourage a great and solitary dolphin which undulates twenty feet off the beach. My wife and the twins swim alongside it.

Everyone's a nature observer. The man at the gas station mentions, 'That osprey is sitting in the tree right across there, looking out to sea. He'll be going fishing soon. It's his eating time.'

On the eastern side of Captiva is an extensive area of mangrove swamp and salt water lagoons, letting out onto Pine Island Sound, and called somewhat uncomfortably the 'Ding' Darling Reserve. J. N. Darling was a cartoonist who signed himself 'Ding' in the *New Yorker* and other journals, and as a project in retirement bought and developed the reserve. Cartooning must have paid well.

It is the sort of place where with luck, you might see wonderful creatures. Or you might drive at a snail's pace for five miles along the dirt road and have to make do with a few cleric-like cormorants and the antics of pelicans.

At evening is the best time when the brackish water is slightly polished and the rosette spoonbills, their legs and feathers glowing pink in the sunset, gather to feed with the heron, the ibis and the ubiquitous white egret. The ibis, with his arched beak, struts along the beach too, picking out morsels from the sand, jumping comically as the wave comes in, to save his feet from getting wet. Sandpipers scurry in formation like teams of emergency workers, and a solitary heron stands in a line of fishermen, staring out to sea, now and again helping himself from the bait bucket.

But it is the pelicans I enjoy. They seem to me living proof that God has a sense of humour. Nothing appears to fit; body, beak and wings somehow out of symmetry and synch, the legs left over from some other creature and added as an afterthought. There are many patrolling the shores of both islands, brown and some white. They are like flying basset hounds. Of an evening they clank up and down looking for fish, flinging themselves idiotically into the sea, wings all askew, every dive looking like the first time.

Mike Dooley comes from the Florida Keys but likes to fish off Captiva Island (so does his son, Casey, aged four, who while we were there caught a snoek only slightly smaller than himself). Mike, a lean and humorous man, was with me on the offshore sandbar. We were both fishing. I did not get a bite. He pulled a silver and yellow pompano from the water. Two pelicans cruised close by eyeing his catch. 'Now and then they'll go for it,' he said in his Deep South accent. 'And then sure they get the hook as well as the fish. Catching one of those birds is something you have to see. It takes three men. One to get the hook out and two to hold the pelican.'

On the white scarf of beach that runs the entire western flank of Captiva, the loggerhead turtles lumber along to lay their eggs in the sand. The strand is sparsely populated by humans but the buried caches are detected and marked by more devoted conservationists. A small notice is displayed threatening imprisonment or at least a fine for the disturbance of the eggs. The lady loggerhead returns to the water and leaves the eggs to hatch themselves. When they do, the baby turtles come out like a crowd leaving a football ground, scampering towards the sea. People with seaside houses are asked to extinguish any illuminations facing the beach because the tiny turtles, not knowing any better, scramble towards the lights and the living-room instead of going to their proper home in the gulf.

But the truly mysterious creature of this warm coast is the manatee. There are said to be only a thousand remaining and these are helped and cossetted with all the concern that American conservation can muster. They are encouraged to keep within the immediate waters because it is feared that should they venture out into their natural home, the open sea, they would not long survive. It is difficult to see the whole animal because only the puppy-like nose and mouth ever break the surface of the water. The remaining *three thousands pounds* or so of the animal, which looks like a type of walrus, only more ungainly, if that is possible, rarely appear. They live mainly in the harbour at Plantation – a glossy vacation resort, on the upper end of Captiva, where a thoughtful hotel management provides them with outlets of warm water which they enjoy.

It is from Plantation that a bright, imitation riverboat *Jean Nicolette* (the 'Jean' is pronounced the French way, the captain informs passengers) voyages almost the length of Pine Island Sound to Cabbage Key. The entire trip is on water so shallow you could walk it keeping your head above the surface. Even the flat-bottomed vessel has to keep to a marked channel. 'She's pretty, but she can be tough,' said one of the crew. 'In difficult weather getting her berthed at Cabbage Key can be like shutting a barn door in a gale.'

There has never been a mishap, however, and it is a satisfying journey of a couple of hours on a good day, in the company of seabirds and dolphins. If anyone has any doubt that the endearing dolphin likes human company, then a trip on the *Jean Nicolette* should dispel it. They come pounding across the water at the sight of the vessel's bow and perform their tricks all around the hull. They seem to appreciate blasts on a whistle, shouted approval (the 'whoops' at which the Americans are so practised) and even sedate applause.

So low-lying are the barrier islands that little can be seen of them from the navigation channel. They lie like carpets on the sea. North Captiva is reduced to a few pointed roofs and a water tower and on the Pine Island side the sole distinguishable features are the stilted huts built years ago by Cuban fishermen, sometimes now occupied by adventurous squatters. It was in these waters and along these shores that the CIA rehearsed (insufficiently it would seem) its forces for the Bay of Pigs invasion of Cuba in 1963.

Cabbage Key is what counts as an observation point in these latitudes. It rises all of thirty feet above sea level, the remnant of an ancient Indian mound (either a midden or a monument) surmounted by a house, now an inn, built by the American novelist Mary Roberts Rinehart in the 1930s.

Before that it had been occupied by a series of people who fancied the life of a castaway. One owner, known for his miserly ways, a mixture of Robinson Crusoe and Ebenezer Scrooge, received a tax bill for ten dollars from Lee County, of which Cabbage Key is a part. 'Ten dollars!' he bellowed waving the piece of paper at the distant mainland. 'I'm not paying ten dollars. You can keep the place!' Whereupon he packed his belongings, rowed over to Florida and never went back.

The most extraordinary thing about Cabbage Key is apparent as soon as you walk into the inn. Once your eyes become used to the dimness you see that every wall is covered with dollar notes. They are everwhere, in every room, like wallpaper. Most are inscribed with the names of visitors. I found an inscription from a man who lives half a mile away from my house in England.

'It started with the Cuban fishermen, years ago,' said the barman surveying the room. 'They would have a good day and sell their catch well and they would come to Cabbage Key for a drink. They got into the habit of pinning a few dollars to the wall against the time when they *didn't* get any fish. And the habit sort of caught on. Nobody's counted but I guess there are close on 30,000 bucks hanging up there now.'

There was a fit and friendly man, who jogged three miles along the sand and shingle on Captiva every day while his dog ran ten. He used to pass our house to go between the trees and he always called something to us. One morning he shouted, 'We got Andrew coming!'

My first reaction was to assume we were to get a visit from a member of the British Royal Family. 'Hurricane Andrew,' he corrected. 'He's coming at force five. And they don't come any harder than that.'

I was not alarmed. I had long suspected that the people of Florida overreacted to the warnings of hurricanes. There was a marked 'Evacuation Route' along the only possible way off both Captiva and Sanibel, the single main road leading to the causeway; there were area wardens in charge of emergency measures; every house had a list of dos and don'ts posted on the wall – have a supply of fresh water and tinned food – torches, batteries, etc; and only that week the local newspapers had splashed the story of the island's new toy, a device which would interrupt television to allow the mayor to broadcast the portentous evacuation order. I had a notion that everyone secretly enjoyed all the excitement and anticipation in the way that in wartime Britain there was a *frisson* about the air raids and the threat of invasion. After all there had only been two major hurricanes in that area in the last half century, the second more than twenty-seven years before. The sun shone steadily and the sea was amiable. We decided not to store water and canned food.

But the television commentators were becoming increasingly emphatic. They kept showing satellite pictures of the Bahamas, off the east coast, enveloped by a nasty looking blodge. Hurricane Andrew was heading for Florida.

A million people were reported to be fleeing Miami. On Captiva householders began to batten down the windows. I kept looking at the sky. It looked back innocently.

Someone told us that the risk was the causeway. Big seas could easily sweep over the top. Waves could reach *eleven* feet. The island was scarcely eighteen inches above sea level. Joe and Charlie, the seven-year-old twins, were three feet high. I began to feel anxious.

Then it was settled for me. The mayor, who must have been itching to use his new machine, did so. We were watching the main newscast when a noise like a police siren came from the set and the picture blanked out. On the screen came the mayor's grave voice, the words reinforced in outsize letters on the screen. 'Sanibel and Captiva Islands must be evacuated within the next three hours.'

The twins looked excited. 'What are we going to do?' they asked together.

'We're going,' I said decisively. Diana nodded and made for the suitcases. 'Get your teddy bears.'

Almost everyone got out before us. When we drove out at seven o'clock on a broody evening, with the sea flat and copper coloured, there was hardly a soul on either island. The only islanders remaining were the police (for some reason in anti-riot gear) and a lone jogger wearing earphones and a steadfast expression. I wondered if he had heard.

The road was empty. It was uncanny. We were on the mainland in no time. I was unwilling to join the traffic on the main routes north, spectacularly jammed according to the radio, so I merely drove into Fort Myers and went to the Sheraton, which looked more or less stable, where I got two rooms on the twenty-second floor.

I was not sure what a hurricane would be like up there but people from the South were coming in all the time trying to get rooms. I decided to stay put. At eight o'clock the next morning the edge of Hurricane Andrew pussy-footed by the window. I said I had played golf in worse weather.

But ten degrees south tens of thousands were already frightened and homeless. It was being called America's worst natural disaster. A week later, I was in Miami and there was still no drinking water, some places were without electricity, the traffic lights were out of action and thousands were sleeping in the open.

Matthew and Sophie returned to the island that night. There was no power but little damage. A big surf was running.

On the following morning, Diana and I returned with the twins over the causeway and then the bridge to Captiva. The sun was bright. The beach shone. The pelicans flew. It was almost like going home.

Sanibel situated latitude 26°26′N and longitude 82°10′W; area 22 sq. m (57 sq. km); population approx. 5,000. CAPTIVA situated latitude 26°31′N and longitude 82°12′W; area 9 sq. m (23 sq. km); population approx. 500

Saba, St Maarten, St Barthélemy
The Surprise Isles

Look stranger, on this island new
W. H. AUDEN

Of all the many islands of the world I have come to know, Saba in the Dutch Antilles of the Caribbean is the most astounding. A slab of rock rising 3,000 feet to meet a cloth of cloud, its houses clinging like seabirds to its ledges. It is a wonder anyone lives there at all for until recent times it was all but inaccessible; there was no harbour, no airfield, no road. And yet it has always had a population of some hundreds, white people living in the hamlets of Hell's Gate, Windwardside and Booby Hill, and in the tiny red-roofed town quaintly called the Bottom.

The large message outside the airport on St Maarten, the nearest island meant well, but read ambiguously. 'Have A Good Flight,' it said. 'Hope You Come Back.'

As the twin otter aircraft banked tentatively alongside Saba I began to believe they meant it. The island climbing like a wall on every side, cloud-wraithed, with a zig-zag scrape down its flank that I knew was its single, all but vertical, road. At the foot of the road, the size of a piece of sticking plaster, was the airfield, a place so minute that I thought the best policy was to close my eyes and hope the pilot did not do the same.

We curled over the purple-troughed sea, thudding against patient rocks; we rocked in the cross-currents of air, engines shrieking, cabin bucking, and bounced onto the only flat piece of ground for many miles. The wheels bumped and squealed, the plane pulled up like a car at a sudden change of traffic lights and there we were at the Juancho E. Yrausquin airport (its name longer than its runway), and one of the world's astonishing places.

Saba (pronounced 'Say-ber') is a Dutch colony populated mainly by the descendants of settlers who came from the Shetland Islands north of Scotland and possibly from Jersey in the English Channel. One of them, Wilf Hassell, a gingery fair young man with a brick-coloured face, met me in his yellow taxi. His family have been on the island since 1672. How many Hassells were there now? 'Nearly 400 out of a thousand people,' he answered as we started up the almost vertical road.

It was one of his family, Josephus Lambert Hassell, who was responsible for the building of that road. Before 1940 the only way from the wild landing beaches to the villages far up in the quiet mists was up hundreds of steps hewn into the rocks, wriggling up through boulders, ferns and forests. It took hours to travel the couple of miles from one settlement to the next and all goods and water (and sometimes boats) had to be borne on the heads of the people. Will Johnson, editor of the once-a-month *Saba Herald* and a member of the island's second largest clan, remembers that his grandmother was fifty years old before she ever travelled from her home in Hell's Gate to the main town, the Bottom, lying as its name suggests in the cup of a cooled volcanic crater. She could see no good reason for making the walk.

After Dutch experts had said that the building of a road was impossible because of the steepness of the terrain, Josephus Lambert Hassell sent to the United States for a correspondence course in civil engineering, read it thoroughly, and with his fellow islanders hacked out the highway over the mountains and over the next twenty years.

'Today,' said Wilf Hassell in his West Indian English, as we curled around the tight elbow bends, 'you arrived at an important time. This morning they have begun a new road over the hills. The people still have to walk with their goods on their heads from that place. In a year they will be able to ride.' And we both saluted a gang of men digging the first rocks out of the mountain.

Every turn, every gradient, every new angle of the road brought another amazing aspect of this vertical place into view. How they built the road, even in twenty years, could have been nothing short of remarkable, especially from instructions received by post. 'Now,' said Wilf as we backed tightly into a corner to let another car go down (the pleasant habit of everyone waving to everyone else on this road is disconcerting for a stranger), 'these days we have more than 200 cars on Saba. The first came ashore in 1947 lashed to two rowing boats. The crews had to judge the waves and they came into the beach on a good roller. Then fifty men lifted the car, which was a jeep, ashore. That was a great day for this place.'

The jeep had scarcely a mile of road at its disposal, but it was growing daily. Then came the airstrip. It was a small tongue of land, a lip of lava from the ancient volcano, called the Flat. An intrepid pilot, a Monsieur de Haenow, mayor of the neighbouring French island of St Barthélemy, landed to much excitement. After that they built the harbour and the road to join the two.

Wild goats ran through the thick cover of growth over the rocksides. It was cool and misty, like a summer morning in Scotland. Little houses up there have chimneys and fireplaces and once, so several people told me proudly, hailstones fell. 'Windwardside,' announced Wilf stopping the car. I looked over a precipice onto a thick green valley that ascended beyond into frail clouds. The houses of the village, red-roofed, white-faced, hung onto the side of the mountain. A cock called across the valley and smoke curled from a chimney to join the clouds. It was a place apart.

The Dutch Antilles consist of the islands of Aruba, Curaçao and Bonaire, which are called the Leeward Islands, and St Maarten (shared with the French), St Eustatius and Saba. During the roving days of the early sailing colonists, these islands saw many changes of flag as the English, the French, the Dutch, the Spaniards (and even the Russians) sent their ships into the Caribbean to see what could be gained. Sometimes islands were sighted, by men such as Columbus (who was first on the horizon during his second voyage of 1493), given a name and marked approximately on a map only to be rechristened by the next adventurer to heave to. This confusion is today made no easier by the fact that the Windward Islands of the Dutch Antilles lie almost in the lap of what the British still call the Leeward Islands – Antigua, St Kitts, Nevis and Anguilla. The Dutch Leewards, Aruba, Curaçao and Bonaire, sit on the shoulder of South America, while the British-named Windwards are off the same coast a few miles southeast.

All this mattered little to the people of Saba, living in their rocky privacy. The origins of the people are a matter of nationalistic dispute but it seems that the Dutch who claimed the island never stayed for long. Soon the Shetland Islanders arrived, Presbyterians, it is said, fleeing from religious persecution, and settled here. By the beginning of the eighteenth century a Dutch missionary complained that no one could understand a word he was saying. The first Hassell arrived in 1672 from a family widespread in Jersey in the English Channel Islands. The Dutch have remained in possession, and the Princesses Irene and Margariet, Queen Beatrix's sisters, were welcomed in 1962 when they were carried bodily ashore (clad in raincoats) from a pitching, rowing boat in the days before the harbour was built. But there is little Dutch tradition about the strange, enclosed place. The five churches are Roman Catholic, Anglican and Wesleyan and the language is English.

Mount Scenery rises almost 3,000 feet into the West Indian sky, with the Bottom, a splendidly organized little town, sitting with aplomb in the crater of the old volcano. A Dutch government official arrived in the islands in the 1930s and proceeded to tell the population his version of their history. How their names were really Anglicized Dutch, how their traditions and their seamanship went back to their Netherlands forebears, how the Bottom was really the word *Botte*, used in Holland for a bowl. The Saba people listened in silence. They say they knew better. Today they tell you firmly that the Bottom means exactly what it says – the bottom of the volcano crater.

The Bottom, its red buildings spread out across one of the few non-vertical areas of Saba, is a misty, cosy place, with a self-contained life. It has modern schools, a radio station, churches, a fire station, a police house, a two-cell jail (with a roof for sunbathing), a hospital and old people's home, the latter two conveniently joined together. There are stores in each of the island villages, two hotels and a Chinese restaurant.

Hell's Gate rises neatly on another flank of the island and Booby Hill on yet another. On Booby Hill is the grave of one of the renowned Saban sea skippers, Captain Ernest Johnson (buried in his garden as most people on the island were since there is little room for a cemetery). In 1920 he was sailing from Boston harbour in the SS *Atlantus* when he saw through his binoculars a white shirt flying out at sea. On further investigation he found that the shirt was protruding from a hole in the stern plates of the United States submarine S-5, which had become disabled during a dive and was lying helpless below the sea. The shirt belonged to her captain.

The Saban mariner brought his ship close to and lassoed the submarine's propellers. Then they hung on until help arrived. All thirty-eight officers and men of the S-5 were rescued through a hole cut in the exposed stern. Captain Johnson was presented with an engraved gold watch in appreciation by the rescued men. A wonderful capped and bearded figure, he loved to show it to visitors to his island house.

Before that time the sailors and schooners of Saba had become famous throughout the world. Anyone who lived on that place, under constant siege from the sea, was a born mariner. But they always returned to their island of orchids and breadfruit, mangoes, mists and whirling seabirds.

In the little museum Sherry Peterson ('born a Hassell') shows visitors around the house where her husband's grandfather was born. The four-poster bed with its turned uprights, the kitchen stove with its iron implements, the fine needlework of the island women and photographs from the past, are all exhibited. 'This one,' she said, holding up a frame, 'was taken outside the school at the beginning of the century.' A smocked group of round-faced and content-looking children smiled for the photographer. She pointed to two. 'Only this boy and this girl are still alive,' she said. 'They are over eighty, of course, and they have been in Saba all their lives.'

People do not, very often, leave from choice. The men went to sea, but Saba, even when it had no harbour, was their home port. Others went to work in the oil refineries in Curaçao and Aruba, and I first heard about the island from a Saban in Bermuda. They always yearn for home, though; they write poems and songs about it and send them back to Saba with love.

At the airstrip once more, waiting to fly out to St Maarten, I sat among the parcels and passengers at what could easily have been a country railway station. Despite its grand title the Juancho E. Yrausquin Airport appears just like that: wooden seats, porter's room, weighing scales, and a little undercover section of carved wooden beams. The airport manager wears a trilby hat and the people watch the aircraft come in with affection. 'Here come that Charlie now,' they exclaim in their strange Caribbean English. A few people left the little aircraft and I climbed aboard. The others had only come to watch or to load on packages. They waved as we took off and then went back, up the steep and amazing road, to their red-roofed homes in the island hills.

There is a story that when the Dutch and the French arrived simultaneously on the island they now call St Maarten, or St Martin, they decided to divide it peaceably – thus it was arranged that a Frenchman and a Dutchman would walk around the coast in opposite directions until they came face to face. All the land within the area walked by the Frenchman would belong to his country and all that circumnavigated by the Dutchman to the Netherlands. They set off, the Frenchman decently supplied with wine and the Dutchman with gin, and eventually met. The Frenchman had covered a greater area, but the Dutchman had found the best harbour and the more accessible countryside with valuable salt ponds. So the island was divided, roughly two-thirds to France and one-third to the Netherlands. It remains today the smallest territory in the world governed by two nations, something that used to be called a condominium until that word came to mean an American apartment and was hideously shortened to 'condo'.

The Princess Juliana Airport is on the Dutch side, however, and the Dutch capital is called Philipsburg; the French capital is Marigot. Despite the two nationalities the people speak mainly English and the local patois called Papiamento, which is a mix of Dutch, Portuguese, Spanish, English and the odd African phrase.

It's a prosperous little place, enjoying its good fortune as a free port and its fine natural accessories, lakes, salt flats, white-sand bays and a brilliant sea, with loaf-shaped mountains looking down on the commercial activity with ancient calm. Its restaurants and shops, in both the small capitals, are a relief after some I had experienced on other Caribbean islands.

There is an inlet called Cay Bay where the great Dutch adventurer Peter Stuyvesant lost his leg in a brush with the Spanish. This was in 1644 when there were strange bedfellows in the Caribbean as the maritime nations decimated the poor Carib Indians and battled each other to seize the best islands. Sometimes nations that were at war in Europe would temporarily ally themselves to fight another foe in the West Indies. On Palm Sunday, 1644, the Dutch, the French (and, it is thought, the English from St Kitts to the south), sailed into the anchorage at Cay Bay under the command of Stuyvesant in his ship the *Blauwe Haan* – 'the Blue Cockerel'. There was no resistance from the Spanish and, after consolidating his positions, Stuyvesant wrote a letter to the occupying commander calling on him to surrender. He then, unwisely, underlined the threat by walking out to the limit of his fortifications and, with his own hands, placed a Dutch banner on his forward battery. The Spaniards fired a single shot hitting the brave Dutchman in the leg. The limb was amputated and thrown into the sea.

All this was before Peter Stuyvesant became governor of the Dutch colony, New Amsterdam, now New York. He died there in 1672 and is buried in St Mark's Church in the Bowery. (His age is given incorrectly in his epitaph. He was sixty at his death, not eighty as stated on the tombstone.)

Over the years the Dutch and the French have rarely quarrelled in their small island. Once when the countries were at war in Europe, an 'army' of sixteen Dutchmen conquered the French side but French sovereignty was later restored. The Dutch side of the island is busier with Philipsburg, three streets wide, stretched along a narrow neck of land between two bulky shoulders. I stayed at the Pasanggrahan, once the seaside guesthouse of the Dutch Governor. A portrait of Queen Beatrix of the Netherlands hangs in the reception hall. The streets in the town all have Dutch names although few people speak the language. The voices all around are English-American and patois. Here, as in many of the West Indian islands, there was once a Jewish colony. The Jews who lived here had probably fled from Brazil. Their tombstones, brought from Europe as ballast in ships, with their Hebrew inscriptions, are to be seen on many of the islands (particularly in Nevis and in the Dutch island of St Eustatius). In Philipsburg are remains of what is thought to be a 300-year-old synagogue – to find it you have to look on the vacant land behind the West Indian Tavern.

The bay off Philipsburg was full of idle white hulls, with a cruise liner lying like a shadow on the misty skyline. Japanese and Korean fishermen work their boats out of the bay here. There is a modern fish factory with ancient cannon and anchors set among its refrigeration plant. Beside the port a silver tank reflects the sun. I took it to be for fuel storage. I was wrong. It was for rum.

The island has a spine of smooth green hills, rounded like men's heads, running beside its salt lakes (an important industry), its bays and its pastures. Most of the farming land is on the French side. Immediately you cross the 'border' – the sign says, *'Bienvenue Partie Française'* but there are no frontier guards or customs officials – you find yourself in a gentler more pastoral setting. The next sign to this welcome, in English, says uncompromisingly 'Keep Your Goats Out'.

There are meadows here, deep and cool like the pastoral lands of France, the Normandy *Bocage* perhaps, trees in clumps, streams and low farmhouses. The first village into the French sector is called Orleans. At Cul de Sac, a serene vale ending at the sea, there used to be thriving sugar, tobacco and indigo plantations. Now everything is green and quiet. The village school has the word *Ecole* fashioned in sea-shells on its wall.

It was a sweet day, fine sun, roaming white clouds like islands themselves and, as I drove, segments of the ever-blue sea showing between the hills. Two islets lay offshore, Flat Island and Penal Isle, now both uninhabited but for sheep and goats. Black boulders and black cattle, so similar in size it was difficult to tell them apart, stood in the fields by the sea. Turning inland the hills and then the mountains fold against each other. For such a small island St Maarten looks to have a large interior.

In Marigot, the French capital, an appealing, wooden place, with balconies and unofficial pavements, with a restaurant every few yards, I saw some Black West Indians listening ardently to a cricket commentary from distant Barbados. They said they were from Antigua and cricket, despite the French and the Dutch, was their game. When they could gather two teams they arranged matches in the countryside – exiles enjoying a taste of old times. Baseball and softball are the usual summer games, imported with the American tourists, and soccer is played. The two segments of the island had just played an 'international' match and had drawn one goal each.

But the 'money' sport is cock-fighting. It is legal and popular in St Maarten. I watched a farmer with two of his fighting cocks, pampering them like pets, and at La Savannah, just beyond Marigot, I saw the dusty arena where the men in the cock-fighting season gather to watch the bloody matches.

St Maarten or St Martin is flourishing. A staple industry of the island has always included smuggling and it remains increasingly so today, including the trafficking of drugs. There are Mercedes and Mustang convertibles in the streets, the shops are resplendent with goods, and the sun shines on some of the finest beaches and most lofty scenery in the Caribbean.

Evening came down with much exaggeration – soft light, a finger of wind on the water, boats nudging each other in the swell, music drifting. I looked out to sea, and thought that still perhaps, somewhere out there, were the bones of Peter Stuyvesant's leg.

The small French colony of St Barthélemy is one of the most delicious islands in the whole of the West Indies. To reach it is another adventure in a bouncing aircraft but it's worth every air pocket and every bruise (I failed to tighten my seat belt sufficiently and received a lump on my head to prove it). From St Maarten it is a flight of only a few minutes, but on the approach to St Bart's, as the isle is known, the pilot seems to take utter leave of his senses and aims the nose of the aircraft at an escarpment of rocks. Nervous shouts rise from passengers who have never before made the flight, increasing as the plane abruptly rears and leaps across the top of the plateau like a hunter over a fence. Then if front of you the runway rolls out like a white carpet to the sea. The French call it the *Aérodrome la Tourmente*, and it is well named.

Once there, however, all is delight. Two little huts, one labelled, 'Immigration' and the other, 'Merchandises', make up the airport buildings. A wind-split tricolour flies above them and the luggage is conveyed on a squeaky handcart officially marked 'Air Guadeloupe'. After St Maarten everything is blessedly small-town. Around the airfield the island hills rise green and sunny and there is the inevitable floating aroma of French cooking.

St Barthélemy was first seen by Columbus and named after his brother. It has the curious history (although, in the Caribbean, not so curious) of having its main town named after a King of Sweden, and streets with names like the rue de la République and the rue Général de Gaulle (sometimes with the old Swedish name attached), and the exquisite harbour called the Port de Plaisance.

The island was one of Sweden's rare ventures in colonialism in the eighteenth century, when the capital was named Gustavia. The people, however, were French colonists from Britanny and Normandy, and were astonished to hear one day that they had been traded to Sweden by Louis XVI in exchange for berthing and warehouse facilities in the Swedish port of Göteborg. The Swedes renamed the capital (previously Carenage) after the King, declared it a free port and proceeded to make their fortunes.

In those adventurous days trade, piracy, and war went hand in hand in the Caribbean. Off the neighbouring Dutch island of St Eustatius, the English Admiral Rodney captured 150 loaded ships, and a further forty out to sea. He sacked the bulging warehouses, and sent his booty, worth four million pounds, back to England. Within a day's sailing of home the ships were captured off Brest and the loot reappropriated by the Dutch and the French.

Gustavia managed to avoid such mishap, although hurricane and fire ravaged the town. The Swedes stayed for almost a hundred years before handing back the island to the French.

It is astonishing to drive around St Barthélemy and to realize the complete Frenchness of it. The people are white-skinned with blue eyes, and the language is entirely Gallic. Only a few Black families live there for slavery was never the terrible industry that cruelly prospered in other islands. At Corosol, a village by the sea, the older women still wear the *calèche*, the white pleated bonnet of northwestern France. They are very shy and run to hide at the sight of a stranger, particularly if he happens to have a camera, as I did. Their days in their tidy, hamlet village on its hill by the ocean are spent in making fine straw baskets and hats which they send to Gustavia for sale. The people of the rural places are quiet and devout. On the Eve of All Saints they light candles on the graves in the island cemeteries; it is a ghostly sight.

The island has wonderful curly roads with ancient stone walls dividing the fields. There are steep – often hilarious – hills which joyfully give out onto vast white and blue panoramas of sea or bright green plains illuminated with sunshine. Houses are red-roofed and scattered among the greenery. The oldest homes are like red huts and are still to be seen, shyly concealed, in places close to the sea with a boat drawn against the shingle, a few chickens and goats about the door. What a place for a castaway.

Gustavia is the best sight of all. An oblong inlet between green headlands with toothy off-shore islands, it comes into sight from the hill road, like a revelation. When I arrived it was late afternoon and the sun was going home. There was a warm yellow light on the sea and on the town. The many masts caught its final gleam and the hulls of the anchored vessels reflected the sunset from the water. The last of the original Swedish families here died about two years ago, but there are those who have arrived since, their names above bars and shops, doubtless thinking, on a winter's day, how different the weather must be in their far homeland.

Gustavia, being French, is a blessedly civilized place. On many occasions I have felt that although I enjoy being a traveller in out-of-the-way places, roughing it is something else. This explorer likes a glass of wine and a good dinner. Here there was choice enough and I found myself in the warm breeze of the evening in excellent French company sitting on a terrace high over the harbour.

The place was called L'Hibiscus and was set just below an ancient wooden clock tower which chimed twice, five minutes before the hour and five minutes after. Steeples, red roofs and flowered streets led down towards Gustavia's purple harbour. It was as comfortable an evening as you would wish to discover anywhere.

Henri, who runs the place and was once an international soccer player, pretended he had not noticed the clock struck each hour twice. He certainly did not know the reason. As it struck seven once and then again, he shrugged a Gallic shrug and said, 'That, monsieur, is just a crazy clock.'

You feel that it will go on being a crazy clock for ever. Nobody is going to get around to putting it right. Not on St Barthélemy.

SABA situated latitude 17°30′ N and longitude 63°15′ W; area 5 sq. m (13 sq. km); population approx. 1,000; The Netherlands. ST MAARTEN latitude 18°10′ N and longitude 63°10′ W; area 20 sq. m (52 sq. km); population approx. 4,500; France. ST BARTHELEMY latitude 17°55′N and longitude 62°50′W; area 37 sq. m (96 sq. km); population approx. 6,000; The Netherlands

St Kitts and Nevis
First of the Caribbees

In the little isle of Nevis . . . I have remained a good time, to gather
wood and water, to refresh my men and replenish stocks. Also to hang
two mutineers.

CAPTAIN JOHN SMITH of Virginia

It was Sunday morning on St Kitts and in every hamlet along the coastal road
the people were singing in church; Anglican, Wesleyan, Methodist, Catholic,
all at the height of their voices and enthusiasm, through doors and windows
(wide open as if they were singing too), so that the hymns sounded unbroken
along the seashore. At Middle Island Village the Church tower was toppled
by an earthquake in 1974 and remains a ruin, but inside the congregation was
letting fly with such verve that the stranger feared for the rest of the
building.

Old Town Road, a nearby wooden village, has the distinction of being the
first settlement established by Europeans in all the Caribbean. Not that you
would know it. The landing beach where Sir Thomas Warner and his
colonists came ashore on 28 January 1623 is marked only by a public
bathhouse and a rusty cinema, with a few rough boats drawn up on the
scrubby beach. St Kitts may have been the Queen of the Caribbees at one
time but no one shouts about it. The island which, some say, Columbus
called after himself, is a brooding little place, half-overlooked. Some say they
like it to be that way.

Perhaps its image is not improved by the fact that the peak which
dominates it is called Mount Misery. It looked indeed doleful from the plane,
clouds like winding sheets threading the peaks, the sea wind-blown, the
town of Basseterre lying beside an all but empty bay, a downcast January
evening, 360 years to the day after Sir Thomas Warner's arrival. It almost
made me feel at home.

The next morning was ragged with a sun looking like lemon curd pushing
its way through skirts of lugubrious cloud. But below my room an apparently
cheerful cage bird whistled one tune – 'Colonel Bogey' – and Radio Paradise
brought reggae music to the room. Brown pelicans roamed the bay like lost

dogs, every now and then belying their awkwardness by flopping down from twenty feet or so into the choppy water and emerging with a fish in their bill.

The previous evening Big Mac had appeared with his band, a little knot of nondescript musicians playing quaint instruments, more or less together. They grouped tightly, pointing inwards like plotters. A tiny man squeaked on a penny whistle and a long fellow blew down what appeared to be a neon light tube, but turned out to be a roll of plastic, an instrument called a bass pipe, which makes a bass sound (and is rudely called an ass pipe). Big Mac plunked a minuscule ukulele at the front.

'They've had offers from all over the world,' muttered Tony Meston, a pilot with Leeward Islands Air Transport, keeping a serious face. Mac, a formidable Black man, came by and they shook hands. 'Have you told the Vienna Opera House that you can't make it this year?' asked the young Englishman. Mac shrugged. 'We had no practice,' he said.

Meston is another islandman. He lives with his wife in Antigua and dreams of Bembridge, Isle of Wight. 'It's the long evenings in England in summer I miss most,' he said, 'sitting outside the pub.' He was flying Britten-Norman Islanders and Tri-landers between the little Leeward Islands, a case of *déjà vu* for years previously he had worked for the company and had helped to build the aircraft he now pilots. The tough and tiny planes, which have carried me to many islands, are flown to the West Indies from the Isle of Wight via Scotland, Iceland, Greenland, Newfoundland, down the Eastern Seaboard of the United States and then in hops across the Caribbean to Antigua. 'We've just had a new plane delivered with my name written on the side,' he related with some pride. 'It came from England, from the Isle of Wight, and they knew that I would be flying it so they painted my name on the door.'

Big Mac returned and asked if we needed his services any further. I had no objection to the band playing but it turned out that he was also a taxi driver and that is what he meant. If nobody wanted to go anywhere then he was off to the Saturday night service at his church. He went. As he did so he called over his shoulder, 'It was just a scratch band.'

It occurs to me as very odd that Columbus should have named St Kitts after himself but this is the generally accepted story. Certainly it was called St Christopher's and truncated to its present form, but had the time come when Columbus thought he deserved some recognition for all his almost daily discoveries during 1492–3? Or was he running short of names?

It is said he named the neighbouring St Barthélemy after his brother Bartholomew, but it's the prefix of 'Saint' that worries me. Was Columbus looking forward to an even more illustrious future?

No. I believe the *other* story. I believe he named it St Christopher's because, when he peered at the highest peak, he saw that cloud cut it at the neck and it appeared to be carrying another small mountain on its shoulder – just as St Christopher had carried the infant Jesus in the story. I like that much better than the thought of Columbus mumbling, 'It's time I got some recognition for this job.'

Columbus's interest in clouds is borne out on the next island of Nevis. He named it after *las neives*, Spanish for 'the snows', because of the white vapour lying on its peaks.

Mount Misery (no one remembers from where this doleful appellation came) was thus crowned when I made my Sunday journey around the coastal road of St Kitts. Like Tahiti, like Kauai, like many mountainous isles, the only road hems the sea. No one lives in the hills; nothing but goats and howling monkeys.

After Sir Thomas Warner arrived in 1623 at the little beach and walked up the few yards to the site where the cinema now stands, St Kitts underwent the fluctuating invasions and possessions common to most of the Caribbean islands. (I had thought that the rusty gates outside the door of the picture palace, marked Circle Entrance, indicated that it was derelict. It was not. A film called *The Professionals* was showing, a title Sir Thomas would have approved since he was the classic professional colonist.)

Sir Thomas may not have approved of the current somewhat rundown state of his own grave. Approached through a magnificent avenue of royal palms in the grounds of the earthquake-damaged church at Middle Island, he lies in rickety surroundings, the canopy over his tomb as decrepit as an old howdah, the marble stone cracked like a jigsaw and a luxuriant flowering weed growing from where his ancient head must be lying. Poor recognition, you might think, for a man described on the broken stone as 'Lieutenant General of the Caribbees Islands'. He died on 10 March 1648, and the stone entreats the visitor to 'first reed, then weep'. Well, it's not quite that bad, but perhaps someone ought to tidy him up a little.

The coastal villages are haphazard, wooden, with public bathhouses (few of the homes have running water) and the communal wells are inset with a mailbox so that you can post a letter and fill a pail at the same time. In Old Town Road there is a gully that drops through the village from the mountains to the sea. When the crater of Mount Misery floods (the island has eighty-two inches of rain a year) the torrent flows down the slopes and across the ramshackle street so that the people have to take to a bridge especially built for the purpose.

If these places are primitive, and they are compared to, say St Maarten or St Barthélemy, then at least the people lead their own lives and not some life imposed on them by the demands of the tourist. Just to be in the villages is to sense that life is very self-contained there, with its own relationships, jokes, sorrows and excitements. They love their churches (a poster proclaims, 'Another Heaven-sent Gospel Meeting'), their music, their homes and families, their contests of village cricket, and the occasional bottle of Guinness. Halfway Tree Village is, however, noted for its moonshine rum. It's called White Lightning.

It was here that the French and the British frontier was fixed when the two jointly occupied St Kitts in the eighteenth century. At Bloody Point just along the coast they conspired together (a rare alliance) to ambush the original owners, the Carib Indians, and effectively wipe them out.

Such alliances could scarcely be allowed to continue and the two occupants were soon at war again with the British numbering only 800, besieged in the great fortress of Brimstone Hill, with 8,000 Frenchmen trying to winkle them out. Looking at the size of the task even today is to realize that they probably thought it was much more difficult than it proved to be.

Brimstone Hill has been called the Gibraltar of the West Indies, a magnificent defensive rock, dominating the coast and the hills. It rears out of the sky from the flat coastal plain and from the top it is not difficult to believe that you can see half the earth.

It gained its name because of the sulphur fumes which seep through its crust from some place deep in the ground. The British, realizing that since they occupied St Kitts jointly with the French, who were never to be trusted (and more to the point outnumbered them), built the fortress into the rock and sat there watching their fellow occupants of the island moving about below. The building of the foretress started in 1690 and its construction took almost a century.

Unfortunately human frailty often more than cancels out stone walls and when the attack on Brimstone Hill was finally mounted by the French on 11 January 1782, ten large guns with their ammunition, meant for the stronghold, were found conveniently waiting at the foot of the hill and were joyfully seized and used by the attackers. It is reputed that the non-delivery of the guns to the fort had much to do with a group of Englishmen sympathetic to the American rebels at that time waging the War of

Independence against Britain. The French hardly needed encouragement. They had 8,000 troops against 800. The bastion which had taken just short of a century to build surrendered in a month.

The real sacking of Brimstone Hill took place many years later, however, after the British had returned and eventually decided that the stronghold was untenable. The redoubt was simply abandoned and became the prey of vandals and predators. Stone, windows and wood were carried away. So were the guns. A great many ornamental cannons and mortars decorating parks and gardens throughout the Caribbean (and the United States) once had their sights looking out from Brimstone Hill.

Today, however, the great hump has been well restored. From its battlements it looks impregnable. History, and treachery, proved that it was not.

One of the world's shorter scheduled air routes is the six-minute flight from St Kitts to its abutting small island of Nevis. Tony Meston flew the islander down the long peninsula below the main island and across the strait to Nevis, (pronounced 'Nee-vis') forming the dot of the exclamation mark it makes with St Kitts.

The sun was bright, but the wind continued brisk along the coast, although not strongly enough to disturb the tranquillity of clouds on the hills of Nevis, the clouds that gave it its name. There were goats and donkeys grazing just off the runway as the plane touched down at the wayside airport. This was another island Horatio Nelson visited, a place where he discovered fresh water and romance. Nelson's Spring is still bubbling beside the road. It was here, while stationed in Antigua, that he brought his ship to shore and here that he met and married Frances Nisbet, the young widow who lived in a great lonely house on the Montpelier Sugar Plantation.

Fig Tree Church, where they married, stands beside the road now, its nave and churchyard engraved with history, and a notice which welcomes the Tourist With A Clean Smile. Inside, to the left of the door, is the register which Horatio and Fanny signed. Its faded inscription reads, '1787. March 11th. Horatio Nelson of His Majesty's ship *Boreas* to Frances Herbert Nisbet, Widow.' It was a sailor's marriage, as history now knows, giving poor Fanny little happiness. Emma Hamilton was not far over the next horizon.

A mile away at the beautifully named Morningstar Plantation there is a collection of Nelsonia, including a letter written by him, left-handed after he had lost his right. There is also a faded print of the sad Fanny Nisbet and a gruesome little coffin, one of those sold as souvenirs in London after Nelson's death at Trafalgar. Perhaps the most touching exhibit, however, is a grandfather clock which was stopped at a quarter to three on 22 February 1966 – the moment Queen Elizabeth II of England stepped through the door. Florence Abrahams stopped it as a unique and nostalgic memento. Mrs Abrahams later died on a visit to England to seek more Nelson relics for her collection.

Once there was a battle at the estate – poetically called the battle of Morningstar – when 2,000 French troops came ashore to be faced by fifty nervous Nevis militia. It did not last long.

Most of the great sugar plantations, with their round mill houses and their chimneys still standing, like thin ghosts, have been turned into private homes or hotels. The Bath Hotel, however, where thermal springs caused Captain John Smith, on his way to found the Jamestown colony in America, to record that his crew found a 'great poole, where in bathing themselves they found much ease', is no more. The building stands deserted, half derelict, its healing water bubbling unattended, unused.

At the Zetland Plantation I met Richard and Maureen Lupinacci, from a town called King of Prussia, Pennsylvania, acquaintances of Allan Grant, a friend in England who was the expert and commercial brain behind the growth of the philatelic business in St Kitts and Nevis, whose stamps are much prized by collectors. The Lupinaccis had fashioned a delightful resort hotel from the old plantation, with the mill and the odds and ends of the sugar machinery still *in situ*. It was the name that interested me. Zetland is the most northerly county in Britain – the Shetland Islands. Did people from that remote northern place come here as they did to Saba, only a few miles across the Caribbean, to win the freedom to worship as they pleased? It's a tempting thought.

There is no sugar harvest in Nevis now. The island grows coconuts, cotton and breadfruit – which was brought originally from the South Seas. Captain Bligh was on his way to the West Indies with a cargo when the crew of the *Bounty* mutinied. Ginger is grown at a village called Gingerland. The island is a velvet green with flowers lining the roads and the hutted villages where people sit and stare or wave as an occasional car goes by. In the fields there are cattle, each beast with its own attendant white egret, sitting beside it or on its back, picking away the ticks – a good arrangement from the point of view of bird, beast and man.

Jamestown was once the capital of Nevis, but it was smitten with cholera and then washed away by a tidal wave or an earthquake, no one seems quite sure. There are few remnants of its streets now. The new capital, Charlestown, was built not far away – a sunny little town with some lingering curiosities.

It was here that Alexander Hamilton, the poor boy who improved his lot so much that he became one of the Founding Fathers of the United States, was born in a house on the outskirts of the town. All that remains now are a few blocks of stone and a flight of spectral stone steps. Chickens pick their way around the yard.

Hamilton's parents (who were not married) were a Scot, James Hamilton, and a Creole, Rachel Fawcett, a girl who had, at sixteen, been forced into marriage with a Dane. It was, curiously, to the Danish colony of St Croix, in what is now the US Virgin Islands, that Hamilton took his family after becoming an estate manager. Later he went to St Vincent and hardly saw his wife or son again. Rachel died and Alexander was raised by an aunt, worked in a shop on St Croix and, at fifteen, sailed for America where he became a leading rebel against the British and, after Independence, was made Secretary of the Treasury. After such a life he was killed, at fifty, on 11 July 1804, in a duel with Aarron Burr, the Vice President of the United States, at Weehawken, New Jersey.

Another of Charlestown's curiosities is the courthouse which sits on the site of notorious slave auctions. Nineteen Negroes were publicly beaten here in 1810, giving impetus to the slave revolts that eventually resounded through the islands. The slave master on this occasion was one Edward Huggins. Famed as a builder (there is a building company called Huggins in Nevis today) his initials are to be seen over a door at Golden Rock, now a hotel, which he built in 1815. After the construction, Huggins' thanks to his chief stonemason was to incarcerate the poor fellow in a sealed dungeon with a week's food, and then to breezily set sail for England many weeks away. It is said that the hollow blows of the stonemason's ghostly hammer can be heard even now.

In front of the courthouse is a brief triangle of garden, a memorial to the men of Nevis who left their warm unworldly island to die in the trenches of France in World War I. Instead of the traditional piece of artillery – and goodness knows such ordnance is common enough in the West Indies – there is a captured German machine gun, of the sort those brave and probably bewildered islanders had to face in that foreign field.

The third curiosity is the Jewish cemetery. There are also the remnants of a synagogue at the end of a path called the Jews Walk, although the building is now the Charlestown police station. These people had fled from Brazil and found themselves among the Caribbean islands, leaving their traces on several. At one time a fifth of the inhabitants of Nevis were Jews, working in the sugar plantations, and their resting places in the cemetery are marked by stones in Hebrew, Portuguese and English, some dating from 1684.

Nevis lies a little somnolently under its peak and the attendant puff of cloud. It is almost as if its early days in the frantic rush of the sugar trade have tired it. But its life is measured and pleasant, its people calm, kind and devout (there is a church with a Black Christ crucified). It is not solely the natives who enjoy the island's twentieth-century serenity. People from the outside world, from America and Europe, go to find tranquillity in Nevis.

At the airport, where I waited for Tony Meston to pick me up in the islander, were two frail and elderly Americans. They were talking to the airport staff. The old man looked very ill. He had lost an arm and his face was scarred and white, as if he had been in an accident. It was apparent to me that they loved each other dearly. Her arm was about his waist as he took faltering steps. I could see that here was a story, but I could not bring myself to disturb them. 'Here comes the plane,' she whispered to him as the islander hovered and came onto the runway. 'Now we'll go home.' I worried how he would survive any sort of journey, but I need not have. As Tony taxied in she took the old man's arm and led him out – to the exit. Back to the island.

ST KITTS situated latitude 17°18′ N and longitude 62°48′ W; area 65 sq. m (168 sq. km); population approx. 35,000; Britain. NEVIS latitude 17°10′ N and longitude 62°35′ W; area 36 sq. m (93 sq. km); population approx. 9,300; Britain

Antigua
A Tale of Nelson's Bed

. . . port after stormy seas.
EDMUND SPENSER

English Harbour, Antigua, is a fortunate anchorage, located almost privately from the open sea, with high headlands on either side. Even before Nelson's days on the island the British knew they were secure here under the powerfully fortified heights. Standing above the harbour now, looking far down at it and then miles out into the Atlantic, it is easy to appreciate what a prize place it was. British guns pointed in all directions, the look-outs had a splendid horizon and Nelson, when ashore, could sleep soundly in his small bed. Antigua, as it happened, was unique in the Caribbean in those boisterous days. It was never attacked.

Today, walking around Nelson's Dockyard at English Harbour, is to see something of what it was at the end of the eighteenth century. After years of disgraceful neglect, when it was reduced to rubble and weeds, it has been finely restored and is now working as a port and shipyard again.

It is one of the most satisfying places in the West Indies. The serene Admiral's Inn is constructed of stone and brick carried from England as ship's ballast (how many useful things were transported as a make-weight in those days – tombstones, ironwork, paving, cobbles). The inn's beams were once ships' timbers, with the initials and private jokes of sailors long dead visible on them. After a night in a deeply beamed room, with three-foot thick walls, I sat on the terrace at breakfast and watched the many vessels lying in the waterway, with coloured birds in the foliage around me and an Antiguan girl arranging hibiscus in a vase. Considering it was January and I had flown from a London racked by stiff, cold winds, I began to feel extremely pleased.

The birds became, it is true, a minor annoyance. There were tiny bananaquits, finch-like fellows with yellow waistcoats and piercing squeaks, who sat in a line across the backs of neighbouring chairs and took it in turns to make fluttering forays on the butter, milk, sugar, or anything else that could be pecked, except the bread which they left alone. Bread is not very good in Antigua. When another even bigger marauder arrived, they would spit like cats at it. In the end, to gain some peace, I put my table napkin like a flag on top of the coffee pot and that caused some anxiety. I remembered how, years ago, being dive-bombed by gannets and skuas on the isle of Unst in the Shetlands, I walked around feeling very foolish, holding a stick with a handkerchief tied to it. Keeping this aloft, above my head, I must have appeared like the last surrendering soldier from World War II, but it was effective and there was no one in that remote place to laugh anyway.

Strolling in the early sun on Antigua I realized that the boats moored to the wharfs and anchored in the estuary were from the many places I had touched in my long journey around the earth's islands. On their sterns they bore names like Jersey and Guernsey, Bermuda, Nantucket, and one from Capri. It was almost a reunion.

Along the shore West Indian children pretended that the great-armed capstans of Nelson's day were carousels; the satisfying sound of sawing wood came across the sunlight from the mast house where local men still make masts and spars; a stonemason was chipping at the last building in the process of restoration, keeping time with reggae music coming from one of the yachts offshore. Everywhere people seemed to be scraping hulls, painting boards, sewing sails. A pretty girl chopped rust from some ironwork, using a chipping hammer, the same implement I remember my father used for scaling ships' boilers many years ago.

Everywhere the grey stone looked benign and warm. The boat crews said there had been an excess of rain over Christmas and the New Year but there were now only a few cartoon clouds in the sky. Pelicans creaked through the sky and frigate birds, like gigantic slow swallows, cruised. In the shade a group of taxi drivers listened to a cricket commentary and played Warri, a marvellously absorbing game performed with warri nuts and a board with a series of cups in it, beautifully worn with use. We conversed about the cricket and I asked them to explain the Warri game, which they courteously did, leaving me none the wiser. I asked about the earthquake that had struck Antigua in October 1974. The church at Libertia, a village in the centre of the island, still looks decidedly shaky as a result of the earth-tremor. 'That was some excitement,' recalled Winston Thomas, one of the drivers. 'That quake came at six o'clock in the morning. Everybody got out of bed the same time that day.'

The buildings of the dockyards have been excellently restored and put to everyday use, but it seems that some of the smaller relics have been left purposely lying around. The quay, the forecourts of the various establishments, and the small road that winds through the area, are littered with cannon and squat mortars, sitting like wide-mouthed frogs. Guns lie about, sitting up, pointing in a dozen directions, or are buried up to their waists and used as bollards for the mooring ropes of boats. The sturdy columns of what was once the main boathouse and sail-loft march in two ranks into the estuary. It was strange being there, so far from home and yet in such undoubtedly English surroundings. I used to live in Hampshire, near Buckler's Hard, another of Nelson's shipyards, with its reminders of the maritime pomp and greatness of the early 1800s. Nelson's ships were built and repaired there too. For me, being at English Harbour was like being at the landfall of an historical voyage. As if to reinforce the reverie the yacht offshore, which had been playing West Indian music, now reverted stridently to 'Land of Hope and Glory'.

The former Admiral's quarters at the yard, a deliciously cool building, are now a museum. It has some fine model ships, the tracery of their masts and rigging making shadows on the floor, as the sun pours through the ranks of windows. There is a framed proclamation calling for the '. . . royal tars of Old England, if you love your country and liberty, now is the time to show your love, repair all who have a good heart to love their King, country and religion, who hate the French and Damn the Pope, to Lieutenant W. J. Stephens at his rendezvous . . .'

Another enticement promises that those tars who join ship will be provided with, 'bountiful supply of clothing, grog flip and strong beer', not to mention prize money enabling them to 'spend their days in peace and plenty'. It ends with the exclamation 'Huzzaa!' as well it might.

Nelson arrived here as commander of HMS *Boreas* in 1784. There is a record in the museum of him commuting a death sentence on a seaman, William Clark, who was to be hanged from the yardarm for desertion. For his trouble Nelson was admonished by the Admiralty and told that only the sovereign had the power of pardon.

Also in the museum, discovered among the rubble of the old buildings, is a bed, a four-poster said to have been Nelson's own. It had been well restored and placed in a room apart with a somewhat distraught lady figurehead standing outside the door. I mention it now because thereby, as they used to say, hangs a tale, which in good time I will recount.

From the airy summit of Shirley Heights it is easy to comprehend how Antigua remained impregnable when some of the islands in the West Indies changed hands so frequently that it is difficult to trace who occupied them and when. St Eustatius, now firmly Dutch, for example, had no fewer than twenty-two changes of flag in a few turbulent and, inevitably, bewildering years.

Fort Charlotte was the centre-point of the Shirley Heights fortifications, its brow looking over the ocean for many miles. A sentry would only have to turn about and march a few paces for a complete view of Falmouth and English Harbour; another turn would show him Indian Creek and the inlets along the southern coast. Standing there I had no difficulty in looking across miles of apple-green island to the opposite side where the waves of the Caribbean Sea were breaking. Today wandering around the stony ruins is like walking through the remnants of somewhere far more ancient. Arches that might have graced Rome stand against the thick growth of the Antiguan slopes. There are officers' quarters, ammunition stores and gun positions, all now fallen in the sun and lying among peaceful shadows. The real story of Shirley Heights, however, lies in the small meadow-like cemetery where soldiers who died far from home are buried. I saw it from some distance away, a few railed tombs among the grass, and approaching it I found myself in a field that might have been England. The grass was deep and butterflies fluttered about. There were a few unofficial flowers, sweet-smelling weeds and a tangled hedge against a stone wall. Apart from the rusty-railed tombstones, only a handful, there was a plinth with a platoon of names engraved on it, now all but unreadable. The soldiers died not in war but of cholera, dysentery and some of rum-poisoning. The balmy island of today was then far from a health posting. One epitaph tells the poignant tale with stonemason's economy: 'Sacred to the memory of Harriet, the beloved wife of Sergeant Major T. W. Hipkin of Her Majesty's Liverpool Regiment who fell victim to the withering effects of the climate on 28th January, 1851, aged 35 years. The last tribute of her sorrowing husband.' A corner of a foreign field indeed.

How much the villages of this island have changed over the years I do not know but it can only have been a little. The wooden settlements dot the bright green plains of Antigua and sometimes sit among the loaf-shaped hills of its interior. In such a comparatively tight place surrounded by water it is amazing to hear that until a reservoir was constructed in those hills a few years ago there were children who had never seen a boat. It is probably true, for people still tend to walk familiar paths, living out their lives as their fathers and grandfathers have done since they were freed of slavery. I saw a note in a parish baptism register recording the end of that iniquitous era. From a Methodist church it noted, after years of entries which described a child's parents as 'slaves', 'Here endeth all registration in which distinction of civil status is specified, August 1st, 1834, being the glorious day of immediate and entire universal freedom for every human being in Antigua.' What a day that must have been.

Driving through the villages towards St John's, the capital of the island, it is apparent that no one is in a hurry. Weeds grow on the telegraph wires, strangely hanging there like birds' nests. There is always time to sit and stare, or talk, or read the newspaper, or listen to music and the cricket on the radio.

I have mentioned cricket overmuch in my experiences of the West Indies but it is not just because it is the game of my heart, it is part of the life and soul of the British islands. In St John's the prison is located right next to the cricket ground where the big matches are played. Was that part of the punishment, I wondered, to be locked up and to hear the cries of the great crowd as sixes are struck or wickets taken? 'Not at all,' a St John's man said. 'When the big games are on, the prisoners, they sit up on the roof. It's the best seat you can get, man!'

When A. G. MacDonnell wrote his famous and funny book *England Their England* he noted that there was a singular breed of man to be found in odd corners of the world, building machines or bridges or such things, or taking them apart – the British engineer.

Wally Smith, a cherubic man from the north of England whom I met in Antigua, was one of that breed. He had been an engineer in all sorts of places: in Africa, in South America, aboard merchant ships, returning home a couple of times a year to see his wife and play a few rounds of 'civilized golf'. He was in Antigua 'running in' a new power station. He was a cheerful and (although perhaps he would hardly admit it to himself) quietly poetic man. We were watching the pelicans patrolling the harbour at St John's, when he said, 'Saddest thing I've ever seen, I think, was in South America. Some freak thing had happened to the sea, the tides had got messed up or something, and suddenly there were no fish left in the pelicans' feeding-grounds. The poor things ended up walking around the town, drooping and dusty like old, begging men, looking for scraps.'

Wally and I had partaken of a few cordials one evening and at two o'clock he dropped me off outside the Admiral's Inn at English Harbour. He drove away and I climbed in through a tight little door into the hotel. All was silent and a shade ghostly. Lamps glimmered but there was no one around – nor was there a key in my pigeon hole behind the reception desk. I am often absent-minded to the point of eccentricity and I thought I must have left my key in my room which was in an annex on the waterfront. I walked across the moonlit grounds but my door was firmly locked. After going back to the lobby and failing to raise anybody who might help I went out into the dockyard again – and there saw before me the museum. And in the museum, as I had seen only that day, was a fine four-poster – Nelson's bed!

If it had not been for the aforementioned cordials and the fact that I was desperately fatigued I might have thought twice, but I didn't. Mooching around the side of the museum I perceived that the old shutters, held with a single swivelling bar of wood, could be opened quite easily by the insertion of a stick. It took only a minute – and there was the illustrious four-poster standing in the moonbeams. I climbed over the sill and carefully and quietly stretched myself on the counterpane and slept.

Nelson was a short man, for my feet dangled over the bottom, but it was not a bad night's sleep in the circumstances. No ghosts walked. Or if they did they must have been disappointed because I did not wake up until the Caribbean birds were whooping and whistling in the trees.

ANTIGUA situated latitude 17°3′ N and longitude 61°48′ W; area 108 sq. m (280 sq. km); population approx. 73,000; Britain

St Thomas and St John
A Visit to Two Virgins

There were so many islands I scarce knew to which one I should go.
CHRISTOPHER COLUMBUS

Travelling to St Thomas and then St John, in the United States Virgin Islands, is to visit two different ages in the same day. Three miles of blue but boisterous Caribbean and many years of time separate them and the arrangement appears to suit both.

The islands, with the third member of the family, St Croix, lie forty miles east of Puerto Rico, the first in the long rainbow of small places that curves between and separates the Atlantic and the Caribbean Sea – what in the roaring days of history was known as the Spanish Main.

Drake hid his ships among the hundred isles of the archipelago, loitering in what is called today Drake's Passage, and pouncing on the fat treasure galleons plodding home to Spain with the loot of South America in their holds. The superb natural harbour on St Thomas was his base as it became for privateers and freebooters through the centuries. Captain Kidd and Blackbeard the pirate were familiar with the tides, creeks and inlets.

Today the deep harbour town is known as Charlotte Amalie – surely the most felicitous name for a port anywhere in the world. It was called after the Consort of King Christian V of Denmark, for from 1666 the Virgin Islands were a lucrative colony of Denmark. It was not until 1917 that the United

States, seeking a barricade to protect its interests in the Panama Canal, purchased them for the sum of $25 million. Now the Stars and Stripes, the white cross of Denmark and the banner of the Virgin Islands fly side by side in St Thomas, although the presence of the Danish flag is nothing more than an acknowledgment of the past and a tourist attraction.

Flying over the islands is a scenic experience for they spread, velvet, hilly, lying among turquoise shoals and channels. In the distance the British Virgin Islands rise in the form of the broad back of Tortola, but St Thomas leaves you in no doubt that it is American, even if with European undertones.

American, though, in quite a small-town way. I had half expected a concrete city like Honolulu, the buildings trying to outstand the mountains, and to see the sprightly red roofs of Charlotte Amalie lying among the green below was reassuring.

Along the waterfront the traffic was solid in the sunshine. A police siren squealed. After journeying through the quiet islands of the Caribbean I knew I was back in the real world.

The town, however frantic (it's a free port and the streets are thick with tourists buying cheaply things they would never buy at home), has its past to thank for its charm. Stone warehouses, with their arched entrances, their fine door carvings and their cool interiors, have been converted into shops and arcades. Where the loot of pirates and traders was once stored side by side (the port was always ready to turn a blind eye on irregularities providing it profited by them) are now display counters.

It's a fine place to walk about though, for its streets and alleys remain full of character, courtyards and cuttings. The great warehouses were bisected by broad, short avenues, where trees gave respite from the sun. Palm Passage and others remain, cooled by fronds and branches, with restaurant tables set beneath them. In one of the courtyards two English girls, twins Irene and Geraldine Carr, run a restaurant (called the Twins) where they serve steak-and-kidney pudding, Lancashire hot pot and roast beef and Yorkshire pudding, much to the mystification and frequently to the delight of Americans.

Charlotte Amalie was once a town of 'ladder streets', steps climbing up into its three hills, the trio known to sailors as the Foretop, Main and Mizzen-mast, for from the sea they look like sails. Some of these cut steps remain, joining the roads that travel on the flanks of the uplands. I climbed one, known as the Ninety-Nine Steps, to arrive at my hotel, called the 1829, an endearing and extraordinary place built by a French sea captain named Lafayette in the year that it now uses as its name. His initials A.L. were worked into the beautiful ironwork of my balcony overlooking the breathtaking harbour. A three-masted schooner lay poetically offshore and bougainvillaea and hibiscus cascaded over the walls and railings around. Outside the door was a machine gun, a novelty on wheels, dating I imagine from the Spanish-American war and coming from Puerto Rico or Cuba.

The house was built in Spanish style around a courtyard, with tiled steps and flowered landings. It was a good place for drinking and playing backgammon. The owner, Vernon Ball, would play anyone of a good standard. He was world champion in the 1970s.

Below the Ninety-Nine Steps is a small park where slaves were once auctioned, for St Thomas was the biggest slave market in the West Indies in the early part of the nineteenth century. Now, alongside a full-sized replica of the American Liberty Bell, Black schoolchildren were dancing to rowdy radios. A moustachioed bust of King Christian of Denmark sat disembodied above it all, not looking particularly approving.

Sometimes as many as six cruise liners a day lie in or just off the port, bringing their eager passengers to the even more eager shopkeepers. One morning I saw them approaching one after the other, like battleships of old advancing in line-ahead. A noisy seaplane split the everyday cacophony of the place at intervals, rising to make the forty-mile journey to St Croix, the larger but quieter brother of St Thomas.

Much mention is made in Charlotte Amalie of the Red Fort, a Danish construction on the waterfront, the hue of raspberry ice-cream. That it has history is certain, for malefactors have been tried and imprisoned there for many years and it still has cells in use (some for prisoners, some as a museum). It looks rather a reduced fortress now marooned by honking traffic. Its clock, which has stopped, is the only still and silent thing around.

Its red walls, however, do add a startling background to the bright yellow engines of the Charlotte Amalie Fire Brigade. The firemen were grouped outside, around an ornamental cannon, as if awaiting a somewhat different fire order. They have a sign over their station, almost like a pub sign, of a dependable-looking rescuer carrying a child from a blaze.

In this maritime town, in 1830, was born Camille Pissarro, the father of Impressionist painting. His parents, Spanish Jews, worshipped in the synagogue which still shines its lamp at the back of the town. Today the synagogue (the second oldest in the Western hemisphere) preserves the ancient custom of having its floor scattered with clean sand, marking the flight over the desert of the Israelites out of Egypt. Pissarro was born Jacob Pizarro; the boy worked, like Alexander Hamilton, also to find fame, in a

Virgin Islands shop, this one his father's store in Charlotte Amalie. His parents are buried in the Jewish cemetery and some of his paintings are hanging in Government House, once the Danish Colonial Council building now the US Governor's residence. It is only a short walk away from the synagogue where the shopkeeper and his wife went to worship.

Of all the multi-nationalities who knew St Thomas, one minority group settled in quietly but firmly more than a century ago – French people from St Barthélemy Island a few miles to the southeast. They left their isle when it was summarily handed to Sweden by urban politicians in far-off Paris, and sailed to St Thomas where they remain. They speak a Norman-French that would be recognizable in the English Channel Islands. They live by fishing and selling straw-work to tourists, as do the French people of Corrosol on St Barthélmy. They wear peaked *chapeaux* made of straw. Their little enclave is officially called Frenchtown, but it also answers to Cha-Cha Town for the cha-cha is the name of their special hat.

While waiting for the ferry from Red Hook on the eastern edge of St Thomas I sat in the sun and watched the somnolent activity around the odd jetty. What looked like a World War II landing barge came in from one of the out-isles and discharged a truck and a man on a donkey. At the jetty men were loading a stubby cargo boat. The consignment was entirely alcoholic, crate after crate and cask after cask. The men sweated in the mid-morning warmth. 'If that sinks the fishes are going to be drunk for a month,' I mentioned to one of the loaders. He smiled, a slow one that moved carefully across his face. 'Just refuelling,' he answered. 'Just refuelling.'

The ferry arrived and set off again jauntily from the inlet, clearing the protecting capes and then bouncing and bounding over long humps of blue sea that came straight from the Atlantic to meet the Caribbean. St John was always near, a pyramid island, tree-coated, a collar of beaches and a few buildings like squares of paper against the green.

We were at sea only twenty minutes and then we eased into a harbour and an island so unlike St Thomas that it could have been in another far-distant age and ocean.

Cruz Bay village, with its wooden jetty and its beach, idled beneath its trees, a definite Saturday-morning look about it. It was Tuesday. I walked ashore and felt the pleasure of the place come gradually over me. A few wooden buildings, a café, a shop and a wonderful lopsided green construction like a beached Noah's Ark bearing the legend 'United States Immigration And Naturalization Service'. It set the tone for the island.

With a couple from Montana, who showed me photographs of their children, their cattle and a brown bear who had called at their door, I boarded an open toast-rack truck and set out to explore St John. For a small place it is full of history, from the arrival of Columbus in the channel that divides it from Tortola in the British Virgin Islands, through to Drake and a pride of pirates; to battles between the French, the Danes and the British, who then became allies to crush a rebellion of the slaves.

Columbus, gazing about at the many islands, called them the Virgins in honour of St Ursula and her 11,000 virgin followers. Drake provisioned and armed his ships for his final battle, his failed assault on the Spanish in Puerto Rico, and the pirates sportingly buried a large treasure on Norman's Island where it was uncovered recently.

After the red roofs among the green of Cruz Bay there is little of St John that is not bay-forest, beautiful beaches, silent coves and curling hills. It has become a US National Park through the efforts and the money of the Rockefeller family.

There are 3,000 people on St John, compared with 45,000 each on St Thomas and St Croix. Here, in the wooded sunshine, the zebra butterfly, the wild donkey and the mongoose (introduced in the sugar days to kill the rats) live together with the golden orb spider whose web is as strong as a fish net. Orchids, hibiscus, the oyster plant, the lipstick flowers and the flamboyant bloom together with the yellow-trumpeted Ginger Thomas, the emblem flower of the Virgin Islands. Nests of termites, as large and round as footballs, bulge from trunks. The bay tree casts its shade and so does the manchineel, whose fruit is poison and whose sap, which drips from its branches, burns the skin. Its 'death apple' killed some of Columbus's men.

Limes grow by the sea at Lameshur, a Danish version of Limeshore, called so by the British seamen who came there to eat the fruit as a precaution against scurvy (which is why they were first called Limeys). The old Danish roads across St John are still favoured footpaths and go deep into and over the top of the island where there are meadows alive with blue morning glory.

St John, however, for all its sweetness, has an unpleasant past. It was here that the slaves imported by the Danish West Indies and Guinea Company (Guinea being in effect, Africa) were first landed to be 'acclimatized' before being transhipped to sugar plantations on St Croix and St Thomas. The shadow of this tragedy still lurks in the sunlit ruins of the

Annaberg estate – the tight slave houses, the mill, the dungeon, the sugar crusher and the spirit crusher, which had a grim double-entendre. A contemporary account relates, 'Slave auctions were the most exciting events of any month. When the slaver entered port, the white inhabitants rushed to the water's edge and took to boats in order to get a preview of the living cargo . . .'

The inevitable rebellion flared in November 1733. The slaves marched and overcame their guards and their owners. It took months and a combined force of Danes, British and French soldiers to subdue them.

In the schoolyard at Cruz Bay, after returning from those haunted ruins at Annaberg, I watched the descendants of those slaves, infant children, hilariously trying to play volleyball with a White teacher and a solitary White boy. In the end the rebellion was worth it.

Evening came down with its customary spectacle on the harbour at Charlotte Amalie. The flying-boat was pulled out of the water for the day, the liners trooped out obediently, their lights joining the sunset, a honky-tonk piano sounded from a bar somewhere in the streets. Lying flat out on a bench by the harbour was a tramp; a real tramp, whiskers out of control, battered hat, two coats, shoes open in jagged grins, trousers which looked as if they had exploded at the bottoms. Across his chest was a plastic shopping bag with the names Rio de Janeiro, New York, Paris, Vienna. Another travelling man.

Well, as for this traveller, I was going home. At the airport next morning, boarding my flight, I saw a woman carrying five cotton bags in each of which was a live and complaining chicken. At security the metal detector was passed solidly over the bags and their owner permitted through. I smiled at the security lady and nodded at the bags. She sniffed. 'She from St Croix,' she said, as if that explained everything. Perhaps it did.

ST THOMAS situated latitude 18°22′N and longitude 64° 57′ W; area 28 sq. m (72 sq. km); population approx. 45,000; USA. ST JOHN latitude 18°22′ N and longitude 64°47′ W; area 20 sq. m (52 sq. km); population approx. 3,000; USA

EUROPE

Isles of an island. Vlacherna and Pondikonisi, Corfu.

Gotland and Bornholm
Treasures and Battles

> We have this treasure
> in earthen vessels.
> *II Corinthians, Chapter 4 verse 7*

The world's most surprising treasure island is Gotland, the Swedish island in the Baltic Sea. No palm trees and pirate coves here, but lavish finds of silver, gold and ornaments – the majority of them emanating in the Mediterranean, Asia Minor and even riches from the Caliph's Palace in Baghdad.

A sturdy race of merchant-adventurers inhabited this northern, green island in the Middle Ages and they reached the warm lands of the Near East in their ships, but not by taking the long and dangerous route around the outskirts of Europe. They crossed the Baltic, entered the Russian rivers and followed them down to the Black Sea and to Constantinople, the gateway to the East. The Volga, the Don and the Dneiper rivers were their trade routes, pioneered by the Vikings before them. The Russian cities of Kiev and Smolensk were established as trading centres by these northern nomads.

Gotland – today a summer-holiday island for Scandinavians – was once an independent state, a market place for Arctic traders who sold skins for Eastern gold and jewellery. It is littered with chambers and tombs dating from the Bronze Age through to the dark mediaeval times. In these tombs and in secret caches have been found amazing treasures.

In Stockholm Museum there is exhibited the great treasure uncovered in 1881 at Dune Farm, Dalhem, in the centre of the island. Here are cups and spoons and bowls of silver, filigree gold plates, gold coins minted for Moroccan princes, magnificent belt ornaments and an Oriental drinking cup of thirteenth-century silver.

To date there have been almost six hundred separate finds of treasure in Gotland. School children playing in a quarry in 1936 uncovered a cache of 2,600 Arabian coins, which ranged over two hundred years of Baghdad caliphs, and were probably concealed by some successful merchant returning from the East in the tenth century. At Asarve, on the southwest coast of Gotland, another hoard of silver ornaments was found, these the product of smiths in central Russia, on the Volga trade route.

At the fishing village of Holm yet another find of silver coins was made, this time Swedish in origin, from the reigns of Charles XI and XII. They were said to have come from the wreck of a ship carrying pay for soldiers. In 1963, in the bleak area of Gotland known as Havor, among some Viking age graves and the remnants of fortifications, was discovered a storage jar containing Roman wine ladles and strainers and a sumptuous gold ring, from the Crimea. These can be seen today in the island museum at Visby.

Across the grey Baltic lies the Danish island of Bornholm where three years after the Battle of Trafalgar, Nelson's flagship, HMS *Victory*, refitted at Chatham Dockyard, became engaged in a campaign that brought her somewhat less glory.

It was not overwhelmingly surprising that the British fleet failed to record any sort of victory because from the days of the Vikings, through years of piracy and invasions, the Bornholmers had become used to attack. They built great round churches, which are the island's pride today, with walls like bastions. The roundness was designed, it was said, to give the Devil nowhere to hide, but the practical uses were more convincing. At the first sign of attack the population would barricade themselves in the huge upper rooms of the churches (taking cows and goats with them) and stay there until their enemy had departed. They built their windmills on wheels so that they could be removed the moment a marauding ship was sighted.

Bornholm (whose migrants are said to have settled in France and named Burgundy after their island home) is nearer to Sweden than Denmark. The Swedes have not let this go unnoticed. One attempted invasion, so the legend goes, was thwarted when a dog belonging to the Swedish King picked up an invasion plan from his desk and obligingly dropped it at the feet of a gardener who happened to be Danish, and who quickly alerted his own King.

In October 1808, at the behest of the King of Sweden, their ally, a British fleet led by the formidable HMS *Victory*, approached Bornholm. The fleet was under the command of Sir James de Saumerez, who instead of attacking, believing that Bornholm was heavily garrisoned, lay far out to sea and contented himself with bombarding the off-lying islets of Christiano and Graesholm, the latter uninhabited. The ships were so distant that the guns on the Danish island could not reach them. The only casualties among the defending troops were two wounded who had tried to fire a long-range mortar at the British ships which split in two, plus six Swedish prisoners who were playing cards when a cannon ball from their British allies landed among them.

The British fleet sailed away and left Bornholm in peace. Today the defending cannon which never fired can still be seen and on Christiano the soldiers' barracks have been converted into a main street for the village. The battle that never took place is remembered as a notable victory.

GOTLAND situated latitude 56°50′–58° N and longitude 18°30′–19°E; area 1,167 sq. m (3,022 sq. km); population approx. 54,000; Sweden. BORNHOLM latitude 55°5′N and longitude 14°41′E; area 227 sq. m (589 sq. km); population approx. 50,000; Denmark

Ameland
A Touch of Winter

Lord, Thou hast given me a cell
Wherein to dwell,
A little house, whose humble roof
Is weather proof.
ROBERT HERRICK

In winter, in the deep and bitter days, the shallow sea between the mainland of Holland and the low Frisian Islands freezes and the daily ferry boat has to be preceded by an ice-breaking tug. At this time of year the very air is gaunt, trees turn to iron, solitary birds cross the muslin sky, and the islands are beneath snow and silence.

People in distant days used to pull their boats from the water, drive their livestock into barns, and hibernate, sleeping in beds set into warm cupboards in their cosseted houses. It was not until the ice had cracked and melted, the island fields had greened, and the flowers and springtime birds appeared, that life began again.

Standing in one such house, in the village of Hollum on Ameland, one of the middle islands of north Friesland, you could imagine how they lived. The house had belonged to a seventeenth-century Frisian whaling captain. When he came home from the ocean he hung an anchor from an upstairs window to announce his presence and settled in for the winter. The fires were carefully fed, for wood was precious, and no method was neglected that could conserve the domestic warmth. The bed for the commander and his wife in the wall cupboard was like those I had seen in some Scottish islands but much shorter. 'These people,' explained my guide, 'slept sitting up because they feared that if they lay down the blood would rush to their brains and they would surely die.'

They were, however, more realistic in other matters. There was a shelf at the bottom of the cupboard for their baby and another for the chamber pot. When they were all settled the commander said goodnight to his wife, they kissed the baby and then closed the cupboard until the morning.

The Frisian archipelago runs in a straggle along the Netherlands shore into Germany and then, after a long stretch of sea, is continued up the northward coastline to the Danish border. The most westerly is the largest, Texel, throughout history an important maritime defence-work and harbour. From the port of Den Helder I watched, from the point called Land's End, the coming and going of ships out to the island, lying low and white, like a grin on the horizon. The next island eastwards is Vlieland, where *La Lutine*, the legendary treasure ship, lies sunk. She was carrying money to pay British troops occupying Texel during the war in 1779 against France and Holland, and bullion valued at more than a million pounds, bound for Hamburg.

In tempestuous weather she was caught between Vlieland and Terschelling, the next of the Frisian group, and was lost. Only one man survived the wreck and he died before he could tell his tale.

Over the years there have been many salvage attempts on *La Lutine* but only two have yielded anything. The Dutch, soon after the disaster, succeeded in recovering ninety gold and silver bars and in 1860 another hundred bars were brought to the surface together with the ship's bell and rudder. The latter were taken to Lloyds of London where the rudder can be seen today, fashioned into a unique table, and the Lutine Bell, hung in its cupola, is still rung to give news of a loss at sea.

Beyond Ameland is the island of Schiermonnikoog, a wild place of dunes and drifts; further east still the final island, Rottumeroog, has only one house and looks across a watery frontier to the West German island of Borkum.

It was not quite winter when I journeyed to Ameland, but the year was venturing towards it and a wind chafed across the low sea. The ferry was like a large and cheerful bumble-bee, round nosed, yellow and black. It came into a solitary jetty a few miles west of the little red-roofed town of Holwerd. We set off across the short sea in the early evening, with the daylight seeping away and the ship guided by an odd grove of thin, dead saplings thrust into the mud only a few feet down. This reached far out into the dim sea and the vessel followed it until the jetty of Ameland was in sight.

Seemingly homeless birds sat on the shoals, waiting for a bed perhaps, and a formation of black and white geese droned across the dying sky. A cormorant dived near the jetty as if specially carrying out the performance for arriving visitors. There were few people on the boat, a clutch of ornithologists with their travelling eyes and thick clothes and some Ameland people returning from a visit to the mainland, peering out, as islanders always do, to spot familiar landmarks from the sea.

The island has four villages and I spent the evening beside a high fire in a small hotel at Nes, the capital settlement, in the entertaining company of two North Sea gasmen who had been working offshore. Tom and Caspar, both Dutchmen, had been sailors and we talked of the places of the world we knew, and we were eventually joined by a young man from Dublin who runs a restaurant in West Berlin. 'I come over here to Ameland to get a few days' peace and quiet,' he said.

It was a comfortable place. In the dining-room, where I had as good a *Bamijoreng* as you would get in Bali (the cook came from the former Dutch East Indies), was a piano and, standing against it, a fine dark cello. At weekends a pianist and a man who played the cello went in and everybody had a singsong. Tom described to me the steely days of winter when the sea froze. There had been a plan to build a great dyke joining each of the Frisian Islands to the next from Texel to Rottumeroog, much like the amazing damming of the Zuider Zee, but the ecologists and other environmentalists had succeeded in bedevilling the scheme. In a low country like Holland where the land and the sea are lip to lip people are cautious about up-ending nature. 'They do not like modern windmills,' Tom said. 'The old windmills turn silently but the streamlined things they build today make a terrible noise. Some think it is better to be without the cheap power.'

There has been little change in the families of the islands since the days when Ameland was an independent country (it was neutral during Cromwell's war against the Dutch). 'Many people here are called Brouwer and Bruins,' said Casper. 'Six out of every ten men in the crew of the ferry have those names.' The old, independent flag of two crescent moons and six horizontal bars, blue and yellow, still flies in the villages.

That night there was true island weather, a rattling storm of rain and wind, the sort of night when the deeper one's bed is the better. It was like being in a typhoon at sea, except I was spared the heaving of the ship.

By daybreak the ill wind had gone on its way, leaving a washed-out sky. I went down to the little port near Ballum, now virtually disused and the last resting place of some old forlorn Frisian ships. The harbour looked more of a wreck than the ships. Its moribund jetty was crumbling, the sea ate at the planks, and all that moved there were a few gulls. Even the village from which the harbour takes its name is half a mile inland – as if it has edged away on the quiet.

Within the sea-dykes that rise about it like a rim, the miniature countryside of Ameland is green and pastoral, at least until the dead eye of winter settles balefully upon it. Frisian cattle graze in meadows below a fine nineteenth-century windmill called De Phoenix, performing its silent gymnastics in the North Sea breezes, and a lighthouse, standing like a tall football player in a red-and-white striped jersey.

Beyond the westernmost village of Hollum are fields, adjoining the sea, the home of the powerful horses trained to launch the Ameland lifeboat – the only lifeboat in the world then that used real horsepower for its launching. Ten horses, two pulling the carriage of the boat along the lanes, and eight to pull it into the waves, were used, summoned in an emergency by a farmer furiously blowing a whistle. They knew the call and galloped to their stations. The lifeboat, housed in the village, was tugged to the shore as quickly, or even faster, as any tractor.

On 14 August 1979, an abrupt North Sea storm caught a German yacht in difficulties off the island and she sent out distress signals. The horses were whistled and harnessed, but then came tragedy. The team of eight that pulled the lifeboat into the pounding sea were drowned by the waves as they sank in the treacherous sand. In vain island men tried to cut them loose from the harness. They died within a few yards of the shore and the whole island grieved. The crew of the yacht was saved.

Today you can walk that duned shore and see, in the marram grass, the grave of the horses. Its gravestone is inscribed and tells of their death with an etching above it. Normally it is a rule that any livestock dying on Ameland must be taken to the mainland for burial or burning in order to keep the island cattle free from the risk of disease. In the case of the horses, however, an exception was made and they are buried on the wave-washed shore, near the place where they lost their lives.

In the cobbled, red-roofed, wide-windowed village of Hollum itself, the house of the whaling commander I mentioned earlier has a garden fence made of whalebones like whitened planks of wood. It is now part of an intimate and delightful museum. Harpoons and drawings of fights against large polar bears, and the heroic death of a whale, surround the stern portrait of Commander Hidde Dirks Kat, an expansive and expensive-looking man in a fur coat and top hat, who was famous as a whaler from this little village to the shores of Labrador in Canada. He may even have been on shouting terms with the whalers whose homes and pictures I had seen on the island of Nantucket off Cape Cod.

The house, its distinctive yellow brick coping denoting that it was the home of a commander, is enclosed and warm, the rooms decorated with blue tiles and the cupboard-beds in one room. Family furniture includes a chair for the baby with a little cubbyhole beneath it where a bowl of hot coals was placed, to keep the infant constantly warm.

There are drawings and photographs of the bone-hard winters that regularly visit this coast; people standing in slightly self-conscious groups on the ice, aircraft and more recently helicopters that have brought relief when the ships could not break through. (The inn at Nes has a photograph of barrels of beer being unloaded from an aircraft that landed on the ice, bringing a look of obvious and happy relief to the faces of the men unloading it.)

In what was the commander's front room is another relic of those frozen days, a boat-like sledge as delicately carved as fretwork, fine enough for a pantomine fairy queen, but once used daily by postmen to bring the mail across the frozen sea. It was last used in 1925. At the back of the sledge is a saddle upon which the man used to sit while a horse whirled him across the ice. What fun it must have been to be a postman!

In the main village of Nes the clock on the square church tower sounds the short day away. The tower is decorated with three dates, marking its various changes and additions – 1664 at the base, 1732 at the top and 1890 over the door. Many of the houses of Nes display dates from the seventeenth and eighteenth centuries and, not abashed, there are several dated 1974 and 1975 as well.

Large grey clouds, like the heads of old men, moved from the sea, casting their shadows over the farms, the fields and the villages, and then voyaging on towards the Dutch mainland. There was a sense of completeness about Ameland, the year was almost over; women had begun to knit, the visitors had gone, even the birdwatchers were now reduced to a few shivering, but patient, souls.

Nowadays the island is not completely cut off in severe weather. Once the storm clears the helicopter will always get through. But there remains in such places an inward instinct; they will always remain islands. The villages of Ameland have their rivalries and their winter joys, one of which is the December night, the Feast of St Nicholas, when the men of the island, reaching back into a dim past, dress in homemade white costumes and white hats and wear sinister masks. These costumes are made by their wearers in dead secret throughout the year so that no one, and especially no woman, will know who is beneath the disguise. On the Eve of St Nicholas the men roam abroad, in their own village and others, drinking and dancing and taking advantage of their disguise. When I asked at what age these male frolickings were permitted I was told that in the village of Hollum it was a rule that a boy had to be twelve years old before he could partake, whereas boys from the eastern part of the island wore their costumes as soon as they could make one for themselves.

In the village of Buren is the only memorial to a wrecker I have ever seen on any island where wrecking was once often listed among the most active of occupations. It is a bronze figure, a witch-like woman called Ritskemooi, hook-nosed, wearing clogs and a flying cloak, and carrying her wicked lantern. It is reputed that she used that lantern once too often to lure a ship onto the shore and that she found her own son lying drowned on the beach. On wild, ghostly nights, even now, they say you can hear her crying his name in the wind along the shore.

Night came on as I went to the Ameland jetty to leave the island. The ferry blustered into the harbour on a sea serrated with foam; the wind, blowing from the northeast, brought rain with a touch of snow about it. Winter was on its way.

AMELAND situated latitude 52°38′ N and longitude 5°45′ E; area 35 sq. m (91 sq. km); population approx. 3,000; The Netherlands.

Borkum
The Last Serenade

The setting sun,
and music at the close.
SHAKESPEARE, *Richard II*

It was the last afternoon at the Kurhalle. Outside, the pigeon-coloured day was diminishing, the long sands stretched out to touch the October sea. Inside, the mustachioed orchestra was playing for the final time that season, the last *Kaffe* was being drunk and the ultimate cream cakes munched; the sounds of Schubert drifted out to the spot where fat gulls stood or strutted along the promenade. Soon they would have the place to themselves.

Borkum, in the German Frisian Islands, has preserved, indeed even revived, the art of spa gentility. Its visitors, on that final autumn day of the season, enjoyed gentle walks, ample food and violins in the salt air. There were some young people about, one of them sailing a land-yacht far out on the sand-spit, others walking in brisk jeans and heavy sweaters along the bricked streets of the small, proper town. But the wheeled bathing-machines drawn from the water's edge, the coloured tents, sad now they had been abandoned, Herr Ackerman's sedate horse-and-buggy rides to view the seal colony, were all as shadows from another time.

Even the journey there had an old-fashioned touch. The port of Borkum is far out on a sand-and-marshland arm of the island. Leaving the ferry, which takes two and a half hours from Emden, passengers embark onto a miniature train, with an orange engine and coloured coaches, which chugs towards the town.

The train journey of seven kilometres takes twenty minutes, rattling through wild dunes and windy marshes, and sheltered copses and gardens too. On the fringes of the town are some practical-looking houses. The tentacles of suburbia reach far out into the North Sea. But, at once, the disappointment is lifted by a jaunty striped lighthouse at the end of a street.

At the end of its brief journey the train clangs into a pretty railway station, tiled and roofed and be-potted with plants, the line running at right angles to the main street once known as the Bismark Strasse. The station does not have much of a platform, its underfoot blocks make it like a street itself. Shops and a café with a pleasing window stand along it. Outside are some large hotels, with peeling paint that somehow adds to their charm.

Before Borkum became a resort it earned its living from the sea – whaling, fishing, trading, and as a naval outpost. In 1902, Erskine Childers wrote a novel centred on the German Frisians, *The Riddle of the Sands*, now accepted as the first published spy story. Childers, a tormented man (in 1922, in Ireland, he was executed for treason by a British firing squad), purported in the story to warn of the dangers of a German invasion of Britain 'by a multitude of sea-going lighters' from bases behind the islands. This novel was produced, as evidence, in 1910 when two young British officers, Lieutenant Vivian Brandon and Captain Bernard Trench, were arrested for spying on Borkum island. At their trial they admitted sending secret information to London on picture postcards and that their Whitehall contact was called 'Reggie' whose code address was 'Sunburnt London'. They were sentenced to four years 'in a fortress'.

The fashion for sea-bathing, which began for Germany on the neighbouring island of Norderney in the middle of the nineteenth century, brought people and prosperity to Borkum but today there are constant reminders of the maritime past. The most prominent of these is the giant lighthouse (not the one I saw from the train, that was only a satellite). Unlike most of its kind, it is not set on some remote and rocky cape, but is established as the very centrepiece of the town, crowning a grass knoll and looking out over the entire flat island.

Viewed in the day it would not be judged among the most pleasing of lighthouses. It is built of dark brick and has the dire aspect of a prison watchtower. But at night – what a transformation! Its vivid beams sweep around and above the island and far out to sea like the spokes of a great wheel.

In the tidy town and gardens are more reminders of the seafaring life. Red and green buoys mark the streets, and there is an anchor standing among the shops. There are buoys and harpoons, masts and spars in people's gardens, and careful models of ships in the windows of houses and in restaurants.

As in Ameland, in the Dutch Frisians, the former home of a sea captain is now appropriately a museum – it houses the old Borkum lifeboat resting on its great-wheeled cart. There is a whalebone arch outside the museum door and immediately within a photograph of an avuncular Hindenburg. Bewhiskered sailors and shawled and bonneted ladies gaze from frames upon the domestic implements and the maritime tools and equipment that would have been familiar to them. There are some robust relics of the old bathing days too, when Germans seeking salt air and sunshine flocked to the island beaches, first changing into striped long drawers in the secrecy of wheeled bathing-machines.

A short walk from the museum is the brick tower of the old church, now bereft of the church itself, and in the grassy churchyard is another reminder of the former days – a sailor's tombstone made into a sanctuary by a fence of whalebones.

In the summer Borkum is famed for its seaside delights, the widespread beaches, the casino, the concert hall, the Kurhaus, and the swimming pool that provides artificial waves – as if the real thing were not plentifully available.

But now the winds and mists of winter were following each other to the shore. People walked in a manner which told you they thought they were doing something good for their health. A small crowd gathered to watch an intrepid man, in a bathing suit like a circus strongman, wade into the leaden sea. On the promenade those who were brave enough to sit, watched container ships moving down the sea lanes. The spectators moved their stance a little every few minutes as they followed the shadowy vessels along the horizon.

On the beach the coloured tents, set out like hundreds of sentry boxes, were standing awry, some leaning one way, some another – a scene of autumn desolation. An old man in an overcoat, like a last-ditch defender, was sitting to the leeward side of his tent, in a hole he had dug in the sand. Inside the tent his wife, rotund and red, gazed out at the ebbing tide.

The bandstand on the promenade is more substantial than most of its kind, like a large stone birdcage, the music stands of the summer abandoned within the windowed apertures. It was here that I first heard the strings on the cold air and imagined that it might be the echo of a ghostly concert. But then I realized that the sounds were coming from the Kurhalle Am Meer, a nicely poised building, its windows facing the promenade. I went inside and joined the final *Kaffe* takers and cake-crunchers of the year. When the band had finished its programme – detailed on a printed sheet at the door – with a last rendition of Toselli's *Serenade*, it packed up its instruments and went home. I saw the leader, a young man, his spangled coat now replaced by a leather jacket, go out of the front door. I went too. It was all finished for that year.

BORKUM situated latitude 53°35′ N and longitude 6°40′ E; area 14 sq. m (36 sq. km); population approx. 7,750; Germany

The Lesser Scottish Islands
Isle of My Heart

'O, these endless little isles'
T. S. MUIR, *Ecclesiological Notes
on some of the Islands of Scotland*

Those outriders of Britain, the smallest, tallest and most remote of the
Scottish Islands, lie out there in their distant tides like shadows on the
northern horizon. St Kilda, Mingulay, the Flannans, North Rona, Fair Isle,
Foula. The poetry of their names is matched only by the romance of their
wild situations.

On midnight evenings in summer, they sometimes stand on a sea of
tranquillity with the dusk dying around them; on winter days, when it is
barely light before it is again dark, they are awash with the most powerful
waves of the world. Some still have habitations and people, but others gave
up the struggle long ago and now remain silent and vacant except for the
birds, the Atlantic seals and the wind.

Using the old measurement for an island (in these waters anyway) – that it
has enough pasture to graze one sheep for a year – the Scottish isles are said
to number one for each day in the calendar. The Orkneys and Shetlands sit
like a mitre above the head of the mainland, with the closely-grouped
Hebrides a cloak on its back. But far out in the big seas are other places.

St Kilda presents the most awesome rockscape of any in Europe. Four
islands rising abruptly from the Atlantic, a hundred miles off the coast of
mainland Scotland: Hirta, Soay, Dun and Boreray, the latter rising a sheer
1,200 feet from the sea, and with their attendant rocks, Stac Lee, 544 feet,
the home of 40,000 pairs of gannets, and Stac an Armin, 627 feet, the highest
single rock in Britain.

Once here was a community cut off from the world for much of the year, a
village alongside a sheltered bay, a scoop in the fearsome landscape. The
people lived, mainly, on seabirds and their eggs, for these islanders were
renowned climbers. Young men had to scale the 300-foot Maidens Rock, and
stand on one foot at the top before they were permitted to marry. It was
proof, said the elders, that the husband could provide for a family.

Unfortunately the little group could not provide for itself. The men met every day in a 'Parliament' to decide on important issues, but sometimes the talking took so long that nothing was done about anything. Babies died of tetanus because of the primitive ritual of smearing the navel with dung after birth. Pneumonia and tuberculosis were killers and there was no doctor on the island. Eventually, after a winter of great hardship, the St Kilda missionary wrote to the British Government in the spring of 1930 requesting that the thirty remaining islanders be taken off to the mainland. On 29 August, the fishery protection cruiser HMS *Harebell* and a cargo vessel arrived in Village Bay and the St Kildans sailed away from their island for the last time. Romance and reality are often poor bedfellows.

St Kilda was left to the storms and windy sunshine. Its houses fell, its little gardens grew over. The sheep on Soay, brought there first by the Vikings a thousand years ago, hardly noticed the departure of the humans. The island has an army contingent now, a tracking unit for a missile range in the Hebrides, and the National Trust for Scotland takes parties out there in the summer to restore the houses. But it will never be the same again.

The Gaelic-speaking people of Mingulay, on the southernmost tail of the Hebrides, used to call it Eilean Mo Chridhe, the Isle of My Heart, for they dearly loved it. Many lived and died there without ever leaving. They did not believe there was any better place to be. But today this is a haunted island too, no peat smoke from the chimneys, no voices calling across the water, no winter stories by the fireside.

Other islands are haunted too. The Flannans, or the Seven Hunters as they are also called, remote and beautiful; their sole habitation the lighthouse where three keepers vanished. One night the light had failed and when a boat was sent to investigate it found no trace of the men. No one has ever been able to resolve that mystery.

Even before that the Flannans held simple men in thrall. When fishermen from Lewis went ashore there they observed a whole catalogue of superstitious rituals to keep evil away and refused to mention certain places and things by the usual names. A custom that lingers even now. In some islands a clergyman – called an Upstander – is considered to be an unlucky passenger in a boat and the hull will be washed out after he has left.

There is another ghostly island too, North Rona, lying north of the halfway point between the head of Scotland at Cape Wrath and the Butt of Lewis. But in the seventeenth century a book written about North Rona by Martin

Martin Gentleman, who had also travelled to St Kilda, describes life on the island as idyllic. There were, he observed, '. . . five families who lived a harmless life being perfectly ignorant of most of the vices which abound in the world . . . They have an agreeable and hospitable temper for all strangers. They take their surname from the colours of the sky, the rainbow and the clouds.' He describes how one man, wanting a wife, sent a shilling with a missionary to Lewis and a wife was sent to him by the next yearly supply boat.

North Rona suffered depopulation and it was not until 1884 that it had further inhabitants – two men who had quarrelled with their minister at Ness went into exile on the island. They lived there, like castaways, for a year. In the summer of 1885 a boatman found them dead, one with his plaid laid reverently across his body. They had kept track of the days by marking notches on a stick. The last notch was for 17 February.

Most of the little out-islands are now only home for howling seals and sheep, and the roaming seabirds of the north, the arctic skua and the gannet, the fulmer, the comical puffin, the oyster catcher and the tern. Today the most remote inhabited place in Britain is Fair Isle, lying south of Shetland, with neighbouring Foula to its north, which lacks a good harbour. Even Christmas is a movable feast there, depending on the arrival of the supply boat.

Fair Isle was always beckoning me (to hear it named every day on the radio weather forecasts was enticement enough) and it was a happy time when I looked out from the south of Mainland island, in Shetland, and saw it, far off, like a shade on the skyline. I made several journeys there, each one three-and-a-half turbulent hours in the sturdy little boat *The Good Shepherd*. It takes the course where the Atlantic seas surge in to meet those of the North Sea. The boat's size is limited and it has to be taken from the water at the end of its journey.

The voyage is wonderfully worthwhile. For here is the outpost of birds, the landfall for the migrations from the Arctic. The sound of wings and bird calls are all over the island. Fair Isle rises spectacularly from the waves, the pinnacle of Sheep Craig dominating everything else. The Craig is the nearest thing to a vertical meadow and sheep are grazed there throughout the year, being taken over on a set day and then, the men having climbed a chain, hauled to the grass at the top.

Within the fastness of the majestic cliffs is a mild, smiling, open island, with its houses and two churches, its post office and shop, and its village hall, spread over the gentle landscape; everything within sight of everything else, but no neighbour too near another. It is an arrangement that has worked for generations.

It was the dream of a man called George Waterson to own this fine but remote island (given to Scotland as a dowry for a Norwegian princess). While he was a prisoner of war in the 1940s he thought about the island constantly and, on his repatriation from Sweden, Fair Isle riding on the sea was his first sight of his homeland. He paid £5,000 for it in 1947 and dedicated it to the birds. Now the National Trust for Scotland administers it and a comfortable bird observatory with accommodation for visitors (not only ornithologists) has replaced the old and shaky wartime huts which I remember from my early visits.

The island is famous for its Fair Isle knitting, a cross-pattern, the secrets of which are still guarded by a select group of Fair Isle women. Legend says the secrets came from a wrecked Spanish galleon. The composition of the dyes which go into the wool is still only known to a few. The women meet regularly to inspect the garments knitted before they are sent to exclusive customers all over the world but demand for Fair Isle knitwear far exceeds supply today. Some garments are sent back for repair after many years of wear.

I remember one evening in summer – the long late light they call the 'simmer dim' – talking to a lady called Mrs Busta (named after her house since the majority of the population have the same surname – Stout) about her island. She was shy about her love for it, but then she said that she liked it because it was clear and treeless. Trees spoiled the view, and anywhere else she would not be able to feel and see and hear the ocean all around her. In saying that she spoke for so many islanders everywhere. They are a special people.

FAIR ISLE, SHETLAND situated latitude 59°32′ N and longitude 1°40′ W; area 6 sq. m (15 sq. km); population approx. 75; Britain (private ownership). ST KILDA, HEBRIDES latitude 57°50′ N and longitude 8°32′ W; area 1 sq. m (2.5 sq. km); uninhabited; Britain (National Trust for Scotland)

Isle of Man
A Picture from Childhood

Come for a while
Back to your isle
Of dreams.
1930s popular song

If happiness is an island, then, I suppose, the Isle of Man meant that for me. It was the first island I ever set foot upon; that was at the end of World War II and the end of my childhood.

In the summer of 1945 I was fourteen years old. The immediate years behind me had been in disarray. My parents had died – my father in a ship on the ocean and my mother six months later – and I had found myself in an orphanage. This, however, had its compensations and one of these was a summer camp on the Isle of Man. It was wonderful; the war was over, the sun shone (with the constancy that only occurred when you were young) and there was I sailing, with forty or so other boys – and girls! – from Liverpool to Douglas, the island capital, aboard a jaunty-funnelled ferry called the *Ben My Cree*.

We camped in the grounds of a house at Lezayre, a hamlet with a dark church, two-thirds to the north of the island. There was a shallow cold river called the Sulby, where every day we swam. We explored the limpid glens, climbed Snaefell Mountain, saw, from its summit, the countries of Scotland, Ireland, England and Wales, went to the seaside at Ramsey, and surveyed in wonder the great water-wheel of the old lead mines at Laxey. I also fell in love.

I discovered early what a distress that can be. One translucent evening I went with my beloved, who was thirteen and had a sharp turn of phrase, to the beach. Determined to impress her I set out to swim to the sunset. I swam and swam, far out where the cormorants were diving for fish. The water became grey and cold and my loved one had diminished to a dot on the distant shore. Enough was enough. I turned and stroked my way back. It was a long way. The water became colder and the air darker, and I was relieved when at last I staggered on my skinny legs up the shingle. She stood there, my heart's object, looking at my thin shivering skin, my eyes, misty and reddened, and at the water dripping down my somewhat long nose. 'You know,' she said eventually, 'you've got a face just like a crow.'

I've got over it now (even the nose has fallen more or less into place as the flesh around it has increased), but on the several times I have returned to the isle since that boyhood summer I have remembered it a little ruefully. Once, long after, I drove over the silent mountain and down along the shady, remembered road, stopping outside the house at Lezayre. It was late twilight and the white walls were as pale as people's faces at dusk. I did not go in, but merely looked over the gate and then through the hedge into the field where we had pitched our tents. You can never call it back, can you? It's gone. Everything seemed much smaller and somehow sad, but the evening was so tranquil that I could hear the Sulby river bubbling over its stones in the distant shadows.

I remembered that hedgerow especially. In that first post-war summer they restarted the famous Isle of Man motor-cycle races, the Tourist Trophy, and the road alongside the hedge was one of the fastest parts of the course. The riders took a sharp bend at Sulby Bridge and then rushed down the straight at 120 miles an hour. Practice runs were made at six in the morning and we boys stood in the hedge and watched the riders turn the bend and rush by, leaving the air full of fumes and our ears full of roar. Now, at that time, there was a lot of military clothing and stores on the civilian market (I used to wear an army tunic to school!) and at the camp my bed was warmed by a red blanket, the sort used in hospitals. One morning, to watch the TT practice, I put this around my shoulders and the daredevil riders skidded and braked in a terrible tangle. Fortunately none was hurt and I stood puzzled by the occurrence until an official approached and asked me to refrain from draping my shoulders with the 'Immediate Danger Ahead' signal!

When I was on the island again, I drove along part of the TT course, out of Douglas and towards Peel. Every bend and wall and post was sandbagged and padded, giving the route the appearance of preparing for some impending war. In 1945 the whole seafront at Douglas looked like that, bulwarks and bastions, the tall Georgian houses and hotels painted grey, for the whole stretch was officially a ship – HMS *Valkyrie*. Aliens were detained on the Isle of Man during the war, some of them with little justification; some, indeed, had only just escaped from Nazi Germany.

There is another wartime story associated with the island which concerned the very ship *Ben My Cree* (named after a character of the island writer, Hall Caine) that had taken me on that first romantic voyage. In June 1940 she was in the fleet of nondescript vessels sent to evacuate the beleaguered British army from the beaches at Dunkirk. One of these soldiers, in a letter written many years later to the English magazine *Country Life*, described how he managed to board the vessel after tramping for miles across the battlefield. He was dirty, hot and exhausted, so imagine his delight when, on getting aboard the ferry, he found a properly white-coated steward, polishing the bar. The ship was rocking from bombs and shells, wounded lay on her upper decks, but this phlegmatic orderly was ignoring it all. The soldier approached gladly and asked for a large drink. As the explosions rocked the vessel, the steward shook his head: 'Sorry, sir,' he said with a pained face. 'We are not allowed to serve alcoholic drinks while the ship is in port.'

The Isle of Man is a place of garrisons, glens and ghosts. There are powerfully built fortresses at salient places on its coast, the greatest being on St Patrick's Isle, across the fishing harbour at Peel. The ghost of the Moddy Dhoo, the black dog, still pads the towers at night. Long ago I remember hearing at the campfire how it sent a soldier raving mad – and I looked around to see the wide, utterly believing eyes of my childhood companions. The sylvan glens that run through the island hills, with streams and waterfalls tinkling through the woods, are, naturally, the haunts of elves and goblins. On the road between Douglas and Ronaldsway Airport is the Fairy Bridge (marked with a proper road sign) where all passers are obliged, as they cross, to call, 'Goodnight Little People.' Most do.

As you approach Peel, at the foot of the Greeba Mountain is the church of St Trinian's, with walls and tower but no roof. A bad fairy called a Buggare was blamed for the roof being blown off.

Peel is a staunch little town, houses facing directly across to Ireland. The piled castle protects the harbour from the worst of the ocean weather, which comes in at any season with a dark and disturbing enthusiasm. It was June when I was last there. The coloured fishing boats bounced and creaked against the jetties, gulls screamed against the wind and the houses of the town were dark across the bay, a darkness broken by an occasional and romantic shaft of wan sunshine. It is a fine place; I went into an inn where there was a summer fire burning in the grate, bought some famous Manx kippers – smoked herrings – and marvelled at the strange names above the old shops. The island has the oddest collection of names in Britain – Quale, Quinlan, Quiggin and Quirk, and suchlike, to families rejoicing in the title of Looney.

From distant misty history, the Isle of Man has had its own Parliament, Tynwald, which makes independent laws and levies taxes. The Manx language flickers and there is hope of its revival. Some street signs and direction posts are in Manx and English, often erected above or alongside a standing-stone dating back to pre-history. These relics are so numerous that they stand casually about attracting (from the locals anyway) as little attention as a post box.

The north of the island, towards the Point of Ayre, becomes, surprisingly, a flat plain after the glens and uplands of the middle island. I remember going up there one day and discovering the wreck of a ship made of concrete. She was one of a number cast like that – to save steel – during World War I. She certainly looked the most permanent shipwreck I have ever seen, although it is possible that she has since been blown up or dismantled with pneumatic drills.

In the south is marvellous green scenery. Sweet hills patterned with some trees and pastoral valleys. At the end of the island are Castletown, Port St Mary and Port Erin, little folded places of stone, shingle and sand. When the tide is out the wide beaches, flat and shiny, seem to mirror the sky. Cregneish village, a collection of cottages and a lovely small church with an open belfry, is down there too on the way to Spanish Head and the offshore island, the Calf of Man.

Spanish Head is reputed to be the place where a galleon of the scattered Spanish Armada finally came to grief, after an escape that took her from the western English Channel right around the head of Scotland and almost back to where she began. The Manx cat, which has no tail, is said to be the descendant of the cats that climbed ashore from the rigging to the cliffs.

I wanted to see the Calf of Man again because I could not recall how it was shaped. It was much broader than I had thought, green plateaued, lying close inshore across the fretful Calf Sound. It is uninhabited except for bird wardens and the coastguard who with the seabirds and wild creatures keeps it as their safe, protected home.

The heyday of the traditional North of England holiday on the Isle of Man is, they say, gone. At one time the steamers used to come to Douglas loaded with workers who had earned a holiday by the sea from the cotton, steel and coal towns, but now the numbers have diminished.

Douglas retains its tall, elegant appearance around one of the finest bays in Britain; its buildings haughty, its horse-trams still clopping along the promenade. The red funnels of the ferries stand out against the grey-green of the headland.

I walked along the sea edge and tried to imagine myself back in that golden August when the war was ended. It is for that reason that I will always love this island. I was happy there once. Even if she did say I had a face like a crow.

ISLE OF MAN situated between latitudes 53°3'–54°25' N and longitudes 4°18'–4°47' W; area 227 sq. m (572 sq. km); population approx. 64,000; Britain

The English Channel Islands
A Family of the Sea

They are fragments of France which fell into the sea
to be gathered up by England.
VICTOR HUGO

It was early afternoon when the storm arrived. The morning had been too bright, too brittle, a sure portent for bad weather, with the off-lying islands clear as cut-outs against the flat sky. Deep clouds moved in, pushing the sun aside; the wind began to sneak around the streets, like a man shiftily whistling from the corner of his mouth. The sea ruffled; then came thickening rain. By two o'clock it was like ten in the evening. Gulls turned up in the port in apprehensive hundreds; the coastguards had long issued timely warnings.

Then the storm rushed up the English Channel like a ruffian, barging and banging, whooping around the harbour houses, whirling the cowls of chimney pots. The wind was drubbing doors; I could hardly see from my window for the onslaught of the rain. It was a wonderful day to be on an island.

The window faced St Peter Port Harbour in Guernsey. I sat for an hour and watched the show. The fortress at the anchorage entrance was half blotted out. Was it rocking in the wind? Moored boats cringed. Sometimes a gull would try to fly but was flung like a rag and soon returned to the sensible sheltering beneath the wall. Outlying rocks were frothing with foam like a fleet trying to voyage on a violent sea. The other islands, Herm, Jethou and Sark had vanished. Perhaps they had even been washed away.

It was a Saturday. Shoppers reported being toppled by the wind in the stony streets of St Peter Port; a surprised man was lifted from his horse. At an island football match the game was abandoned because the referee complained he was soaked to the skin and the ball kept blowing away.

By night-time the worst – or the best, depending on your sense of the dramatic and how sheltered you were – was over. The wind fell to sulky gusts, the rain went to France or somewhere, only the sea sounded louder and that was because the other noises had quit. Later even the waves diminished, the sky cleared and a blameless moon came out. It was as though nothing untoward had ever happened.

They lie in the crook of the arm of France, this little company of islands. Britain, to whom (with one exception) they belong, is many miles over the sea. France is so near people joke in Alderney that you can smell the cooking when the wind is right. When the Queen is toasted by the islanders there is added the appellation, 'Duke of Normandy'.

I lived in the Channel Islands for a year and they have been dear to me. I have thought of them as a family – Jersey and Guernsey, the larger pair, as father and mother, the older children, Alderney, Sark and Herm; a gaggle of toddlers, Brechou, Lihou, Burhou, Jethou, with the infant islands, Les Ecréhous, Les Minquiers and Les Casquets. To the south of Jersey lies their demure French cousin, so shy as to be almost unknown, the Isle of Chausey.

The proximity of the archipelago to the Cherbourg Peninsula, with Britain out of view over the northern horizon, means their possession by the English crown could have only come about by some sheer carelessness on the part of the French or some extreme cleverness on the part of the British.

That the roots of these swept scraps of land are still very much in their Norman origins can be seen today in the ancient laws, the names of districts and streets and, less now, in the language of the insular people. Breton-

French is spoken in the green hinterland of Jersey although, curiously, the English-speaking Jerseyman has an accent that is not far off the sound of Dutch-South African – a linguistic conundrum. In Guernsey the voices are quite different, as are the islands, and the patois is a sort of Norman-French. With the sharp rivalry and sharper vernacular that is common to most neighbouring islands throughout the world, the Guernseyman refers to his Jersey neighbours as '*crapauds*' – toads. In turn the Jerseyman calls the man of Guernsey a donkey.

As is the way with collections of islands, each one of the Channel Islands is distinct in character, topography and atmosphere from the others in the group. Having lived among them I now gaze down from an aircraft passing south and see them sitting in their private blue sea, each a small solitary, tight place, living its life away from the others and, not infrequently, from the world at large. When I lived in Jersey a ship cut the submarine cable that carried the telephone and telex cables to England. For four days we were as isolated as it was possible to be in these technical times. The only people who appeared worried were the offshore financial houses (Jersey being, among other things, a tax haven) who, cut off from figures, averages, percentages had their clerks queueing night-long for every available aircraft seat.

One windy winter I lived with my family in a stone farmhouse on Jersey. All the visitors had gone home to their cities and the place was left to its inhabitants, the sea and the weather. There were thrilling January days when gales would hoot through the modest valleys, when the long beaches would be rolled by great waves; when the sky was wild. Then there were other days, even at that remote time of the year, when yellow sunshine would clothe the islands and we would spend the day on the beach among the rocks, the sand and the periwinkles.

Jersey is the most pastoral of the islands. It has farms and folding fields and you can be inland, away from the sea for a while. Its face is turned south, towards the sun, so that it does not have to rely on great shining acres of glasshouses that make Guernsey, on the approach by air, appear like a place of lakes or ice-floes. Jersey's mild air encourages the gardener, the botanist and the arborist.

When the Civil War broke out in England Jersey stood by the King and Guernsey became an outpost of Cromwell's Roundheads; the two islands were at war. Even today the silver mace given to Jersey by a grateful and restored Charles II is brought out and displayed at ceremonial times. The island sheltered the fugitive King in Elizabeth Castle between the little port of St Aubin and the capital, St Helier. Today the pile still stands beyond the tides, marooned when the sea comes in. When Charles was restored to the throne he made his silver token of gratitude to the loyal Jerseymen, sportingly pardoned the people of Guernsey, and gave George de Carteret, Jersey's bailiff and the Governor of the former island, a tract of land, 8,000 square miles of it, in the new colonies of Virginia. It is called New Jersey.

Today in the churchyard at St Helier are buried two opposing commanders who fought the last battle ever to take place on British soil. One is Philippe Charles Félix Macquart, Baron de Rullecourt, who invaded the island with a French force in the early days of 1781, and the other Major Francis Peirson, the British officer who, after his superior commander had cravenly surrenderd, decided to ignore the order, attacked the invaders and defeated them. Both commanders were killed in the skirmish and now rest in neighbouring tombs. The battle is also commemorated on Jersey banknotes and stamps, and in the name of a pub in the centre of St Helier.

It was 160 years before Jersey was next invaded. This time there was no battle. After a preliminary bombing attack a lone, German aircraft landed (at the pilot's own initiative) at the newly opened airport – out stepped Luftwaffe Lieutenant Richard Kern who was taken to a telephone box where he telephoned the bailiff and ordered the island's surrender. There followed four years of privation not only for the inhabitants but, eventually, for the isolated garrison as well. The islands were not liberated until the rest of She
Europe was free, in May 1945, when Nazi Germany had surrendered. They were bypassed by the D-Day forces. Months passed while Paris, Brussels and Copenhagen were freed, and the little British islands remained prisoners. The stories of those days still abound in the Channel Islands but, for me, the whole extraordinary episode was brought into focus by some copies of the *Guernsey Star* published in 1940 which I bought for a couple of pounds at an auction in Jersey.

The newspapers, sear and brittle now, show, as few things can, the plight of the poor islanders during those hopeless days. A German-inspired communiqué about Allied shipping losses leads what little news is presented, alongside a much longer item about a man who stole someone's bicycle. There were messages, passed through the Red Cross, from relatives in England, a recipe for swede soup, and – intriguingly – alongside an advertisement for a German film at the cinema, one for a Hollywood musical. America had not then entered World War II.

There was little underground resistance in the Channel Islands. They are so confined that anyone causing trouble would have had difficulty in hiding and such adventures as cutting telephone wires irritated and inconvenienced the local populace as much as the Germans. A handful of tragic Jews were sent away to a nameless fate. Another group of people were ordered to St Helier Harbour one morning with, ominously, only the personal possessions they could carry. Nothing happened. The boat that was supposed to come from St Malo to fetch them failed to appear and they were sent home for another night of agonizing. The following day the boat did turn up and the pathetic group were shipped to France and thence by slow train to Germany. They spent the rest of the war in a not uncomfortable camp, a German castle where, among other things, they formed an orchestra. I was shown the programme of one of their concerts. As the war drew to its close they were guarded by ancient and infirm German soldiers to whom they gave shelter during Allied air raids. At the end of hostilities they were carried immediately back to their island homes.

Strange things happened to many people. Signor Valli, for many years the dignified headwaiter of the Hôtel l'Horizon in Jersey, having lived in Britain for much of his life, was nevertheless told by the Germans to return to his Italian homeland to join the army. 'I made all the excuses I could think about,' he said. 'But eventually they said I had to go and with another Italian I was shipped across to St Malo and given a rail ticket and enough money to get to Lyons where we were instructed to report to the Italian consul. It took us days to get there because the French railways were in a bad state and were being bombed. Eventually we arrived and went to the consul which was jammed with people. After a whole day a woman assistant told us to go to a hotel and gave us money to pay our bill and for food. We returned to the office the next day and the same thing happened and this went on for several days until eventually the lady took us out into the street where she waylaid some German officers who were going to lunch. She asked them to sign some papers, which they did. Then she gave the documents and rail tickets to us and said, "Go on back to Jersey." We did, gladly.'

Alderney was an out-and-out slave labour camp with uncounted numbers of prisoners from Eastern Europe and elsewhere dying cruel deaths. Outside its small airfield today is a sundial which has an inscription, 'Do as the sundial does – count the bright hours only.' Despite the philosophy, and the amiable character of the island's inhabitants, most of whom live in St Anne, the most delightful town in the Channel Islands, the past still broods over Alderney in the shape of great concrete blockhouses and bunkers, so strong they can never be removed and which all the climbing wisteria and honeysuckle cannot disguise. A great pity.

Herm, the low, pretty island lying to the east of Guernsey, had a strange war. Throughout most of the occupation its only inhabitants were the caretaker and his wife. They were instructed to look after the island for the owner Lord Perry and that is exactly what they did. The Germans in the main respected their function although they did stage a mock invasion on the famous Shell Beach, an exercise filmed and shown in Berlin as representing the invasion of Britain itself.

But undoubtedly one of the oddest results of the German occupation is to be seen on the island of Sark today in the person of its recent Constable, Herr Werner Rang, who first arrived there as part of its German garrison. He is a round-faced, easily smiling man whose friends from Germany joke that he now speaks his native language with a Sark accent. Apart from his responsibility for keeping law and order on the tiny island he and his wife Phyllis keep a guest house and have a jewellery shop. 'I was a medical sergeant here in Sark,' relates Werner. 'And since there was no civilian doctor on the island I used to do what I could when people were sick. One day I was called to Phyllis's house because she had the 'flu. My first words to her were, "I want to take your temperature." '

When the war was done Werner was shipped to England and spent the next three years in a prisoner-of-war camp. He remembered Sark with affection and he and Phyllis began to correspond. When he was released he forsook Germany and returned to Sark. He and Phyllis married and they had a family and now have five grandchildren. He showed me his silver and ebony mace, his symbol of office (he has no uniform). 'When Her Majesty the Queen came to Sark,' he said smiling, 'I had to present her with this mace and she handed it back to me. It was the proudest moment of my life.'

Victor Hugo lived in the Channel Islands having been banished from France with others for criticizing Napoleon III – Napoleon the Little as he was derisively called. After settling first in Jersey, where he was seen, a black encloaked figure, looking out over the sea like a man haunted, he was then banished a second time for the same reason. He and other exiles published a pamphlet which attacked the French ruler and furthermore libelled Queen Victoria for her support of the regime in Paris. Hugo, who never wrote or spoke a word of English, was expelled from Jersey.

He was, however, welcomed in Guernsey in 1855 where he lived until 1870. His house in the rue de Hauteville in St Peter Port can be visited today. It is literally heavy with memories – his books, his awesome four-poster bed, the bulky furniture and drapes, the wooden crucifix upon the wall, a screen said to have been the handiwork of Madame de Pompadour herself. In the ornate dining-room is the oak chair he kept reserved for the Great Unknown Guest. A chain across it prevented any other person sitting there.

Hugo wore the sadness of his exile as heavy as his cloak. He wandered through the islands, taking many local scenes for his novels. He wrote *Les Misérables* there and on Sark he found the inspiration for *The Toilers of the Sea*. His heart, however, was forever in France. The windows of his study, built on the roof of his house, looked towards his beloved, lost, homeland. Today a French flag flies above the house where he lived.

I first went into the marketplace in St Helier, Jersey, just before Christmas in the year I lived on the island. Among all the fruit and holly and Christmas flowers I saw at once a stout sight, a Victorian post box, and into it went my Christmas cards. The first post boxes erected in the British Isles appeared in Jersey, designed by Anthony Trollope, a post office surveyor before he took to writing. It stands as a cheerful and ever-used memorial.

In the churchyard at St Saviour's is another memorial, more beautiful and poignant – a bust of the actress Lillie Langtry, the lovely Jersey Lily. She was born only a few steps away, the daughter of the Dean of Jersey, the Reverend William Corbet Le Breton.

She was called the Jersey Lily after her portrait was painted by Millais, himself from a Channel Islands family. She had black hair and stone-white skin. He painted her holding a flower and entitled the work, which was exhibited at the Royal Academy, 'A Jersey Lily'. It was her name forever.

Wherever she went, to America, throughout Europe, as the guest of the great, the mistress of a king, she knew that one day she would go back to the small place that gave her birth. She died in Monte Carlo in 1929 and her dearest wish was answered; she was buried at St Saviour's.

Although they are all collected in the Gulf of St Malo, the Channel Islands are well scattered, sometimes twenty miles between them. Jersey sits apart, a Victorian father in his sanctum. It is Guernsey, the mother island, that has the company of the family about her. From the splendid harbour at St Peter Port you can see that she is cast about with other islands, islets and colonies of rocks. Herm, Jethou, Brechou and Sark are there on the immediate horizon, Alderney is just beyond. One of the great joys of that place is at evening – to see the sky spread across the patterned sea and to see the bright red and blue ferry steamer from the mainland, making her entry into the setting, on her way to her berth at St Peter Port.

Sark is a surprising island for it rises high from the sea and is surrounded by a skirt of difficult water and many outlandish rocks (one looking like the Loch Ness Monster). To navigate the notorious current can be a difficult feat, but its reward is to arrive into the enclosed harbour that is the smallest registered port in the world. A tunnel, carved out in the sixteenth century, leads the passenger from the quay to the interior, a curious experience in itself. At the distant outlet of the tunnel he will find the island transport awaiting him – tractors towing 'toast rack' carts. There are no cars on Sark. The tractors, the horses and carts, and the many bicycles are the only means of getting around.

Feudal rule has held sway since 1565 when Elizabeth I presented the island to Helier de Carteret, a nobleman from Jersey, to fortify and to cultivate. One of the battery of cannon she sent for this purpose is still to be seen. The ruler, called either the Seigneur or the Dame, has wide power. Only he or she is allowed to keep a bitch, a dove or a duck. A levy of a chicken a year is paid by householders. During the German occupation in World War II the Dame, Sybil Hathaway, made it clear to the conquerors that she was still to be counted. She would receive German officers in a long room at her official residence, her desk raised on a dais at the far end. They had to walk a long way to approach her and only then would she deign to look up from the work on her desk. They were left in no doubt as to who was giving audience to whom.

Herm island is ruled, although not by title, by another singular person, Major Peter Wood who, with his wife Jenny, came to land there not long after World War II and found the whole place a sad, overgrown wilderness. Their years of work and organization have borne fruit for today it is a quiet and lovely place, rich with flowers and scents, puckered with fine bays including one, Shell Beach, which is an object of pilgrimage for conchologists from many countries. The island has its own hotel and farm. I have known Peter Wood for some years and on my last visit we walked slowly around the entire island in an hour. Every now and then he would stand and point out some view or some curiosity with the enthusiasm and sincerity that you imagine he felt all those years ago when he first arrived there.

He is so familiar with every inch of that enclosed landscape that he even notices when two small boulders are in different positions from the places they occupied the previous week. He is concerned that the island should remain as it is. Herm is packed with wild flowers, scenting the deep lanes, and visitors are requested, on landing, not to pick them.

There was a stray white duck in the harbour. It had been there for about a month waiting to be fed at appointed times, quite solitary, swimming in the water of the new tide as it eddied in. 'I can't ever see us wanting to leave here,' said Peter looking across the sea that was the colour of a peacock. Guernsey, the nearest civilization, looked very far away. 'In more than thirty years we've become as much a part of this island as the rocks. People ask us what we get from it, don't we get bored with it? The answer is that we get tranquillity – and that is something we could never be bored with.' The duck on the harbour wall, with a short quack, flopped into the water and paddled around. He apparently agreed.

Small yellow aircraft hum between the islands; operated by Aurigny Airlines – Aurigny being the ancient name for Alderney which was the site, oddly, of the first airport in the islands. The planes are the subject of many legends and a few jokes. But they are sturdy, safe, and their high wings allow the passenger a lyrical view. They link the islands with Dinard in France and with Southampton and despite the fact that their longest flight is only a little over half an hour the airline boasts its own in-flight magazine.

In the first days of flying to the Channel Islands the service was operated by a De Havilland Dragonfly, a wonderful plane which, it is said, was the only aircraft ever to be retired because of woodworm – the pest got into the airframe! Before the construction of Jersey Airport the plane used to land on St Ouen's beach (and on one occasion just off the beach – in the sea). There is still a story about a jolly pilot who used to sit in the passenger seat wearing a civilian overcoat. He would look grumpily at his watch and announce that if the pilot did not arrive soon he would fly the plane himself. Other passengers would laugh at the little joke until he got up, sat behind the controls and started the engines. Consternation had to be stifled by letting them in on the joke.

Today's small planes buzz like wasps between the islands and nowhere is the landing more interesting than on Alderney, where the runway is just inland from the grey cliffs that look as formidable from a height of 1,000 feet as they do from below.

St Anne on Alderney is the sweetest town in the Channel Islands; cobbled streets, coloured houses, wisteria drooping from gardens, window boxes bright along the pavements; it has the undoubted air of having been somehow wafted from the Normandy *Bocage* region just across the water. The Germans took the bells from the church (and chopped up the pews for firewood) but they were found in Cherbourg after World War II and returned to their rightful belfry in the church which is said to have no equal in the islands. To hear those bells calling over the fields of Alderney, across the bays, the harbour, the cliffs and over the sea, is to hear a lovely sound – the sound of an island.

*

Chausey is the shy French cousin. People who think they know the Channel Islands well confess to never having heard of it. But it is there, not just one island but more than fifty, poking their noses from the sea, eight of them with grass and salty trees.

It took a verdict from the International Court to decide that Chausey was truly part of France and that the smaller islands – Les Ecréhous and Les Minquiers – belonged to Jersey. Marmotière, on Les Ecréhous, has a little 'town' – a single short street and a customs post. On Blanque Island there once lived a hermit called Pinel who received a present from Queen Victoria, a grand officer's uniform coat – but no trousers. He was there for forty years, sometimes wearing his coat as he sat outside his house. He was followed years later by another voluntary castaway, a jolly gentleman called Le Gastelois who, wrongly accused of a crime in Jersey, took himself off to Les Ecréhous and remained there until proved innocent.

I went from Granville in Normandy to Chausey on a blissful summer's day with a company of French fishermen who were sailing to gather the pickings of the lowest tide of the year – an amazing drop of more than forty feet which brings the rocks and islands out of the sea like the scaly backs of a herd of monsters. The men spent the day among the pools and inlets while I wandered about the delightful Grande Ile, drank and ate at the inn, looked over the school wall at the island children and sat in superb isolation on the beach. Glowing with the happiness that such a day can bring I boarded the boat with the fishermen again. They were well satisfied. Their buckets and creels were full.

Back to France we went, across the silk evening sea. Sausages, thick bread and wine were produced. With some difficulty I attempted to tell my neighbour of the effect that beautiful and peaceful place had on me. I ended my recitation, *'C'est paradis.'*

Through a mouthful of bread and sausage, which he cleared with a swig of wine, he acknowledged that judging by my French I was English.

' 'Eaven,' he nodded. *'C'est* 'eaven.'

ENGLISH CHANNEL ISLANDS situated between latitudes 48°52'–49°43' N and longitudes 1°49'–2°35' W; total area 75 sq. m (194 sq. km); approx. population: Jersey 82,000, Guernsey 55,000, Alderney 2,000, Sark 600, Herm 37, Jethou 8; Britain. Chausey, approx. population 110; France

Capri
An Island in Autumn

Only by coming back to the island people can understand what rewards
life grants to those who stay.
EDWIN CERIO, *On Capri*

October morning came to the Bay of Naples with a soft brush of sunshine
touching Sorrento, the great mountains hung with cloud, Naples itself still
wet from an overnight thunderstorm, and the islands calm and composed in
the pale sea. Ischia and little Procida blinked in the new sun and on Capri I
opened my windows, stepped out on to the terrace and, looking around,
knew at once that all that is said about Capri is true. It is one of the world's
beautiful places.

I had arrived on the previous black night in the very clutch of the
thunderstorm – Wagner rather than the expected Rossini. The ferry from
Naples plunged and jumped through the surprising waves, lightning smacked
the sea and heaven rolled horribly. It was impossible to remain on deck and
stay dry, so, with my fellow travellers and sufferers, I sat stoically trying to
watch an ancient cowboy film on the saloon television. It was so old even
Gabby Hayes looked young. To see him do his famous monosyllable-and-
spitting act in dubbed Italian might have been engrossing had not the small
ship been going up and down like a rocking horse. The Italians have an apt
way with words for useful things – the *vomitario* on the vessel was well
patronized.

All through the bumpy voyage of an hour and twenty minutes the land was
never far away. Sorrento's stationary lights seemed within grabbing
distance and Capri itself, upon hopeful investigation, appeared only a couple
of cable lengths ahead of the ship. What could we be doing out on that bumpy
sea for so long?

Eventually, in the full sense of that word, the pitching eased and our little
vessel emitted a relieved toot, high like a hunting horn. Stepping out onto the
deck I experienced that incomparable feeling once more, that sensation
known to those chosen people who love islands and can go to them. There it
was directly ahead of us, 10,000 lights climbing the black form of a hillside.

The mole of the harbour slipped by, the waves quietened at once like chastened children, the air felt warm, the scent of pasta drifted from the port. All was well.

Twice happy now, for being there and for escaping the ill-temper of the sea, the passengers hustled ashore. I had made no definite plans, but my immediate future was fixed for me by fate and a young man with a pencil moustache and a peaked cap sporting the legend Savoy Hotel. I am, as I have previously confessed, a traveller who can stand anything but discomfort and the name on the cap was the reassurance I needed. I handed him my bags and we set off at a good gait along the quayside. I was immediately glad I had discovered him, and him me. 'Capri,' he said somehow managing to spread one hand theatrically although still humping the cases, 'she is like a ship, *signore*. Me, I was a steward on the liner called the *Galileo*. It was no difference to me for all my life I lived in this place like a ship at sea.'

It was not a matter of getting into a taxi. Briskly he led me through a big cave in the rock face. He paid at a kiosk without putting down the luggage and led me busily on. It was like going into one of the rides at Disney World. The aptly named *funivia*, a cable car, ascends from the cavern. We climbed into one of the compartments and at once the doors clattered shut and we were clanking splendidly up the flank of the dark mountain with the lights of the harbour spreading out below. It was a brief journey. The doors opened and the man from the Savoy bustled out with me in his wake. It was all I could do to keep up.

He bounded up some steps from the *funivia* with me in pursuit. He opened a door and we set out into one of the most lovely and surprising situations I can ever recall. We were in the miniature town square of Capri, enclosed, with old butter-coloured buildings, and café chairs and tables set around, warmly lit, and a splendid set of stone steps rising from the back. It was like a large stage, the set all ready for the opera. All that was lacking this night were the performers. The rain had stopped but a wet-nosed wind pushed through the crevices of the buildings. A solitary, elderly lady sat, rather regally, at one of the café tables sipping a drink and looking around as if wondering where everyone else had gone.

The man from the Savoy had plunged into a narrow alley, all tight shadows and curves, with lights seeping from small windows and courtyards. Music, smells and voices came from the windows. The further my friend went the faster he walked; perhaps it was the scent of home. He turned right like a soldier and down another flight of worn steps. I could smell the overhanging flowers in the darkness. Now we were there, the Savoy Hotel. It was patently a good deal less grand than its title. My guide, like a man performing a quick-change act, shuffled quickly behind the reception desk and took off his peaked porter's cap which he placed in a drawer. 'Welcome to the Savoy Hotel, *signore*,' he smiled expansively. 'I would like that you meet the owner.' He thrust out his hand. 'Gianni Tarantino. It is me.'

There are two towns on Capri, each one small, each charming, each different. The island is like three steps with the Marina Grande harbour on the first, Capri town on the one above and Anacapri, the second settlement, on the top step. At one time a ladder cut into the soaring rock of this limited but lofty place, gave the only access from the haven at Marina Grande and from Capri to Anacapri. There were more than 800 crazy steps called the Phoenician Staircase. Communications between the two towns were understandably few. Until the road was built in 1874 they regarded each other with suspicion and dislike, usual between neighbouring states or nations.

During my first night on the island I could hear the thunderstorm still tramping around the mainland mountains. It was like having a drunk in the room upstairs.

But by morning I knew he had gone. I lay listening to the private sounds of birds in a garden, somebody calling up from a valley, or down a hill, a single bell sounding. I opened the shutters and looked out with the surprise that is no surprise on a new scene on a new island.

My room was perched half way up the arm of a valley, looking out over flowers, trees, ochre buildings, and beyond that the ruffled blue sea. There was that well-washed smell and balmy feel that comes after a storm. I watched a man warily pulling the coloured sun awning down over the front of his shop, cautious in case it was harbouring a reservoir of rainwater. He pulled. It was. Over the canvas the water gushed and he jumped away. Two other men laughed and shouted late advice. To one side, heading inland, the hill curved like a brandy glass, with the tiles of houses and the neat cupola of a church rising above its greenery. On the other side palms and cypresses fell away cosseting more sunny walls. Flowers dripped everywhere, the splendid bougainvillaea (first brought from the Solomon Islands to the Mediterranean by Bougainville, the explorer), vivid hibiscus, the frangipani of the tropics (although named after an Italian family), alongside clusters of quiet familiar roses. Below my balcony was a banana tree in fruit.

Had I expected, as most travellers to Capri expect, a place of super-sophistication, with every sleek tourist delight on view, everyone a society name, a jet-setter, an aristocrat of the world, then I was mistaken. Capri, despite the fashions of decades, still belongs to its own people. They have seen everything and everybody, right there on their doorstep, and they are no longer amazed or impressed. Their lives, in the main, are simple, village-like, with the tourist industry floating slightly above their heads. Even the delights for the visitor here are modest: there were no fine yachts in the harbour, no grand motor cars (no grand roads either), and the only way to reach the island is by the frequently bumpy boat or the hydrofoil. The islanders started a helicopter service from Naples but it was not a success. The landing pad is now a mass of wild flowers.

Naturally the hub, nub and hubbub of Capri town is the miniature square into which I had emerged on the previous night with such pleasure and surprise. It is splendidly called – entitled – the Piazza Umberto, an appellation which, while it sounds impressive, gives no feel whatever of its delights. Sitting in one of the cane chairs of the three cafés whose tables elbow each other for space on the cobbles, I took it all in, on that first morning, and saw that it was hardly bigger than a couple of tennis courts. And yet so much has been crammed into that space. Shops and the cafés, the municipality, the cathedral with its steps and the lovely campanile and happy clock which are across the street. Flowers spill from walls and urns, a stone prelate sends out a blessing from a small niche, like a saint sheltering from a shower; the clock of the cathedral (its bright face formed by polished tiles and figures) chimes according to its own peculiar pattern. Each quarter it strikes not only the quarter but the hour as well, to remind drowsy people of the exact passage of time.

Around the Piazza the walls of the buildings are old and rich in colour, ancient reds and cheesy yellows, with every iron balcony tendrilled with flowers. To sit there of an evening is to watch the little world of Capri. There are no cars so that everything for the shops in the surrounding alleys has to be transported by small trolleys and carts, some motorized, some pulled by men or boys. Wine, vegetables, bread, boxes, crates and carboys are trundled across the square by dark muttering men, or lads who are inclined to collide with obstacles while eyeing the local maidens. Mere visitors stand back and watch the scene for they are not included, only as bystanders. The lights come on to illuminate it all, the sounds of a debate issue loudly from the council chamber on an upper floor. You can see the councillors' backsides on the window sills. Music and perfume come from the windows. The Capriots stand and chatter in groups, children play, dogs, cats and the occasional smirking goat, wander obliquely. Tourists sit back like an audience. More people gather on the rising steps at the back of the square. The lights are bright. You realize you are watching a stage. It is the beginning of an Italian opera. At any moment you expect the activity to be stilled by someone in a doublet entering right, throwing his arms out, and singing loudly that 'The King is Coming!'

The delights of this island have been obvious through the ages. Capri has known a cavalcade of the famous from Thomas Mann to Gracie Fields to Krupp, who manufactured guns for Germany. He studied the biology of the island (particularly *lamprey larvae*) and built a nice shady seaside walk to commemorate his sojourn, the Via Krupp. Perhaps the arms and the man were two different things.

Capri's lotus-life so attracted the Emperor Tiberius that he made the island the capital of the Roman Empire between AD 27 and 37. His step-father had discovered it first and built no fewer than twelve sumptuous villas upon its balconied cliffs, among the olives and the ilex trees. According to the legend a dead ilex began to grow again when Augustus looked on it and this seemed a good portent and an excuse to establish himself there. He called the island *Apragopolis*, literally 'A Place of Lazy People'. All the excesses of Rome were repeated there in Tiberius's reign, including the tossing of human sacrifices over the huge cliffs. Part of the crazy Caligula's childhood was spent on Capri with Emperor Tiberius in those wild and bloody days.

One of the villas built by Augustus, reduced to stones now with the roots of columns protruding from grass and flowers, is perched on the sheer and beautiful drop almost above the famous Blue Grotto. I wondered if the Romans knew the cave was there, right under their feet (it was not officially 'discovered' until 1826). It would be difficult to believe that they did not, for the low entrance is exposed on good sea days. Perhaps they used its eerie blue reflection as part of their odd ceremonies and enjoyments, although if they did they kept it a secret. It was the one place in Capri that remained inaccessible to me. During my visit the sea was always too heavy.

I went to the Villa Imperiale, above the Blue Grotto, in one of the entrancing taxis which wriggle around the narrow confines of Capri. Some are old and grand, saloon cars with wonderful descending convertible roofs like those of a large perambulator. My driver, Gerardo, was extremely proud of his vehicle, which was nearly new but just as picturesque as the others. He told me how much it cost and not only brushed the seat before I sat down but *after* I got up.

We left from the top of the abyss just outside Capri town where the motor vehicles have to stop. The island's bright orange buses, crawling like ladybirds over the steep roads, also depart from here. In Capri every road seems to ascend. At once we began to climb and soon were circling like an open aircraft high and wonderfully above the town, looking down over the roofs among the trees, onto gardens and vineyards, and beyond to the Marina Grande, its splinter boats and the corrugated sea. Boats made seams across the bay of Naples, the island of Ischia looked content, and there were fluffy clouds over Mount Vesuvius.

It is at this point that the Phoenician Staircase, as the steps are called, the rocky ladder of 800 rungs rising from the harbour to the high streets of Anacapri, are incised at the side of the road. They drop sheerly down over the terrible rocks that go to the shore and rise high into the fir trees and cypresses collaring the heights that lead somewhere to the clouds and the second town. There is, naturally, some argument as to how many steps there are; the legends vary between 777 and 800. It is probably some time since anyone carefully counted them.

It was the centre of the day when we reached Anacapri and the air had warmed. The shy town, uncaring that the settlement on the lower slopes has taken all the glory, is touched with quiet beauty. Houses so mellow they look almost mouldy, clutter courtyards and alleys and the patterned streets. I sat under the vines in a café, drank the cool local wine, and watched the traffic which consisted of two schoolboys in smocks riding the same bicycle and a man solidly trundling a barrow upon which was a fat basket of olive oil.

Anacapri would be just that, another shaded, pretty town overlooking the Mediterranean, if it were not for one extraordinary thing. In the church of San Michele, an otherwise unremarkable eighteenth-century building, is the most amusing and amazing mosaic floor I have ever seen. The wonderful scene – the disgraced Adam and Eve being sent from the Garden of Eden – occupies the entire church floor so that the church is rarely used for services for fear that the feet of the worshippers would damage it. The visitor must creep carefully around the perimeter by means of a treadway, rather like going around an ornamental pond. The best way to observe the entire mosaic, however, is to mount the spiral stairs to the gallery of the church and look down on it in all its coloured wonder.

The tiles are the familiar shiny Mallolica squares; the colours browns, yellows and blues. Sturdy Adam and stocky Eve, the man already running, the woman, naturally, trying to have the last word with the banishing angel, are in the bottom right-hand corner of the scene. The angel sits on a small convenient cloud on the bank of Eden's river. In the middle of the picture is the apple tree with the suitably smirking serpent curled around its trunk.

It is the supporting cast, all lovely animals, that give the picture its fascination and its fun. There are crinkly crocodiles and happy-looking bears, cats and idle dogs, a wandering white horse and a lost-looking elephant. A cat sits pleasantly beneath a camel, there is a griffon, and a beaming lion who appears to be eyeing a brace of chickens and considering lunch. On the water and in the trees are many birds. An eagle watches the scene haughtily and an owl squats in the plundered apple tree wearing an 'I-told-you-so' expression. In the sky the sun and all the stars shine together. You could gaze at it for hours and still find something new. If it were the only thing to see in Capri it would still be worth the journey.

A few streets and squares across the town is the villa where Axel Munthe, the great physician and benefactor, lived, and about which he wrote in his famous autobiography *The Story of San Michele*. He died in 1949 but the house with all the taste and treasures that were his is still kept as it was and is open daily. The people he cared for, and who loved him, look after it with a concern that indicates that the great man might at any moment return.

High above the villa and the town stands Monte Solaro, the highest viewpoint on Capri. The view is commanding in a place of outstanding scenery, but the reaching of it is just as worthwhile. You gain the summit by chairlift, a journey on looping cables slung up the side of the mountain which measures just under 2,000 feet. Sitting on an open, oddly childish seat, being whisked to that height was, I thought, only for the intrepid or the foolhardy. But old ladies do it and come down laughing, so I had to risk it. It is not as fearsome as it sounds for the passenger travels with idyllic lack of speed up the green and gradual slopes, never being more than twenty feet above somebody's roof, vineyard or market garden.

At the bottom end of the cable I bought a return ticket. (Single tickets are available, but how do you get down again?) The attendant instructs you to place your feet on two foot-shapes on the floor and you stand there, feeling mildly foolish, watching the chairs swaying down the mountain towards you and the explorer in front of you being transported on his uphill journey. You study the arriving passengers' faces for signs of terror or relief. There are none. They smile smug smiles that say, 'There's nothing to it really.'

An attendant detaches the passenger as he or she arrives back to earth and they leave the chair with a brief run. Then it swings the corner and comes towards you. The drill is brisk and easy (if you don't panic). The chair curls around the bend and you wait, knees slightly bent, like a skier, so that it catches you and drops you into a sitting position, and away you go. Clipping the fragile bar across your middle, you find yourself being eased aloft at a lullaby speed. You pass an ominous and, for me, unnecessary notice which says, 'Don't Swing'. You look up and examine the single cable upon which you ride: it bumps disconcertingly over the wheels on the pylons spaced at yawning intervals up the mountainside. But it looks as though it might hold. Below, the earth is sliding away. The streets and roofs of Anacapri fan out, the sea is silver. Rocks and gorges change form as you travel. You suspect that you are going to enjoy it.

Despite the widespread view, the real fascination is nearer, more intimate, right beneath your travelling feet: all the way up the terraced slopes are olive groves, vineyards and crowded vegetable patches. There are small horticultural houses almost hidden in vines, and as you dangle past the windows you can see the people inside. It must be very odd sitting there and watching a foreign pair of legs go by every twenty seconds. I tried waving with my foot as I progressed but there was no reaction. They must be used to it by now.

The other pastime, during the twelve minutes to the summit, is observing the people coming down. It is strangely embarrassing to pass a stranger in mid-air; it's difficult to know how or whether to make a greeting.

Some people stare setly ahead. The British and the Japanese are good at this. Others give a small yawing smile and perhaps add a wave, and you, of course, return the courtesy. The embarrassments come into view as they descend towards you. Some summon up a laugh or a comment, although conversation is, of course, limited. Some people play jokes. As I went by one jolly chap called, 'I knew your father!' Before I could question him he had gone forever.

After twelve varied minutes, during which you have seen the beautiful island from a series of unique angles and met twenty or thirty new people, you reach the flattened pate of Monte Solaro. As the cable levels and you run in towards the disembarking point an attendant stands, legs astride, hand thrust out as though ready to shake yours. It is both a greeting and a release for he tugs you clear of the chair and you are there. If the passenger is a pretty girl he grabs her with both hands. It is one of the perks of the job.

At the top the scene is so lavish you have to laugh. Warmth and loveliness spread themselves from your toes to the edge of the world. Misted mountains, brilliant sea; islands, headlands, roofs and sky, near and distant.

It is almost too extravagant. The man who runs the café at the top is used to it all. He goes to work every morning on the chair lift and returns home by it at night. No rush-hour for him. I asked for a glass of wine but he said he could only provide me with a whole bottle. I hesitated and glanced over the parapet to the dizzy descent of the cable. I decided to have a small beer instead.

Capri is a small place and it is the small things that remain with the traveller; two men tuning the organ in the old and broken charterhouse of La Certosa while the woman caretaker went out on the ramparts to watch the sunset. It was not poetry which took her there, but duty and punctuality. She had to lock the place at sunset and when the last red bar of the sun had gone below the sea that is what she did, locked up.

In the unending entertainment of the main square of Capri town, that small theatre, there occurs a regular moment of comedy. There is only one public convenience. The key is kept behind one of the bars and the needy have to request its use. It is attached to a chain and, so that it never gets mislaid, on the end of the chain is a hefty rubber ball, larger than a tennis ball. Some people transport it with some attempt at secrecy and decorum across the crowded square; others, with bravado, swing the ball and chain as they go.

One morning I was sitting on the flowered and urned terrace of the Piazzetta watching the track of the great hydrofoil that journeys between Naples and Salerno. It stood out like a racing liner across the bay. (The Italians, with that blissful touch they have with names, call it *Il Jumbo del Mare* – The Sea Elephant.) A group of American tourists approached and one pair, a man and wife, rounded, elderly, their faces as bright as their clothes, detached themselves to take yet another photograph. The man posed against the beautiful background while his wife fiddled with the camera.

'Do you want the ocean or the mountains behind you?' she demanded.

'Just make it good,' he shouted back. 'This one is for my girlfriend.'

She saw me laughing. 'Listen,' she confided, 'we been married forty-two years. If he can get a girlfriend at his age then he's better than I think.'

She took the pictures. He returned and they laughed. Then he put his arm around her, hers went about him, and, embraced, they waddled tubbily away. All at once I, the lone traveller, felt very solitary. And I realized one last important thing about Capri. It is a place to be with someone you love.

CAPRI situated latitude 40°33′ N and longitude 14°15′ E; area 4 sq. m (10 sq. km); population approx. 12,000; Italy

Corfu
The Green Eye of Greece

. . . the splendour of olive grove and orange garden,
the blue of sky and ivory of church and chapel . . .
EDWARD LEAR on Corfu

At 4.30 in the morning the plane flew in from the west, between dark-shouldered mountains, over the sleeping bay, its lights blazing as it approached the airport, making its own moonlight on the water.

It is said about Corfu – an island like a green eye in the blue Ionian Sea – that you only have to look around and you will see some new beauty. This was mine; a different time, a different viewpoint, standing on my balcony watching the approach of the pre-dawn aircraft. Previously it had seemed to me a great shame that the only possible way by air into this lofty and lovely place was over a land-and-seascape so tranquil that even the wings of a bird would disturb it. Throughout the day, fortunately in the autumn at wide intervals, the noisy planes arrived, flattening out over the lambent bay with its two islets, Vlacherna and Pondikonisi, and roared gutturally onto the runway. It seemed a poor return for centuries of stillness and beauty. But, in the early dark hours, it was different. The plane added something new to the wonders of this place and I had made safe my individual moment of memory.

The two little isles below the balustrades of Kanoni just south of Corfu Town, must be among the most painted and photographed places in the world (to which I added my own dozen or so optimistic frames) and there can be no angle left that will lend a new view. The second islet floats like a dream out in the limp water, a few fingers of cypress, a white tower showing above them; the first is not really an island at all for it can be reached by a stone causeway alongside which the Corfiot fishermen potter in their boats.

It was, in the latter days of the British Protectorate in the 1860s, a favourite promenade for society – a 'walk to the One Gun' it was called, for here was a cannon placed by the French during their occupation. The artillery is long gone, but the walk remains satisfying, out to the isle with its miniature convent and single cypress, where birds sing in the stillness. In order to keep faith with the name of the place, Kanoni, the Corfiots later placed another 'One Gun' overlooking the bay, a Russian artillery piece which is still there, looking a little out of place among the parked cars.

The elegant people's Sunday walk was an aspect of the careful structure of Corfu's society for centuries. When the Serene Republic of Venice held sway over the island the names of the local worthies were entered in Golden Books. These were publicly burned when the French arrived, but *they* built an arcade in Corfu Town which became known as the Liston, the place where only the best people – those on 'The List' – were permitted to perambulate. Today's society is a good deal more dispersed and gregarious, but it still enjoys the shade and elegance of the Liston, its arches and iron lamps modelled on the rue de Rivoli in Paris, sitting, watching, drinking, talking, and forever calling waiters whose names always seem to be Spiro.

This is scarcely an exaggeration for sixty per cent of all Corfu's boys are christened Spiro, and eighty per cent of the waiters have this name. In one restaurant I know, everyone is a Spiro!

They take their name from the island's blessed overseer, St Spiridon, who through plague, storm and battle, has lent protection to his trusting people. He lies in a silver coffin in his red-topped church in Corfu Town ('St Spiridon is in there,' the caretaker, collecting candle-ends and pointing to a side chapel, told me in the manner of a butler confirming that His Lordship is at home.) At Easter, and on other feast days, St Spiridon is taken from the coffin and paraded around the town so the people can view him.

Over the years the relic of the saint has become a little ragged perhaps, but the people still love him dearly, and he has not let them down. Apart from his deliverances from pestilence and soldiery, he once appeared in an olive grove and advised a farmer not to prune the olive trees in the traditional way but to let them grow, to desist from beating the trees (it hurt them, he said), and wait until the fruit fell to the ground. Corfu is the only place in Greece where this method is carried out. Travelling through the countryside you see nets beneath the trees ready to catch the fruit – the finest in the Mediterranean. There are three million unruly olive trees in Corfu, some of them still giving fruit after five hundred years.

When the mummy of St Spiridon arrived in Corfu from Cyprus in 1456 (he had then been dead a thousand years) it was transported in a bag on the back of a donkey, along with the headless remains of St Theodora, by a Greek saint-dealer called Kalokheretes. There is a story that St Theodora's head had been sold in Rome. Both saints are still on the island, the lady is allowed to rest peacefully at Mitropoli, the Orthodox cathedral, but St Spiridon receives visitors daily and is still very much at the heart of the people.

*

Corfu Town – known as Kerkira to the Greeks – is like a well-loaded cheese board. Its old buildings, yellow, cream, peach, orange and white, pile one on the other. They open out into random balconied squares and unofficial alleys, and broaden into a mellow tapestry that can be best viewed from the Citadel, the great abandoned hump of a fortress that overlooks the sea.

It is said that the island took its name from the Citadel, from the Greek *korfous*, meaning the 'peaks' of the fortress (although derivations have to be treated with some caution, since a well-liked Corfiot dish *aristou* is said to be simply a corruption of Irish stew).

For at least 800 years there has been a fortress on the huge haunch of rock, although only in a country so rich in its past as Greece would such a prominence be allowed to decay and crumble like an old cake in the way this Citadel has done. It has, however, some good features: cannons and mortars used as gateposts and even lamp standards, and an exquisite canal that cuts it away from the main town. The traveller John Locke noted in the sixteenth century that it had just been 'trenched about by the sea' and this trench has, fortunately, been preserved rather better than the fortress it was made to protect.

From the bridge high above the canal I looked down on its clever sanctuary, small boats moored side by side, and nose to stern, to protect them from winter's marauding storms. A careful old fisherman was baiting some lines down below me, sitting in his sharp boat, throwing an occasional tidbit to any one of a group of five cats who sat in an expectant half circle. On the other side of the bridge five men were gossiping, two of them sitting in the stern of a boat, smoking, the puffs of their pipes rising like signals. When I peered over two hours later they were still there.

The condition of the interior of the Citadel makes you wonder if it is safe to walk about. Crumbling walls, collapsed wells, old gunpowder chambers grinning like openings in a bad set of teeth, weeds climbing towers; and the saddest of sights, a once fine clock, mottled and scarred, its faded golden hands crippled and stuck at three minutes past three.

If one wants to reach the top of this mouldy pile you creep up through a lightless, dripping tunnel, over broken and slippery steps, and out through a small aperture – to a thrilling viewpoint, overlooking sky and sea, islands and the piled and coloured buildings of Corfu Town.

*

It was November (I was the final guest to leave the hotel before it closed for the winter) and there was rain and dazzling thunderstorms that lit the surprised faces of the mountains and danced on the sea. But there were serene days, also, when the light was dulcet, when an hour in a concealed bay, sitting on rocks, looking into the depths of the water, was an hour sweetly spent.

So, equally, was an hour idling under the fine, lanterned arches of the Liston, doing nothing better than drinking *ouzo*, watching the passing people and the dogs sitting like fielders between the fall of wickets on the famous cricket pitch. Cricket arrived in Corfu, naturally, with the British but not because of the influence, as some would have it, of Lord Byron. It was the British Army who laid out the cricket field on the Esplanade. It afforded an open area, a field of fire for guns pointing seawards, and recreation for officer batsmen and bowlers. The private soldier was not so accommodated. 'On Sundays,' wrote Private Wheeler, a soldier whose letters have been collected and published, 'after service the whole garrison march to the Esplanade where the Major General amuses himself for two or three hours in putting them through a field day.'

Life is less regimented now. Royal Navy teams kept the cricket alive after the British garrison left, then the Corfiots learned the game and today there are two teams who play a version of the English summer game against each other and against scratch teams of visitors.

It was facing the cricket field, on one of the warm nights, that I sat eating my dinner when Spiro, the waiter, sidled up and whispered carefully, 'Sir, a stitch in time saves nine.'

Unable to find anything about my person which needed urgent repairs, I awaited his return to question him. He struck first. This time he said, 'It's a long road that has no turning.' He looked at me anxiously. Did I think that was true? Yes, I thought it was. Later he was back with a sibilant, 'Every cloud has a silver lining,' and a splendid amalgam, 'Look after the pennies and tomorrow will look after itself.'

These wise saws, it appeared, he was garnering from a book of English proverbs, arming himself for brighter and better conversation with the tourists he would be serving the following summer.

As I left I thought I would, in cricket parlance, bowl a bouncer at him. I confided, 'When in doubt, do the right thing.'

I was immediately sorry. Bafflement clutched at his face, he scratched his head. But then he smiled surely and leaned close enough to whisper triumphantly, 'But a stitch in time saves nine.'

The Corfiot is cheerful and friendly, provided you have time to talk. One night all the taxis in the town had apparently gone home to bed and I was given a lift by a telephone engineer from Athens who was living on the island. 'Never, never, never, will you be able to understand how the people here think,' he told me sadly. 'They are strange indeed. I know, I am married to one.'

During the summer the common rural scene is of women hoeing the fields, digging the ditches, carrying loads and driving goats and donkeys, while the menfolk seem to spend an inordinate amount of time sitting and talking in the tavernas. In the south of the island, so I heard, the women held a protest meeting about their hard lot and demanded concessions from their menfolk. The only condition they could wring was that, in future, the wife would not be expected to carry the donkey's load so that her husband could ride on the donkey – for a trial period only.

Out of the town the ancient life settles like a cloak over the countryside. Roads narrow and curve into mountain villages where old men sit in chairs in the street (their womenfolk being well occupied in the fields) where the village well and the café television set are the centres of communal activity. One wonders what such people, with their rough floors, their basic life, make of some of today's television programmes.

Costas, the man who drove me out into the northern hills, told me that on his television set he can get programmes from Yugoslavia, Albania and Italy, but not from mainland Greece. The reception is not good enough. Yet the island is in a fluke position for receiving radio broadcasts. They flow loud and clear from the Middle East, the Mediterranean, the Russian bloc countries and from Africa. A man called Michael Gurdus, who listens eighteen hours a day, broke the news of the Entebbe raid to the Western world, and the failure of President Carter's attempt to rescue the Iran hostages.

Albania is Corfu's close neighbour. The channel between the two is only just over a mile wide in the northeast of the island. Looking out from the delightful, warm, busy village of Kouloura across the water, it lies hard, mountainous and deserted, brooding like an ugly sister.

Up through the mountain passes I went, a country bald with rocks, but with slender cypress trees standing like the look-outs of an army. On one lonely stretch of road was a lorry playing pop music from a loudspeaker. 'I've got what you want,' recommended the singer, appropriately since the wonderfully ornate gipsy woman on the tailboard was selling plastic pails and bowls to village housewives.

A priest trudged down the sloping road with a suitcase, ruminating into his beard as he walked, thinking possibly of God, or of the next incline. The faces of the people seemed as lined as the land. Their olive groves cling to abyss and crag and their vegetables are grown on terraces barely wider than balconies. The difficulties of life show plainly.

Over the mountains we came to Paleocastrizza, a creamy church with shining bells, perched poetically above a dragon coast of deep-cut rocks and bays. The sea was ruffled and blue, there were shady trees in the walled garden of the church and relays of women carried earth for another flowerbed in baskets and tins upon their heads. Life is peaceful but hard.

It is said that Ulysses was wrecked on this rugged northwesterly coast of Corfu, and certainly in the museum in the town there is an intriguing Gorgon carved in stone now 2,500 years old. But, oddly perhaps, the island is without the extravagance of archaeological remains that litter most of mainland Greece.

The history of Corfu was much influenced by the French, the British and particularly the Venetians. (Due to a mistake at the League of Nations Corfu was also put, for two days, under the control of Japan. I suppose it does sound oriental.) Just along the coast from Corfu Town at Gouvis, down some muddy roads that lead to the seashore, and in splendid neglect, is a Venetian arsenal, a wonderful geometry of stone arches, now roofless, criss-crossing each other and casting multiple shadows in the sunlight. Here the ships of the Levant Squadron were pulled from the water and repaired. The place has haphazard wire fencing around it now (full of holes so it is easy to gain entrance) and weeds grow plentifully among the foundations, but it is not difficult to imagine the industry of three centuries ago, with the shipwrights working and the vessels of the Serene Republic lying offshore in the Ionian sunshine.

The French are remembered by the Liston, perhaps as odd a transference of culture, bringing the rue de Rivoli from Paris, as the British establishing a cricket ground immediately alongside it. History can also be found in the British Cemetery, a cool and secluded place, cared for by a custodian called Georges, a Greek who lives at the gate.

Here, below the trees, is the grave of The Honourable Charles Monckton, Captain in Her Britannic Majesty's 38th Regiment of Connaught Rangers, who died at the hand of an assassin on 9 August 1857, aged twenty-six years.

Here also lies Lieutenant Colonel William Jardner Freer who fought in all the major battles of the Peninsular War, losing an arm at Badajos, and dying in Corfu at the age of forty-five. Private John Connors of the Buffs is buried a few paces away – he won the Victoria Cross.

More recent history was marked by the Corfiots while I was on their island. October 28 is *Ohi* Day (literally 'No' day) marking the moment in 1940 when the Greeks refused to bow to the demands of the bully Mussolini. All over the nation parades were held and in Corfu the streets were crowded in the pale sunshine with people watching a happy and thankfully nondescript parade made up of a few soldiers but mostly of bands and out-of-step school children. It was an ebullient affair. Three times I was in danger of having an eye poked out by ecstatic parents pointing out their offspring to each other as they jolted by. The bands kept appearing from mystifying directions – twice joining the parade after bursting through the thick crowd from the rear.

Mussolini, like Napoleon, had a fascination for Corfu, although neither ever visited the island. In 1923, the Italian dictator sent a warship to bombard the town in retaliation for the assassination of a Fascist envoy to a boundary conference in Albania. He would have occupied the island if it had not been for British influence.

If history can be regarded as entertainment, and why not, then Corfu's contribution is in the Achilleion, the astonishing mansion and garden built by the sad Empress Elizabeth of Austria. She had stayed on the island in 1861, for once out of sight of her adulterous husband Franz Josef and his witch of a mother. Imagining herself to have found, at last, happiness, she commissioned the house to be built and thirty years later it was complete. But she spent little time there before her death at the hand of an assassin in 1898.

The house is a glaring mixture of styles and parodies of styles, replete with cupids, angels and nymphs (sucking their fingers), terraces, stairs, carvings and cornices, in goodness knows how many varieties. The whole is said to represent Achilles. Henry Moore wrote of it, 'The Palace at Achilleion stands as an abomination in the face of nature and all things lovely.'

Abomination or not, Corfiots rejoice in sending their visitors to view the charming travesty. I went, additionally, to see one of its newer attractions – it houses the Corfu Casino. Roulette being my speciality I played for a couple of hours and, as is my custom, came out with more than I entered.

What riveted me in the Casino was that at each croupier's hand, on each of the fifteen or so tables, and amid all the apparent sophistication, the clicking quiet, the evening dresses, the stuffed white shirts and the diamonds, was a large red, plastic battery-operated flashlamp. The management, with a few million drachmas on the tables, it seemed trusted neither the electricity supply nor the customers. A switch, to paraphrase Spiro the waiter, in time saves a lot more than nine.

CORFU situated latitude 38°3′ N and longitude 20°5′ E; area 231 sq. m (600 sq. km); population approx. 106,600; Greece

Madeira
The Ocean Garden

I do not know a spot on the globe which so astonishes
and delights upon first arrival.
CAPTAIN MARRYAT

In the lofty centre of the Atlantic island of Madeira is a village called Curral das Freiras lying in the deep cup of a dead volcano. Until recent times there was no road to it and there were some villagers who never went to the outside, not even to Funchal, the island town. They were born, lived and died within the rim of the crater, their world bounded by soaring rocks and a single circle of sky. To leave would have been too difficult; it was too far to walk.

The volcano and the peaks that buttress it collect clouds. When Zarco, the Portuguese adventurer – sent by Henry the Navigator in the fifteenth century to explore the ocean beyond the horizon – first saw Madeira he thought it *was* a cloud. He watched from the small isle of Porto Santo, twenty-eight miles away, and wondered why the cloud was always there but did not venture further for a long time. In his heart he thought it might be the place where God brooded.

When he and his sailors finally voyaged the last few miles, past the barren and haunting islands they called the Desertas, they discovered that the cloud was adorning a mountain range rising from the ocean. It was covered with great trees – the Portuguese word for 'wood' is *madeira* – and Zarco charged one of his lieutenants with burning an area clear for the establishment of a settlement. The man, whose name and fate are not recorded, went too enthusiastically about the razing. He set the entire island ablaze. It burned for seven years.

Today the approach to the island by plane is slightly forbidding. The corrugated Atlantic is abruptly broken by a mountain bearded with cloud, its greyness casting a shadow over the land and the sea. The off-islands lie like patrol boats screening a battleship. Attached to the edge of the landmass, like some afterthought, is the airport. It was 1964 before the islanders could contrive a piece of ground flat enough to take a runway. Before that Madeira was reached only by sea and by flying boat. The runway is very short. Passengers blink with apprehension. The pilot doesn't sound too happy. 'If you have a nervous disposition,' he mentions, 'please pull down the window blinds.'

He has a final look at the approach then puts the Boeing 737 down ('made for little places like this,' he confides to cheer us), with a bump like an elevator, a few feet from the start of the runway. 'It's better than having to pull up sharply at the other end,' he chats. We have ample room. We slow and everybody breathes and smiles again and says it was nothing really. Now the plane turns and we see the name of the island, *Madeira*, laid out in flowers.

Years ago there used to be a character in a decrepit peaked cap who stood on the quay at Funchal; he was called, he said, Manuel P. Texas. I met him when I came ashore from a ship bound for Rio and he took me on a tour of which I remember nothing. All that I do remember are his stories – told in an outrageous James Cagney accent – of how he had been on a sailing- ship wrecked off Madeira, his epic struggle ashore and how he had remained on the island ever since. He had tales of battles and storms and fruity love affairs – some of them possibly true.

A quarter of a century later I went to Funchal harbour with the thought that he might still be there but he wasn't. What's more, no one remembered him. There were guides named Manuel but none called P. Texas.

Since that first journey I have visited the island three times, twice only as a stopping place between other ports of the world (Madeira's traditional role) and I do not remember going beyond the streets of Funchal, an old but very much lived-in place full of clatter and fumes. A doctor I went to see on the last occasion (I developed a spectacularly bleeding nose) described it as the most polluted place in the Atlantic Ocean.

*

Despite the almost total absence of roads (even into the 1970s they were limited) the motor car made an early appearance in Madeira. In 1909 an English observer commenting on the first automobiles attempting to travel along Funchal's cobbled and encrusted streets protested that they were 'an outrage perpetrated on the most cherished traditions of the city . . . mushroom things . . . freaks that fitted as ill as a silk hat on the head of a peasant.' He happily concluded that it was a passing fad and that 'the honour of the town is perfectly safe in the lines of its pavement.'

Some hope. Today Funchal is one of the most noisome and congested places I have ever seen. The tortuous jams were not helped, but undoubtedly enlivened, by the fact that the municipal authority was systematically dynamiting the roads in the most crowded parts of the town during the busiest times of the day. Funchal is built on volcanic rock, and each yard had to be blown up. So a policeman halted the traffic, the charge was exploded and when the dust and rubble had subsided, the drivers were waved on.

Yellow buildings with their old courtyards stand with some remaining dignity amid the twentieth-century mayhem but it is no surprise that the fifteenth-century cathedral looks inauspiciously like a railway station. The tight streets, the exotically grubby bars, the market and the port make up for the grit and the din. In the evening, when the cars are less and the dynamiting is stilled, hundreds of young people gather in the street that leads from the cathedral to the sea. They do not parade along tree-lined avenues as they do in the towns of the Iberian peninsula but simply stand and exchange gossip and jokes. When I first saw them congregate I thought it was a particularly quiet riot, a major accident or at least a film being shot. But they were just chatting.

The island city is, as most are, best viewed from over your shoulder, from the steepling hills, as you leave its annoyances and go into the country beyond. It is only a few miles before you are in a different land; an astounding country of green and mountainous silence.

Up there in the secret interior, men and women work in patches of terrace wearing, strangely, woollen hats which enclose their ears but with nothing on their feet. They grow everything from cabbages to yams (such is the climate and the topography), from chestnuts to custard apples, from potatoes to pawpaw. But they have to buy their meat from the town for there is scarcely room to graze a sheep or a cow.

To travel through these placid upland places is to see glimpses of an untouched life: children in smocks dawdling from school; men carrying great loads on their bonneted heads; a journeying coffee seller with his pole and urns; a country funeral, the mourners in carts beneath a mass of umbrellas; women wearing away the stones of mountain streams with their eternal washing. Outside the door of an inn, overlooking one of the most superlative views I have seen, stood a blind man, never to know what he was missing.

Water runs and tumbles in the high places. On one road the traveller passes through eight waterfalls. The water is garnered in the mountains and fed down to the lowland settlements and fields by a spider's web of ancient canals, called *levadas*, cut, like the roads, by the hands of the peasants through hard rock. The country seems to go forever upwards; up to the peaks, to the barren tops sometimes strewn with snow, to the clouds that Zarco saw.

The British, during the assembly of their Empire, proved to be more able and persuasive in colonies that belonged to somebody else. This was the case in Madeira where their military presence was perfunctory but where their influence was profound and long lasting. Today this influence remains more in evidence than in many former British territories.

Captain Cook was one of the first admirers of the island. 'Madeira,' he wrote in his diary, 'is the recipient of Nature's most liberal gifts.' He did not stop for more than a few days. But others did. Two of the novelties enjoyed by today's tourists – the bullock-sledge and the downhill running-sledge – were the respective brainchildren of a Captain Bulkeley of the Life Guards and a Mr R. M. Gordon. Both conveyances were born out of the ready and rough mountain roads. Captain Bulkeley designed a bullock-carro made for himself and had another made for his wife. Mr Gordon used his sledge to toboggan down the bumpy slope from his hillside villa into Funchal. Naturally he had a servant to pull it back up again. English exiles planted most of the early gardens in the island, recognizing that in this equable place almost anything would flourish. The plants, seeds and saplings, brought by calling sailors, thrived in the warm summers and easy winters – the coral tree from Brazil, the poinsettia from the South Seas, the rose of Sharon, the avocado; shrubs and small flowers of the Andes, Queensland silk oak, tree heather from Ethiopia; the strawberry from the English cottage garden. The delicate embroidery which is the art of Madeiran women and passed on only to selected girls was first demonstrated by Elizabeth Phelps, an English gentlewoman. A story that Thomas Chippendale visited the island and had a hand in the founding of the famous wickerwork furniture industry is unlikely to be proved.

The Madeira wine trade was established by a Scotsman. Shakespeare wrote of the Duke of Clarence drowning in a barrel of malmsey, which is normally better as a drink. The distinctive Madeira wines were discovered, literally, by accident. Sailors tossing on the Atlantic discovered that the contents of the casks in the hold were improved by the rough treatment and the hot conditions. They sang a song which went, 'The moon dost shine, And our ballast is old wine.'

The Blandy family sailed from Britain many generations ago and is now the most powerful of the island's business families. Reid's Hotel, which among many other assets the family owns, is slightly more British than the London Ritz. There is a pre-war gentility that is all-pervasive. A band plays palm Court favourites; tea, with Madeira cake, is served on the terrace; and there was a time when the hotel refused to serve Coca Cola. Sir Winston Churchill frequently stayed there and is still remembered by many Madeirans simply as the man in the big hat who spent days painting the beautiful bay at Câmara de Lobos and never quite got it right.

Zarco, who became governor of the island, chose Câmara de Lobos (the 'cave of wolves') as the subject for his coat-of-arms and it is to be seen today, topped by a hungry-looking wolf with two wolves rampant below. The wolves of Câmara de Lobos, however, were in reality sea-wolves or seals, who used to howl from their cavern on moony nights.

There is a legend that the English arrived in Madeira before Zarco did. For in the fourteenth century Robert Machin, a merchant adventurer, fled from Bristol with a lady, Anne d'Arset, whose outraged father was in close pursuit. They set course for Brittany but missed it by a thousand miles, a storm finally depositing them on the shore of Madeira at the place today called Machico. Here they fell ill and died and were buried by their sailor companions on the lonely shore.

Their graves have been lost but in the small boat-building village today is a chapel that contains two crosses. The first cross is the subject of considerable veneration since it was washed out to sea once when the village was engulfed during a storm. The 4½-foot crucifix was found by an American ship many days later, far out and floating placidly. The crucifix was thought to be miraculous and was taken to Funchal where it was displayed in the cathedral until the chapel at Machico was restored. The second cross, much smaller and fashioned from juniper, is said to be the one from the grave of the sorry lovers. It bears an inscription, 'The remains of Machin's cross collected and deposited here by Robert Page in 1825.'

From the business interests of the Blandy family to elderly ladies in print dresses taking tea on Reid's terrace, signs of the British in Madeira are easy to find. There is an English library and an Anglican Church, a one-time chaplain of which, the Reverend Canon Arthur Walters, a poetic, rugby-playing Welshman, I met on a previous journey aboard the ship taking him to his new parish. His church sits among the Catholic churches of Funchal but, to set it apart, it is not permitted a spire but has instead a dome.

In the village of Camacha, the centre of the basket-weaving industry, there is a curious plaque noting that this was the place where football was first played on Portuguese soil. The British influence again.

Not far away, but higher into the pale eucalyptus trees, I discovered something strange and, for me, exciting. I had heard that in a place called Santo da Serra there had briefly been a British garrison, at the end of the eighteenth and the beginning of the nineteenth century. Napoleon was threatening Madeira and the troops were sent to protect the possession of Britain's Portuguese ally. (Napoleon, on his way to St Helena, called in at Funchal – or at least the ship transporting him did – and he was flattered at being called 'Your Majesty' by the British consul who went aboard to see he was comfortable.)

It was said that the British troops had left their marks in several ways, one being a number of fair-haired, blue-eyed children whose descendants can be quietly distinguished today, and the other by carving their names in the masonry of the village fountain.

But no one I asked, even those in the tourist business, could recall seeing the carvings; nor could Arlindo, my driver and guide, who thought he knew every stone on the island; nor indeed could the old men sitting in the threadbare square of Santo da Serra. They shook their heads and we departed.

After a mile down the mountain I decided to turn back. We immediately saw that the old men had been discussing the matter among themselves. Now one sage remembered; yes, there had been a fountain once, but it was outside the village now, down a rutted track, lost under the growth of the mountain. He had not seen it since he was a boy. We followed his directions. A woman in a field near the spot said she had never heard tell of a fountain but then, as we were going to look further, she came running after us to say that years before somebody else had come to look for the same thing. She pointed to a jungle, an overgrown conglomeration of vines, cider apples and cabbages.

There Arlindo and I discovered, all but hidden under the entwined growth, a flight of mossy, slippery steps. Carefully we descended. The air was fetid.

At the bottom was a stagnant pond buzzing with dragonflies. And also there were the remains of a carved fountain, now almost mouldy . . . and there too, in the masonry, were the engraved names of those soldiers of long ago – Selby, Taylor, Smith, Tate, W. Swayne, dated 1798, Anthony W. Seely, E. F. Goodall, Marshall and E. N. Taylor, 1810.

It was a wonderful, satisfying, moment.

Away from Funchal, anchored to the sea, many of Madeira's people live in places of mediaeval isolation. Despite the road system that has prised its way into the bouldered and desolate mountains, there are still villages which have no communication beyond a primitive track. The *hamac*, a hammock slung on the shoulders of two or four muscular and agile men, is still used to transport aged or sick people to the nearest road, sometimes miles over mountains, so they can be collected by an ambulance. On these cots the British once enjoyed being carried to the summit of Pico Ruivo, the highest peak at 6,106 feet, to observe the sunrise.

People to the north live in long thatched houses that, built among the opulent greenery, might easily be in Samoa. The people go about their difficult but placid lives, working their terraces, without the benefits of the twentieth century. Most places aspire to television (Madeira has its own station to supplement programmes from the Portuguese mainland) but some valleys are so deep that little but shadows are seen on the screen. An important football match sees the men of such places trekking to the neighbour with the highest house in the district. He is the one to keep as a friend.

I chose a Sunday to go to Curral das Freiras, the village in the volcano, and it was a good day to choose. The weather had been as moody as Atlantic weather can be, warm with gusty rain, but now the sky quietened and as Arlindo drove up once more into the eucalyptus belt and the chestnuts, the sun robed the flanks of the mountains and crags.

There are various stories of how the village got its name – the Refuge of the Sisters – the most acceptable being that the nuns of a convent at Santa Clara fled there to escape the attentions of rampaging French pirates.

The road, opened in 1959, curls like a spring around the peaks. It was built, inch by rocky inch, cobblestone by cobblestone, by the labour of the people. Arlindo remembers it. 'When I left the school at thirteen,' he said, 'my first job was to carry rocks and earth on the road-making. Even now, when I drive over that part of road, I must smile because I think some of it is mine.'

We stopped on the rim of the crater. There are houses there remote as sentinels, where people look directly from their windows into a green chasm of 2,000 feet. They cultivate every inch they can flatten. Husbandry must be as risky a business as it is at Cabo Girão, in the south, where the second highest cliff in the world soars straight from the Atlantic. Nineteen hundred feet up, and a foot from goodbye, peasants tend their important lettuces with never a second glance down.

From the volcano ridge I could see the orange roofs and the cotton-thread streets of Curral das Freiras strewn in the base of the crater. The habitations spread far beyond the village – and the new road – tapering up into the remote ravines with only a goat-track to join them with the outside world. The people value their shoes and boots above almost anything for they have to walk for an hour and a half before they reach Curral.

They were walking today for it was Sunday. The precise tinkle of the church bell came up through the sunny air. I could hear it easily at that height. It is astonishing how sounds rise from the deepest valley – a river ran across the green floor and I could hear it clattering over its stones, and a dog barked concisely. There was a fire sending a curl of smoke from a terrace and I could even smell that.

As we descended into the crater we could see the mountain folk walking down towards the village and its summoning bell. It was like one of those Disney scenes where cartoon people converge from miles and you see them tramping and singing over the hills.

If there is any piece of earth in my travels that I am glad I have visited it was that little place of Curral das Freiras, and especially on that day for I soon realized that Sunday was the time when all the people met together in the square and in the streets. They went to mass and then talked and drank and paid their bills in the low-ceilinged shops, and went back to their solitary existence laden with supplies for the week ahead.

A barber had set up his stool in a stone courtyard. A small boy was sitting with the normal impatience of small boys in barbers' chairs, while the man shaved off every morsel of hair from his pate. Old men stood around nodding approvingly. In the square was a cartload of puzzled pigs.

To look into the open doors of the church was to see a scene similar to a Brueghel painting. Every pew was occupied and in the aisle children sat on the floor in the company of a dog and a yellow goat. The dog curled up and went to sleep. The singing broke out into the sunlight, followed closely by the worshippers as the mass ended. They poured from two doors, the women from one, the men from the other. They milled about in the stone square, finding their friends, gossiping; small, deep-eyed people, dressed in garments of the most aching colours, showing off their new boots, pulling at the bobbles on their coal-scuttle hats, the children chasing each other, the young people eyeing and flirting. Then, by the wall outside the church, I saw a young woman in black. She stood looking over into the churchyard, weeping quietly for a husband dead too soon. It all went on around her; all this contained life, a pinch of the world.

It was Arlindo's birthday and he had met a friend, Martin Figeras, born in the crater but now living in Funchal. Each Sunday Martin returns to eat with his parents and, as he explained, 'to put right again their television set.' We went to one of the several bars now doing brisk after-mass trade. Martin brought along his father, whose name is João, and his mother who wears a fur coat bought by her other children who have long emigrated to Venezuela.

Old João was a wonderful character; scarcely five feet in height, even in his hat, his eyes so far back they had all but gone. I asked him about his childhood when the crater village was cut off from the world. Arlindo translated. 'He wants me to tell you that he did not go to school, that he used to carry charcoal across the mountains from the north coast to Funchal and it sometimes took two days – and he'll have a scotch please.'

I was drinking *agua ardente*, literally fire-water, made from sugar-cane and the only drink in my life I have never been able to finish. The islanders say it is very good for starting a coal fire. The others, however, and the party had now grown to a jolly group, all said they would like whisky if it was all right with me. The barman took out the bottle.

The bar was an extraordinary place. Low-ceilinged, a bare electric bulb hanging (the village has electricity but no running water – it still comes from a well), a few tattered posters, a Coca Cola advertisement, and a jukebox. Then I saw something else: two old ladies, widows in spider-black shawls, intent on a game of Space Invaders.

Madeira is a mountain that descends into some of the world's darkest and deepest seas. The fishermen of Câmara de Lobos go out with lines two miles long and barbed with a hundred or more hooks. They catch the *espada*, the scabbard fish, which dwells in such deep places no man has ever seen one alive. By the time they are brought to the surface they are always dead. They are all the same size, three feet long, with a sinister black coat, no small fish or large fish have ever been caught; no one knows why not.

Another curiosity. Right here, in the middle of the wide Atlantic, in a church that for centuries has been a sighting mark for inward-bound sailors, on a hilltop where the maritime breezes blow, is the final resting place of an Emperor of landlocked Austria.

The exiled Emperor, Charles IV, died in the village of Monte in 1922 and now lies in a huge and suitably lugubrious coffin in a side chapel of the church which, appropriately, has the aspect of a municipal building in, say, Salzburg. A few years ago the children of the Emperor visited the church and the coffin was opened for them to view their dead father.

The chapel is decorated with Austrian flags and banners and – touchingly – on one wall postcards of Austria sent by royalists in the old country and addressed to the Emperor, care of Nossa Senhora do Monte.

The leaving of Madeira is as exciting, if not more so, than the arriving. For this time the plane takes a sharp run like a hurdler and lifts off with little enough to spare, banking sharply over steep cliffs, houses, terraces, before heading out to sea. Twenty-eight miles away the plane lands again on the island of Porto Santo in order to refuel. The runway at Madeira is too short to allow an aircraft with a full load of passengers – plus fuel – to take off. There are plans, however, to extend it.

It had all been worth it though. This rough and rocky place, full of fascination and stories. As we came to Porto Santo and circled I could look back and see Madeira just as Zarco had seen it centuries before. A cloud.

MADEIRA situated latitude 32°38′ N and longitude 16°54′ W; area 314 sq. m (813 sq. km); population approx. 273,000; Portugal

AUSTRALASIA

Ken Smith, the blind man of Great Barrier Island, New Zealand.

The Queensland Islands
Within the Reef

Run a boat on the sand at high water, and the first step is planted in
primitive bush – fragrant, clean and undefiled.
E. J. BANFIELD, *The Confessions of a Beachcomber*

Some islands lie close inshore, in groups, like ships in outer sea-roads
awaiting harbour berths. They become familiar figures to people living on the
mainland; they see them as hills in the water or shadows against the sky;
they know their names and at times they may even visit them.

Within the girdle of Australia's Great Barrier Reef there are islands like that.
We think of the reef, 1,200 miles of coral shoals embroidering the Queensland
coast, as low-lying, with its contours, its coloured hills and valleys *below* the
surface of the Pacific Ocean. And so it is. But within the coral, from Fraser
Island, north of Brisbane, to Anchor Cay off Cape York, at the distant
northeastern tip of the state, and of the nation, lie many true islands, lofty,
clothed with trees and clouds, sometimes touched by rainbows.

At six o'clock on an early May morning I looked out across the palm trees
and jetties of Townsville, Queensland, out to the bulk of Magnetic Island
sprawled, snout to the sea, like a duck-billed platypus. A few hours later I
was flying above it heading over the fine ocean to a small speck
unromantically called Dunk.

The plane was one of those affectionately known, in the inimitable manner
of Australian nicknames, as Bushies, and it still had BPA (Bush Pilots
Airways) painted on its nose, although it had recently become part of
Queensland Airways, possibly more businesslike but less adventurous.

Beneath the wing the isles trotted by like stepping stones, most of them
small and green with a boomerang of white beach, a turquoise anchorage and
perhaps a single boat. Over to port, gathering to itself the clouds from miles
around, was the large emerald hump of Hinchinbrook. Dunk Island, although
small, rose sharply like a lad stretching to his full height. We went in across
the reef and the lagoon, hooped in various bands of blue, and landed on the
strip beside the palms.

Dunk has its resort hotel, distributed along the fine beach. Some of the islands have confined holiday colonies like this, but the remainder of the land is left to the native wild. Man has had little choice about where to settle, for the jungle has grown through the centuries and it chokes hills and fills ravines. This was once the untouched place where natives used nuggets of gold as sinkers on their fishing lines.

Crowning Dunk, in fact composing the greater area of Dunk, is Mount Koo-Tal-Oo which is nothing less than 900 feet of jungle. It was a heavily hot day and I had no intention of climbing it. In fact, I was rather looking forward to an easy time, almost a day off after weeks of travelling. I thought I might have an idle lunch and a few glasses of wine, swim and perhaps take a trip in a glass-bottomed boat to view in comfort the varied wonders of the deep. But it was not to be.

The trouble began because of a man called Banfield, an English writer, who had lived a Crusoe existence on Dunk Island in the early part of this century and had recorded his experiences in a book called *The Confessions of a Beachcomber*. Like Robert Louis Stevenson, he was buried on his sanctuary and I wanted to see his grave.

'It's just up there,' pointed a young lady from the hotel. 'See?' All I could see was the mass of the jungled mountain towering ahead and I should have remembered that when an Australian says, 'Just up there,' or 'Just along there,' it could mean 500 yards or 500 miles.

Clad in jeans, a shirt, tennis shoes and carrying my camera and tape recorder I intrepidly set out. At once I became lost. The paths that went into the bush doubled back on themselves, there was a notice warning that the 'swinging bridge' was unsafe, and there were muddy rivulets sweating down the flank of the hill after recent rains. I retraced my steps and another accommodating member of the hotel staff showed me a short cut and off I went again.

It was steaming. There were trees fallen across the steep, slippery paths, like dead men on a battlefield, and apart from an arthritic hip, I had a cracked rib sustained when I fell out of the bath in New Zealand. (I ask you, would Livingstone, or Burton, or Scott have fallen out of a bath?) Up and up went the path until it came to the swinging bridge, with branches across it and the warning, 'Closed. Bridge Dangerous.'

There was no going back. It was too far and too difficult. I climbed over and gingerly as a man on a tightrope went across the thing. My God, I soon knew why they called it the swinging bridge. It swayed like a skipping rope at every tentative step. Halfway across, staring down into a chasm with a stream running between a gut of rocks, I wondered briefly if I had done the sensible thing. By that time it was as easy (or rather, as difficult) to keep going as it was to retire, so I continued, the crazy structure groaning and squeaking at every shift of my weight. Gratefully I reached the other bank where I found a pretty young lady dressed in a leopard skin, just like Tarzan's Jane. It turned out that she had come from the hotel, not hand-over-hand through the trees, but by means of a perfectly reasonable set of stone steps which I had not detected. Yes, she confirmed, the grave of Banfield was 'just up there'.

Just up there I went. And just up there . . . and just up there . . . and just up there. Sweat trickled from me like the streams that wriggled down the thick hillside and over the path. I found a notice which said, 'Mount Koo-Tal-Oo 2 kilometres. Allow Two Hours.' That sounded ridiculous. Two hours for two kilometres? Then I saw that some disgruntled climber had amended the two hours to twelve hours. Upwards, onwards I pressed.

After an hour I thought I might be touching delirium because I had a strong temptation to shout for him. 'Banfield! Banfield – where are you?' What an idiotic place to put a dead man.

Another twenty minutes and I had to stop and take off my trousers. They were jeans meant for knocking around English harbours in winter and tramping over windy fields. I sat on a fallen trunk and pulled them down to my ankles. I was wearing a pair of swimming shorts underneath, not that it mattered in that wilderness. There were ants the size of mice living on the tree stump and they became interested in my revealed legs. Jeans still fixed around my ankles, I was struggling to pull them over my tennis shoes when I got that shady sort of feeling that someone was watching. I looked up. Sitting on the muddy path, four feet away, its head raised and its tongue flicking expectantly, was a long brown snake.

It was difficult to freeze in that heat, but I froze. Standing there in that farcical childlike pose, trousers down, shirt dangling, I froze. The snake was waving about, its spread tongue still going in and out. God, I thought, he's looking at my legs! I was too scared to move. They're killers, the brown ones . . . hadn't a man on the mainland been bitten and died only a few days before . . . if only I could pull my damned trousers up! I had a funny vision of lying in my death throes at the side of the track, trying to tell the story into my tape recorder, perhaps adding a final message for my wife, my family and my dog far away in England: trying to pull up the trousers so that I would die decent.

Then (oh, thank you very much God!) the snake apparently remembered something it had to do. It turned and began to slide slowly across the path and into the bush. My next fear arrived immediately – nobody would believe me! I grabbed the camera and, trousers still dangling, fired off three exposures before the snake finally sidled away. Then I pulled up my trousers.

It took me another half an hour to get to the top of the mountain (a quaint sign said, 'Summit – Four Chains' but I couldn't remember how long a chain was). Nor could I see a sign of Banfield anywhere. I was very annoyed with him. It was touch and go that there were not *two* dead authors up there. I turned and began to descend.

In another hour and a half I stumbled out onto the beach and, empty, exhausted and streaming with sweat, walked into the sea and lay there letting it wash wonderfully over me. Then I made for the hotel, gulped a lot of beer and, seeing the lady who had directed me to Banfield's grave, told her of my adventures. 'The top of the mountain?' she repeated incredulously. 'I told you it was just over-there – and I meant just over there. I'll show you.'

She did. It was all of 150 yards, tucked into the fringe of the bush. I had missed it by taking the recommended short cut. I thought I could hear old Banfield laughing. His stone has a version of that quotation by Thoreau:

> If a man does not keep pace with his companions,
> Perhaps it is because he hears a different drummer.
> Let him step to the music he hears, however measured or far away.

I had certainly followed a different drummer that day.

Nor was the day finished with me yet. Back at Townsville airport on the mainland I rented a car for the 250-mile drive south to Shute Harbour from which I proposed to explore the Whitsunday Islands. There's really only one road – Highway One – which goes due north and south. Nothing could be simpler than that, could it? But it was my day for going the wrong way. With no signs, no habitations, and a dark night, it was thirty miles before I pulled into a far-out hotel and discovered my mistake. 'Never mind, mate,' consoled the barman. 'You've come to a bloody good pub.'

There are times when I think I'll never make an explorer.

There are travellers who say that – notwithstanding Niagara Falls, the Grand Canal or Lake Windermere – the Whitsunday Passage is the world's most beautiful piece of water. Cook thought so, cruising in the *Endeavour* between the misty and mystic islands. 'This passage,' he recorded in his log, 'I have named the Whit Sunday Passage as it was discovered on the day the

Church commemorates that Festival, and the Isles which form it, Cumberland Isles, in honour of His Royal Highness, the Duke of Cumberland.' The date was 4 June 1770.

Today the Cumberland Islands are a fragmentary collection to the south and the main spread of isles just off the Queensland shore are now called the Whitsunday Group. When I first saw them from the shore at Shute Harbour they looked positively Hebridean, dark and pinnacled, and curtained with rain. The storm came out of an early, brooding sky and rushed across the harbour, throwing up the waves, and swallowing the horizon. No one at homely Shute Harbour seemed concerned. They were loading the boats for the islands, fruit, vegetables, crates and casks.

The small place was all pleasant activity. The rain retreated and sun swept across the landscape of Queensland, the ocean and the gleaming islands. I could hardly wait to go out to them.

It has to be said that the Australians, with one of the world's most wondrously scenic countries, are sometimes inclined to spoil their delectable places with commercialism. Some of the tourist brochures extolling the islands within the Barrier Reef have a holiday-camp blatancy. There are photographs of hotels, food and people playing bingo, snooker and ping pong. And outside . . . outside is all that!

Among the vessels at Shute Harbour was a 'horror' ship, painted all over with a sort of tawdry graffiti and with, so I was told, imitation grass and palm trees in her saloon! She was once a decent working ferry in Tasmania, but she has now, literally, been tarted up, and has been renamed *The Happy Hooker*. She transports riotous parties of trippers around the dignified islands. I asked one of the Shute Harbour sailors what he thought of the monstrosity. 'I dunno,' he said carefully. 'I hear she handles well.'

A more sober vessel, called *Telford Wanderer*, three decks and a chimney like a kitchen stove, took me to the Whitsunday Islands, coming out of the sheltered clasp of Shute Harbour and into the bottle-green sea. By now the sky had been cleaned up by a sweeping wind that was still running through the passage. It is an enchanting place, the wide channel, hillocks of sea, shapes of the many islands, the silhouette of each one lying across the next, the further the distance the paler the shade of grey. I thought how thrilling it must have been for Cook to have been the first foreign man to have found himself in that isthmus. A small hand of isles, the Molle Group, were on the landward side of the channel, jaunty, camel-backed, with trees on their slopes and bright yellow beaches. There are South Molle, Middle Molle and North Molle; there is also West Molle, which has been damned with the name of Daydream Island in the interests of tourism (like Happy Bay). I was told that Daydream has been renamed because of a schooner which used to call there; well, all I can say is that Daydream sounds less phoney on a ship than an island. West Molle was a decent name. Why change it? South Molle also has a resort hotel but has retained its name and it is none the worse for that.

On the distant flank of the passage, and it took *Telford Wanderer* three-quarters of an hour to make the crossing, are the more muscular islands – Hook, Whitsunday itself and Lindeman, with the smaller isles of Hayman, Haslewood and Shaw. Beyond them are the myriad shoals of the true Barrier Reef.

On Hook Island there is an underwater observatory, a lighthouse in reverse, because it curls down below the sea-bed. There's a nice unofficial jetty and the round tower is at its end. You go down the spiral staircase into the iron chamber sitting on the sea-bed. Through a series of glass panels, rather like the screens of television sets, you can look out at the fish looking in at you. They loiter there in their hundreds, obese, silver, goggle-eyed creatures, long, languid monsters, little lost fish searching for someone among the crowd, and millions of tiny creatures, all moving the same way at once, all turning at the same invisible corner and then going *en masse* off in another direction, as if in the charge of some piscean drill sergeant.

Of late the reef has been grossly overfished, but safeguards are now in force. The fish around the observatory are specially protected, but midnight poachers have been in among them. Coral, in all its colours and forms, furnishes the cellar of the ocean. It waves, red and straggling like a punk rocker's hair, or sits in the form of a crown upon a rock, or looks large and a rather ghastly grey, like Einstein's brain. The crown of thorns starfish has been gnawing at the coral along the Barrier Reef. The starfish live on the coral killing it and causing the conservationists a serious problem.

These submarine wonders can be viewed from Hook Island in a trio of glass-bottomed boats, reassuringly called *Titanic, Poseidon* and *Jaws.*

On the return voyage across the passage we called briefly at South Molle where parrots fly about like sparrows. The island boat was undergoing her annual overhaul and had been pulled from the water and lifted onto a cradle for the repairs. I sat happily doing that most felicitous thing, watching others work, before going back to the *Telford Wanderer.*

Evening light on the water of the Whitsunday Passage; drifting seabirds, the sky wide and pale. On our starboard the hideous *Happy Hooker* made her technicolored return to Shute Harbour. I could hear them singing raucously across the poetic water. Well, I suppose they had enjoyed their day, just as I had.

QUEENSLAND ISLANDS Whitsunday Group situated latitude 20°30′S and longitude 149° E; area 12 sq. m (31 sq. km); resort islands; Dunk Island situated latitude 18° S and longitude 146° E; area 6 sq. m (16 sq. km); resort island; Australia

Lord Howe Island
Betwixt and Between

Oh! What a snug little Island
A right little, tight little Island
THOMAS DIBDEN

After my years of fascination with islands, my journeys to them, my writing and my speaking of them, I am often asked: 'Of all these small places which is your favourite?'

My answer is always: Lord Howe Island.

It lies between Australia and New Zealand, the most southerly coral island in the world, and one of the most spectacular. You can see it from miles away rising over the Tasman Sea. The warm air of the Pacific meets the cold currents drifting up from Antarctica at the summits of its twin mountains, Mt Gower and Mt Lidgbird. Clouds form while you wait.

It is a rare place, rare in many senses. Much of its natural life is unique and jealously guarded; it is the home of the golden whistler and the sacred kingfisher. Also rare is the sense of old-fashionedness, in the steady pace of life, in the good manners and the gentle humour of its 270 inhabitants. They tell a story of the not-so-long-ago – when to reach Sydney meant a long journey by flying boat – of a boy who had never before left Lord Howe. Almost the first thing he saw when the plane splashed down at Rose Bay was a Sydney Corporation bus. 'Look,' he cried excitedly to his father, 'a bus!' He had never before seen one. Another Corporation bus came into view. He looked puzzled. But then, 'Here it comes again!' he shouted.

Lord Howe is a cool island; cool in the sense that it has none of the overripeness of the Pacific, none of the lassitude of the Caribbean. Tropic, crystalline seas surround it and there is fine summer sun, but the trees that hold the eye are the spread and sturdy Norfolk pines, not palms; the close fields could be in England. Only the two pinnacled peaks speak of a more exotic place.

The journey is not by flying boat now, although the islanders loved the bulbous Sunderlands left over from the war which they used until 1974. Before these came into service, the voyage to the mainland by sea took anything up to five, sometimes stormy, days.

Now the 780 kilometre journey from Sydney is accomplished in two hours in a Dash-Eight, short-landing-and-take-off aircraft which houses thirty-six passengers. There was only one stretch of flat land in the island suitable for an airstrip, and Australian army engineers built it in eight months. It is like a gulley, not an easy landing because of constantly veering winds. There are three wind-socks, and pilots wryly joke that on some days they can be outstretched in three different directions.

But the expedition to this lone and small island (it is four miles by one) is worth making. From the moment of arrival there comes an immediate sense of well-being. Someone arrives in a jeep to pick you up, and you ride through one of the world's most enjoyable island landscapes. If there is one drawback it is that the twin peaks, Gower and Lidgbird, present a sight of such power and beauty that the eye is drawn to them again and again, from every angle, doing an injustice to the rest of the island scene, its beaches, coves and out-isles. When these peaks are out of view, you find yourself looking for them, waiting for their appearance, turning the next bend, climbing the next hill, sailing round the next headland, until you see them. They are constantly transforming, changing colour and form, green one moment, blue in another, grey at morning, smouldering red as the sun drops, wreathed in mist or with puffy white clouds touching their summits, a never-closing show.

And yet Gower and Lidgbird were not the first features that the eighteenth-century navigators spied, the beacons that drew them to Lord Howe. Out in the Tasman Sea, nineteen kilometres away, is a great stack called Ball's Pyramid, set on the horizon like a misty Camelot Castle. Its towers of rock taper to 552 metres and it is all but unapproachable. A naval survey party was working around it when I was on Lord Howe, and I inquired if they would be landing. 'Not if we can help it,' said one member laconically. 'You have to swim. And there's plenty of munchies out there.'

Sharks – munchies – have never been seen on the shallow and translucent waters about the Lord Howe beaches, but many less threatening creatures are. Dazzling fish – big silver drummers, parrot fish, scarlet emperors – will gratefully feed from your hand. At nightfall, people gather to see the mutton-birds, the sooty shearwaters, as they shout and fly from the sea to their burrows on the shore.

Fit climbers, with the help of roped tracks, can seek the colony of woodhens that live on the flank of Mt Lidgbird. They are the only birds of this kind in the world. A pair have also nested in the green garden of the Wilson family home at Oceanview. The Wilsons are one of Lord Howe's staunch families. They take guests at their comfortable house but Kevin Wilson, one of the brothers, says, 'The mainstay of this island is tourism and the whole of Lord Howe can only accommodate 400 visitors at a time. When the summer goes, after Easter say, it can be . . . well, difficult.'

Living in a place as remote as this has never been easy, romantic though it may be to the mainlanders' eyes. Once Gower, Lidgbird and Ball had put their navigation marks on the eighteenth-century maps, and named the island itself after the English Admiral, there were few settlers. There had been no sign of any previous habitations. Early and optimistic colonists, individuals who came ashore and lived rough lives, provided vegetables and fresh meat for passing ships. Whalers – some from as far as Nantucket Island – who sailed on voyages lasting years, came to anchor there with a sigh of relief.

The present islanders have sketched out a family tree beginning with Margaret and Thomas Andrews who arrived aboard *The Rover's Bride* in 1842 to live permanently. They brought up their family on Lord Howe and – incredibly – one of their sons Albert, having lived in such a narrow place in the middle of a wide sea, with all its dangers, was drowned on the *Titanic* in 1912.

Nathan Chase Thompson, a roving whaler captain from Somerset, Massachusetts, landed on the island with a twelve-year-old Pacific princess called Bogue in 1853. The aply named Chase had found the girl, from the Gilbert Islands, adrift in a small boat accompanied by two servants Boranga and Bogaroo. She was fleeing an arranged marriage. On Lord Howe the man from Massachusetts decided to settle down. He built a house and married Boranga, and when she died twelve years later he married Princess Bogue – pronounced Bockoo. They had two boys and three girls. Their descendants are still on the island today.

The Wilson family have lived in the same house on Lord Howe since the

First World War. 'Gower Wilson was known as the Father of the Island. He was named after the mountain,' said Kevin Wilson. 'In 1936 he went to Sydney to collect a new boat. He set sail but was never seen again.'

Roy Wilson, an uncle, was awarded the George Medal in 1948 for helping to rescue two airmen from a Catalina flying boat which became disabled and crashed in the paddock just below the house. Seven airmen died. There is a memorial stone marking the spot.

Below the tragic place is a jetty and I walked down in the early morning. The island was green with sunlight. The fortnightly freighter *Sitka* from Yamba, New South Wales, was unloading her cargo. The islanders had searched the world for her – a vessel with a shallow enough draught to come into the reef and to the jetty. They finally found her in the Baltic – an ice-breaker.

On the Saturday night they had a concert in the community hall. It was wonderful – gloriously amateur, the curtains closing in jumps, a deafening pop group ('We haven't got a name') followed by a demonstrative church organist who threw himself across the instrument as if he were swimming the crawl. Kevin Wilson did an hilarious dog act with his basset hound. There was community singing with songs from the First World War and the Boer War. It was old-fashioned and sincere, a real island evening.

'We've always had lively concerts,' remembered Monique Morris, who had lived on Lord Howe all of her eighty years. Her family, the Austics, are prominent members of the 'family tree'. Known as 'Monnie', she liked to sit and play and sing at the piano. For me she played a song she wrote about the sadness of an islander leaving the island. It was called 'Comes the Day'.

Monnie was one of the inhabitants who can remember the extraordinary day in 1931 when a small seaplane – a Tiger Moth with floats – landed in bad weather in the bay and by next morning was a seemingly total wreck. The pilot was Francis Chichester, an intrepid flier long before he was a yachtsman. 'But he was making a record flight,' Monnie recalled. 'And he wasn't going to give up. So the men hauled the plane ashore and everybody set to and mended it – rebuilt it. It took weeks and Francis Chichester was here the whole time. Fortunately all the men were good boatbuilders. Eventually it was finished and, hearts in our mouths, we saw him take off in it. It flew! And he made it to Sydney.'

It is difficult to imagine a more pleasing place than Lord Howe. It has noble scenery, it has lagoons so clear you can see the bottom from the aeroplane.

The sand is white and the hinterland a mixture of the flamboyant tropics and deep, comfortable, meadows. But, in the end, it is people who make an island. This is a place to which I want to return.

LORD HOWE ISLAND situated latitude 31° 28′ S and longitude 159° 9′ E; area 6.37 sq. m (16.5 sq. km); population approx. 290; Australia

Phillip, Churchill and French Islands
Three in the Bay

I scarcely know a place I would sooner call mine than this little island.
LIEUTENANT JAMES GRANT, RN, of Churchill Island

Phillip Island, Churchill Island and French Island, lying in the cup of Westernport Bay, off the city of Melbourne in Australia, share the distinction of having been discovered by a doctor in a rowing boat.

In the Australian summer of 1798, John Hunter, the Governor of the settlement of Port Jackson, reporting to the Duke of Portland in far-off England, said, 'The tedious repairs which His Majesty's ship *Reliance* necessarily required . . . having given an opportunity to Mr George Bass, her surgeon . . . to offer himself to be employed in any way he could . . . I accordingly furnished him with an excellent whaleboat, well-fitted, victualled and manned to his wish, for the purpose of examining along the coast to the southward of this port, as far as he could with safety and convenience go . . .'

The surgeon and his crew in fact voyaged 600 miles in their craft of twenty-six feet, an epic journey lauded by the explorer Matthew Flinders as having 'not perhaps its equal in the annals of maritime history'.

At the journey's westward extremity Bass saw the low, placid islands lying close together in the bay and, beyond, an exposed ocean. 'By the mountainous sea which rolled from that quarter we have much reason to conclude that there is an open strait.' There was. It was named after him, the Bass Strait.

On an autumn day of blowing grey clouds I stood on the shingled beach where Bass first landed on Churchill Island. There is a red rock at the water's edge with the name 'Bas' (minus the final 's' which has presumably worn away) cut into it. It is, by tradition anyway, the surgeon's own incision. Local children have since embellished it with initials and pithy comments.

Churchill Island got its name from John Churchill 'of Dawlish in the county of Devon' who gave a later party, under Lieutenant James Grant of the barque *Lady Nelson*, vegetable seeds, the stones of peaches and nectarines and the pips of apples 'with an injunction to plant them for the future benefit of our fellow men, be they Countrymen, Europeans or Savages.'

The seeds, together with some potatoes, wheat and Indian corn, were sown (with the aid of a coal shovel) on the island and in the following December, Jonathan Murray, now in command of *Lady Nelson*, went ashore and found the harvest. 'I never saw finer wheat or corn in my life,' he reported, 'the straw being very nearly as large as young sugar-cane.'

The sailors cut the corn and fed it to young swans, whose descendants still cruise the island. It was the first crop to be harvested in what became the state of Victoria.

Churchill Island today is kept virtually untouched, recognizable from the initial colony of the early 1800s. It is joined to the much larger Phillip Island by a narrow causeway and Phillip Island in turn to the Victoria mainland by a bridge originally opened during World War II but rebuilt today. French Island, the third of the group, lies in chosen isolation, with no bridge, few roads, and only home-generated electricity for its sixty farming inhabitants. The islanders once had the consolation of a public house called the Never Never Inn but it is now closed.

French Island has its nuggets of strange history, including the origin of its name. When Britain and France were at war in the early nineteenth century, a French scientific expedition in two vessels, *Le Naturaliste* and *La Géographie*, was allowed unmolested passage in Australian waters. On 10 April 1802, men from *Le Naturaliste* went ashore on the largest island in Westernport Bay, named it Ile des Français and took home two of the black swans which nested there (and had never been seen in Europe) as a present for Napoleon's Empress, Josephine.

Today's French islanders live in a place of quiet, where koalas carry their young through the gum trees and where the potoroo, a midget member of the kangaroo tribe, sleeps through the hot days. The sacred ibis picks its way through the salty shallows, the whistling kite and brown falcon roam the air and the white-breasted sea eagle nests with pelicans as neighbours.

The islanders used to grow and roast chicory and some of their kilns still stand, although the industry has lapsed. Now they graze sheep and cattle and harvest sea grass, useful in the insulation of houses. They keep a barge to bring their necessities ashore and to take them to and from the mainland. The roads joining the settlements (their names telling their history – Perseverance, Energy, Star of Hope) were once maintained by convicts from the prison on the southeastern coast. Now even they have gone home, although the prison is still in use as guest accommodation.

Unlike George Bass, I almost overlooked the islands together. Although I had been in Melbourne I had concluded that, lying so close inshore and with a bridge connection to Phillip and Churchill Islands, they would be merely an extension of suburbia. It was not until I had explored the Great Barrier Reef and returned to Sydney that I realized, in the excellent Mitchell Library of that city, just what I had missed. Hurriedly I returned to the southwest.

Phillip Island, it is true, does have holiday homes and retirement bungalows (many on stilts so they have a view of the sea) and commuters cross the bridge in their cars each day. But it has an old-fashioned charm, part pastoral, part marine, with its places called Cowes, Ventnor, Newhaven and Rhyll by the homesick English settlers of the early years. Across the bridge, however, the geographical associations are altered, for its landfall is called San Remo.

Off these Australian southern-island coasts, with their sober homes, tidy beaches, and where the Isle of Wight Hotel looks out with genteel benignity on the sea, are tide-washed seal rookeries with 5,000 honking inhabitants. Penguins waddle ashore to the sand dunes each night in a noisy and comical parade, there are pink pelicans on the rocks and koalas in the gum trees.

It was silent autumn, a dun day, with the visitors of summer gone from the streets and the beaches. You could feel that sense of relief which comes to all such places when the hot days are finished and the inhabitants settle back into winter. A time of contentment and quiet. On the beach below the pine trees at Cowes, a boy ran in solitary enjoyment; a boat was being loaded in a leisurely way at the pierhead; gulls sat on the sea-wall so close together they looked like a layer of snow. There was a tanker out in the bay. The mainland was lost in early afternoon mist and tea was being served in the hotel. I felt it was a good time to be there.

*

The Isle of Wight Hotel, which faces the wooden L-shaped jetty at Cowes on Phillip Island, has all the aplomb of a genteel English seaside establishment. The original building was burned down in 1921, and with it the chair of Captain Tilson of the *Speke*, a vessel that has its story forever intertwined with that of Phillip Island.

She was one of the largest (and one of the last) steel-hulled sailing ships ever built, launched at Milford Haven in Wales in 1891, a monster of just under 3,000 tons. She arrived off Phillip Island after twelve days of gales and tremendous seas in the Roaring Forties, as they call the rough latutudes. The weary Captain Tilson mistook one lighthouse for another and piled his ship ashore at Kitty Miller Bay where, at low tide, the vestiges of the hull can be seen, standing on end and looking, point upwards and with diamond-shaped holes, curiously like the ruins of a church.

There was no loss of life and the islanders, in common with their like in all parts of the world, began enthusiastically to dismember the frame. The wreck was sold for twelve pounds. The timbers were used to build a barge by a man called Kennan, the captain's chair went into the lounge at the hotel and the ship's bell went to the Presbyterian Church. It still hangs outside the old church building today (a new copper-roofed structure has been added to the rustic original and the church is now called the Uniting Church). The bell is still sounded for services. The anchor is in the grounds of the Phillip Island open-air museum.

Spars and masts went to make gates and the beams of houses but the figurehead mysteriously disappeared, a strange occurrence for a lady 9 feet 4 inches in height. Some schoolboys discovered it, mouldy and cobwebbed, behind a decrepit shed in 1940. They told their schoolmaster at the Cowes State School and 'Lady Speke' was rescued. The pieces were put together, but the mounting with its acanthus scroll was missing. The boys went down to the wreck, which had lain below the tide mark for close on forty years – and found the original mounting still clinging to the corroded ironwork.

Reassembled and repainted by the school 'Lady Speke' looked both shiny and regal, all 9 feet 4 inches of her, magnificently bosomed, clad in a flowing white dress with blue cuffs and collar, and carrying a bunch of daffodils. She was exhibited in the island library and then – horror! – someone suggested that 'Lady Speke' might, in fact, be a man! More people came to stare. Speke, it was pointed out, was the man who explored the source of the Nile, so could that be an Egyptian robe, not a dress, the figure was wearing? Perhaps those were not daffodils it was carrying, but a papyrus plant, grown in Egypt for paper making. And were there not bristles on that chin?

There was even a search made through the records of the distant shipping company, Leylands of Liverpool, who said that their ships were always called after a local place, in this case Speke Hall, a sixteenth-century Lancastrian mansion. But many were still unconvinced. Surely those were bristles?

On Churchill Island is another controversial marine relic – a cannon and a neat pile of cannon balls, sitting dumbly in the garden of the old house there. The story is that the cannon came from an American Civil War ship *Shenandoah* in 1864, although this has been so much disputed that scientific and historical expertise has been called for and intricate reports produced, which are not concluded yet.

Whatever the result, the story of the *Shenandoah* itself is loaded with adventure and romance. She was built as a merchant vessel called *Sea King* on the Clyde in Scotland in 1863, a stern-screw clipper of 1,180 tons. She sailed out on her maiden trip to Bombay, loaded with copper – and vanished. It was reported that she had struck a reef and sunk. What really happened was that the vessel had been purchased by the Confederate Navy and sailed silently to Madeira where she was fitted out as a warship and renamed *Shenandoah*. Under Lieutenant James Waddell she roamed the oceans hunting down Union ships, an epic voyage of thirteen months, during which she sailed an amazing 58,000 miles and touched port only twice. During the hunt through every ocean in the world, except the Antarctic, she sank thirty-two Union ships and captured six others.

In January 1865, she arrived in Port Melbourne where, under the terms of International Law, she was entitled to stay only long enough to take on food and water. But her fame had preceded her and the people of Melbourne, and particularly one Samuel Amess, a leading councillor, had other ideas. Amess, born in Fife, Scotland, was lucky in the Australian goldfields, and purchased, among other properties, Churchill Island (where he introduced hares, quail, pheasants and Highland cattle). He led the citizens in fêting the Confederates and lauding their exploits. At Ballarat a ball was given in their honour, attended by 2,000 people, and another 8,000 visited the ship in Port Melbourne in one day. Eventually the romantic raider sailed, almost a month after arrival, with forty-two Melbourne volunteers in her crew.

Once the news reached London there was consternation. Had not the Colonial Secretary warned all British possessions to abide by the strict

international regulations when dealing with belligerents? A stern rebuke was
sent to Melbourne, followed by a £50,000 fine from the Geneva Convention,
which the British Government found itself obliged to pay.

Amess was not concerned. He became a popular mayor of Melbourne and
when he retreated to his house on Churchill Island he could admire the fine,
muzzle-loading cannon which, so one story goes, Lieutenant Waddell of the
Shenandoah presented to him in gratitude for his, and the city's, hospitality.

PHILLIP, CHURCHILL and FRENCH ISLANDS situated latitude 38°29′S and
longitude 145°16′E; area 142 sq. m (370 sq. km); population approx. 2,700;
Australia

Great Barrier Island
The Great Small Place

Of bird song at morning and star shine at night.
I will make a palace fit for you and me.
Of green days in forests and blue days at sea.
R. L. STEVENSON

At Mechanics Bay, Auckland, the yellow amphibian waddled like a duck into
the water, chugged along the harbour and then clambered into the sky above
the Sunday sailboats. It was a mild afternoon of the southern autumn. We
flew across the distributed islands of the Hauraki Gulf, each one down there
like a relief map, some with trees and buildings, some empty, sullenly
volcanic. Then across the cape of the Coromandel Peninsula in view of the
town of Thames. Coromandel . . . Thames . . . The most poetic names are
so often borrowed from somewhere else.

Great Barrier Island was soon apparent. From my seat beside the pilot I
saw it lying across the horizon, its peaks tented, shadows against the sky. It
is a bulky island, fifty-six miles from Auckland. After its final rock the next
landfall is Chile.

The amphibian was a Grumman Widgeon, a bright pot-bellied little aircraft
belonging to See Bee Airlines. It had a cartoon bee painted on its yolk-

coloured flank. I had never before travelled in a plane that ascended from and landed on water. It had seemed a long time before we shook off the last drops of Auckland Harbour and rose clumsily into the sky, and the half-hour chuntering journey across the Gulf was noisy, but enjoyable. There were three other passengers, plus a dog, a rabbit in a cage and boxes of goods. We lost height as we neared the big island, dropping down into an encompassed bay, snorting across the serrated water until we pulled up, just short of the beach. Then we jolted in and waggled up the shingle in front of the petrol pump and general store at Mulberry Grove.

On the shore were a group of people and a clutch of cars. Everyone helped. A set of wooden steps – the sort used in shops to reach the high shelves – came out and were put against the aircraft. Cargo began to be passed hand over hand, dogs and barefoot children ran in and out of the surf. The pilot's hand was shaken several times, as if he had just accomplished a single-handed flight around the world, or the moon for that matter. He then sat on the roof of the plane to do his paperwork. I had climbed out of the hatch after the other passengers, their chattels, their animals and a barrel of beer, and stood on the shingle. The air was warm but there was a sniff of autumn. The island rose green and luxuriant. I could hear birds whistling in the thick trees and the sea nudged the beach with easy familiarity. I thought, at that first moment, I was going to enjoy this little spot, and that is how it turned out to be.

Bill Maclaren, a Scot from Hamilton who had been on the island ten years, and away from Scotland for twenty (although you would not know it by his accent), was awaiting me. I was to stay at his house, called Pigeons, sitting in the crowd of trees above Shoal Bay, an inlet of Tryphena Bay. It had a white iron anchor at the gate (salvaged from the 1920s wreck of the *Cecilia Sudden*, an American collier). Paths wriggled into the woods, to the headland and down to the profound bay. Trees lodging fat, wooing pigeons; roofs on several levels, bright windows, a balcony from which you see a slice of ocean; a dog, a cat, a son, and a fire in the iron stove. 'We built this ourselves,' said Bill, a pleasant, fair-haired man. He patted the wooden wall. 'Maggie and I. We lived in a tent until we had a couple of rooms finished. Then we moved into them and carried on building from there. When we got here it was just trees and earth.'

Maggie Maclaren was a dark, bright, spare lady. 'She kept her figure shovelling cement,' said Bill sagely. They had a ten-year-old son called Roen whom we found on our journey from the amphibian landing, toiling in bare feet up the hill on his way home from school. 'He's never known what it's like to wear shoes,' laughed Bill. 'We went home to Scotland a couple of years ago and it snowed and there he was trudging about in the snow wearing no shoes and wondering why his feet were turning blue.'

They knew each one of the five hundred inhabitants of the fifty miles of bumpy island. They admitted that, as in all such places, there are disagreements and geographical rivalries. Because of the competition between the southern islanders and those in the north around Port Fitzroy, the council chamber had to be built exactly in the middle of the island at Claris. Then, when the vote for chairman took place, the members voted six each for two candidates. The clerk looked up a reference book and learned that the matter could be quite legally decided by a toss of the coin and this was immediately done.

'We had thoughts of seceding from New Zealand at one time,' announced Bill half-seriously. 'New Zealand never did a lot for us – most of New Zealand hardly realizes we're out here. So we discussed breaking away and starting our own country, our own place, and we amused ourselves by selecting the cabinet posts we each would occupy. Unfortunately we fell out over who was going to be Prime Minister.'

There are families on the island who settled there following the wake of the savage battles between the Maori tribes, one of which was fought on a beach on Great Barrier. Hundreds of bones were found there, in the sand of the battleground, and have been stored by an islander called Les Todd, in a cave just up the valley from Mulberry Grove. He has locked a grille over the entrance and he is reluctant to open it (in any case, over several days we could not find him because, even on islands, privately inclined people can keep away from everybody else). Bill showed me the way to the cave, however, and I gazed through the grille at the shinbones, skulls and ribs of the long-gone warriors.

Bill took me to the north of Great Barrier, where the next-door neighbours are literally in South America, and there showed me the grave of a lady with a double tombstone. Her name was Agnes Dalzill LeRoy, known to everyone as Girlie; her family had been on the Barrier, as they affectionately call the island, for a century. The first tombstone is rough and the second is a proper one, but I was glad the islanders had allowed the first to remain as a token of their affection. She is buried on the hill above her family's house and overlooking an eye of the sea. 'Each day,' said Bill, 'she would go down to Port Fitzroy, to the Last Resort, the store, with milk from her cow. One day she did not arrive and so one of the men came up to find her. She was dead. She had died while milking and he found her with her head still lying against the cow's flank.'

At evening the wind nudged through the kauri trees high above the bay. Bill started the generator at Pigeons and Maggie cleared the evening meal. Jessie, the dog, after a busy day smelling everything on the foreshore, was tired; wood burned comfortably in the stove. On the following morning the cat was going – by air – to the vet in Auckland. It was clearly time for talk.

'The day I landed here,' said the amiable Bill, 'I came ashore from the supply barge, after a crossing in a storm of fourteen hours, during which I lay in a bunk in which a man had just died. It was not auspicious. For my first step on the Barrier I decided to wear my kilt and I stepped bravely ashore, full of Scot's pride. There was a Maori girl standing on the jetty and, believe it or not, she asked me what I wore underneath. I haven't worn it since.'

Maggie and Bill arrived on the island by accident. He was a design engineer, an emigrant to New Zealand, but had bought a boat and decided to attempt to sail around the world in five years to Scotland, which they had left on the day of their marriage. Their first stop was Great Barrier Island and, as Bill put it, they were waylaid. They did not go any further. They tried farming first, then, pitching two tents (one for themselves and another for their daughter Angie so that she could study for her school exams), they set about digging and building the house of which today they are rightly proud.

Bill and some of his fellow islanders had notions for developing tourism, for the Barrier has a wonderful dreamlike quality of green hills, meadows and bays with giant and deserted beaches. Pigeons and a few other guesthouses provide the only accommodation at present but perhaps one day . . . They have even discussed the possibility of clubbing together and buying their own aircraft.

They are aware of the chequered attempts at communications and commerce in the past. Shipping companies and airlines have tried to make the island services pay but, one by one, they have given up; there have been hopeful starts at lumbering, gold-mining and whaling. Today, abandoned in the thick hills are rotting wooden dams which once controlled rapids carrying thousands of tons of lumber down to the seashore where it was sawn and taken away. The lumber of the kauri was ideal for ship-building – when ships were built of wood.

In the Barrier's overgrown interior I stood among the foundations of a crushing mill once used to powder rock in the gold-mining days. That dream of successful mining was not realized either and standing there now, looking over a parapet onto nothing but massively conglomerated trees, it is difficult to imagine there was once located here a township of wooden dwellings used by the gold-miners.

Only six miles off the coast is the unwavering route of the migrating humped-back whales. Whaling companies have brought men and ships and harpoons to the island, the latest in the 1970s, but all have gone away eventually, disappointed. After the last failure, when the final whalers had taken themselves off, empty-handed, thirty whales stranded themselves on the beach at Okupu and had to be towed out to sea again because the smell of them was so shocking.

Roads on the Great Barrier struggle single-handedly over escarpments, threading through valleys and trundling along windy shores. So full of holes are they at times that there appears to have been a bombardment; often they sigh and slide in chunks down a chasm under the onslaught of heavy rain.

'This island,' alleged Bill Maclaren, 'is the place where old cars go to die.' A drive of a few miles through the wooden hamlets shows this to be true. There are cars, seemingly held together only by the ultimate stubbornness of rust. There are vehicles which have been in regular use since the 1920s, including a Ford Model H truck from 1921 kept in prime, beautiful condition, despite making a daily farm-run, by its owner Don Woodcock, a Maori forestry man. Road rules and regulations are ephemeral. 'The only two vehicles on the island which are actually insured collided one day,' remembered Bill with a grin. 'And I was driving one of them.'

By one of those outlandish chances that make a writer's life worth living, there was also on Great Barrier Island, until recently, the giant black Chrysler Imperial owned by the gangster Al Capone. It was bought in America, shipped to Auckland by a dealer, and eventually found its way over to the island where it was regularly used as a taxi and was to be seen standing, ready for custom, outside the Last Resort Store at Port Fitzroy. Now, sadly, it has been restored to an American home. The gangster's ghost seems to have followed me to some unlikely places. On Saint-Pierre, the French island off Newfoundland, I slept in the 'Al Capone Suite' of the wooden Hôtel Robert.

Stories seem to grow in such places as this. The island has the distinction of running the first pigeon post in the world. It was used as an experiment by a newspaper for receiving its reporter's impressions of the visit by the survivors of a heart-rending shipwreck, that of the *Wairarapa*. So successful was the post that a regular message service was instituted, with the birds flying the fifty-six miles from the island to their loft in Auckland, each carrying five messages on rice paper, properly stamped at the cost of one shilling each.

The tragedy of the *Wairarapa* happened on a calm, foggy night in 1894 when the 2,000-ton passenger ship out from Auckland ran full tilt into the cliffs, 600 feet high, at Miner's Head, northwest of the island. It was a dreadful drama. Some racehorses tethered on deck ran amuck among the passengers trying to escape to the boats. The ship broke her back and the entire bridge structure toppled over like a falling house onto the boats already in the sea.

Some passengers and crew managed to reach the formidable cliffs and clung wretchedly to their ledges while others attempted to reach land by climbing hand over hand along spars and ropes. One woman was saved only because her long hair became caught in floating wreckage. Even today Miner's Head cliffs (still faintly marked by an arrow showing where the *Wairarapa* struck) are all but inaccessible. Rescuers, among them Maoris in canoes, had to journey through the blind night and around the dangerous indentations of the coast. Others hurried on horseback across the hills. It was several days before anyone in Auckland knew what had happened to the ship.

One hundred and thirty-four people perished and are buried in the sandy shore on the opposite side of the island at Tapuwai Point. An inquiry held in Auckland (and, incidentally, adjourned for a day to celebrate the Prince of Wales' birthday) found that the vessel was thirty miles off course. The bearded Captain McKintosh, a stubborn man who had been warned by his junior officers about the ship's speed in the fog, could not be asked for his explanation for he had been killed when the bridge collapsed.

Tryphena, the blameless settlement in the middle of the bay where the amphibian had landed, has also had its moment of notoriety – the murder of a man called 'Old Tusky' Taylor in 1887, and referred to, even today, as 'The Murder'.

It was a grotesque sequence. A swaggering man, John Caffrey, captained a 53-foot cutter called *Sovereign of the Seas*. Caffrey fancied himself as a piratical figure, a role enhanced by the fact that almost every inch of him was covered with tattoos and that he had one, baleful, eye.

His fancy had fallen on Old Tusky's daughter – Elizabeth Taylor – but her father forbade her to see Caffrey and encouraged her to marry a bushman called Seymour. She did and a year later gave birth to a child.

In the harbour bars of Auckland, and on the Barrier itself, Caffrey had boasted that he would kidnap Elizabeth and take her off to South America. He wasn't merely boasting. One night, the *Sovereign of the Seas*, flying the skull and crossbones, put into Tryphena, and Caffrey, with his mate Henry Penn and Penn's fifteen-year-old girlfriend, Grace Cleary, went to the Taylor house. Caffrey, his good eye gleaming, had a loaded revolver in each hand. There was a fight at the house and Old Tusky ended up dead in a pool of blood. The three intruders fled.

Two Barrier men rowed the channel of eighteen miles to the Coromandel Peninsula to raise the alarm, but no sign of Caffrey or his cohorts was found for four months. Then the wreck of his boat was washed up on the shore of New South Wales and Caffrey was arrested shortly afterwards in possession of a gun and the pirate flag. Penn and his girl were caught within a few days.

The two men, wearing leg irons, were extradited to Auckland with the girl, and all three went on trial for murder. Caffrey and Penn went to the hangman but Grace Cleary, prettily hatted, patently enjoying every moment of her murky fame, was acquitted. Old Tusky lies buried in the small bay, Taylor's Bay, near the house where I was staying with the Maclarens. His daughter Elizabeth lived until 1952.

We took Tinker the cat to the airstrip the following morning and sent him in a basket by plane for Auckland. It appeared to be no more an unusual transaction than sending a letter. The airstrip is on the marshy plain that runs low towards the coast. Mount Hobson sniffs the sky in the background. The Maoris called the island 'The Place of the White Cloud'. The Barrier warriors came to abrupt extinction when their Coromandel neighbours had their canoes *towed* stealthily across the strait by a sly English captain who had also provided them with muskets. They were thus fresh and well-armed when they fell on their enemies in the traditional dawn massacre. But the real winners were the white men who had helped the Coromandel tribes and then took the land for themselves.

Our journey to the airstrip at Claris on the waist of the island and then, having deposited the cat with the pilot of the plane, onwards to the north, was a succession of views both sudden and lovely. At each lofty turn another line of splendid hills descended to a green and sun-crossed land, which in turn gave out to stupendous beaches where massive seas, white-toothed, came unchecked to the shore.. There were chasms and forests and escarpments and then demure enclosed fields with red-roofed houses tucked into corners beneath a parasol of trees. 'Those people who live over there,' said Bill pointing out a distant farm, 'their house burned down so they moved into their barn until it could be rebuilt. But they found the barn was so comfortable they've stayed there.'

William Abercrombie, Jeremiah Nagle and William Webster were the original purchasers of the island from the Maoris in 1838. Needless to say, Captain Cook had already been there first. He loosed some goats ashore and went on his exploratory way. Abercrombie and Nagle stayed and left their names written on the map of the Barrier. Webster went back to the mainland and became a sort of honorary Maori, a blood brother, living with the Coromandel tribes. Port Fitzroy was named after Captain Robert FitzRoy who, at twenty-six, commanded the *Beagle* on Darwin's voyage. He insisted on the capital R in his surname to designate royal, if unofficial, descent. Today's maps, however, only afford him a lower-case letter. At Nagle Cove was built the largest sailing ship ever constructed in New Zealand, the *Stirlingshire*, a three-masted barque which sailed to California during the gold rush and also voyaged to England. She ended her days as a hulk on a not dissimilar shore at Kinsale in Ireland.

Wide areas of Great Barrier Island remain inaccessible, and more are only reached by horse or on foot. The road slips through unseen gaps and along empty and exquisite coasts, like a running boy who knows the short cuts. The sea comes fiercely ashore and then, with wonderful suddenness, enters some flat, shallow estuary or creek, where gulls and shag reside alone. There are people living in the most unlikely and remote places, their lives undisturbed by the rest of the world, some who have not bothered to visit the mainland for years – Maggie Maclaren only goes twice yearly to Auckland for shopping. Children in these remote homesteads are educated by postal packets of lessons received every two weeks. I met a travelling teacher, Mrs Jan Jackson, whose life it is to visit these 'out-scholars' on behalf of the education department, both here and on the mainland. 'It's by car as long as there's any road,' she said, smiling. 'Then it's a matter of using your feet sometimes an hour and a half at a time until you reach a house with a child sitting with a pile of books at a kitchen table. They really seem to look forward to someone coming to see them every six months or so.'

Bill Maclaren and I travelled miles on tight roads, through empty hills and vacant plains. Then, rounding a bend, by a creek of still water, we came across a couple contentedly painting a boat in the autumn sunshine. No one else lives within miles. Bill greeted them and then, as we drove on, pointed out their tree-hidden house, a hair of smoke wisping from its chimney. What a fine place to live.

Mornings and evenings had an enclosed quietness. There would be pigeons about the house at first light and, before breakfast of bacon, egg and Scottish potato cakes, I would go down with the happy spaniel Jessie through the trees to the cobbled beach, stand there and look out on a scene of unaltering serenity. The water had none of the blue blatancy of the Pacific. It was pale and oddly private – like looking into the window of a small shop.

Evenings I remember for the woodsmoke from the jaunty chimney-pot of the house and those of the others about the bay and the daylight drifting west, slowly like a boat leaving the shore. Lone birds would fly on journeys known only to themselves and the sea would rifle through the shingle and pour into rock pools. Then the generators would start and the lights in the houses would shine and you knew it was time for dinner.

One night the schooner came in, the *Te Aroha*, a stocky vessel built in 1914, bringing goods and a few passengers to the Barrier. In the post office at Mulberry Grove is displayed the timetable of her sailings and arrivals at all the small harbours and anchorages up the island coast.

I went down to the jetty with Bill and the dog and watched the crew – including a young and hard-working lady called Maggie Pigeon (pigeons of all sorts seem to have an affinity with the Barrier) unloading the cargo.

Maggie is from Brisbane. Clad in a black singlet and shorts she was operating the winch, regulating the boom that swung out the cargo of everything from boxes of apples to window frames. I sat on a rock and enjoyed the scene. There are few pleasures as enjoyable as watching a boat being unloaded.

Just above the jetty I discovered another extraordinary family: Dick Wheeler, a cray-fisherman and harbour-master of Tryphena, his wife Lynne and their children. There was also a young man there who had come from Lord Howe Island, in the Tasman Sea. Islandmen are always attracted to other islands. On the Barrier until some time ago lived Johnny Laffoley, who came from Jersey in the English Channel Islands, in 1862. He had a little 'bach' (a cabin) above Tryphena and he played the violin at socials. Another of the old settler families, the McMillans, came from Prince Edward Island, Canada.

Dick Wheeler, when he is not out fishing, has been building his own house. It is an amazing place, a sort of great wooden hull – like the interior of Noah's Ark – into which, over the past ten years, he has been fitting comfortable rooms. The living-room looks out over the superb anchorage, and is one of those places that is at once welcoming to the stranger, crammed with books and wine bottles, and with the kettle chuffing on the hob. Not content with building his house, Dick was also constructing a boat. He took me down to his shed and there she was, a splendid 38-footer, each panel and piece lovingly placed and veneered with the touch of a true craftsman. 'Two years it'll take to finish her,' he forecast. 'I've still got a bit to do in the house.' I can imagine him now, working away there on the winter nights, the lantern glowing across the tide below. Fortunate man.

Most of the inhabitants of the Barrier have built their own homes. When I was walking by the shore at Mulberry Grove I met Ken Smith who built his house. He is blind, but his expertise in carpentry and joinery is legendary. His brother Bert lives in a distant part of the island. He is also blind and built his own house too. Jan Jackson, the travelling teacher, had met Bert and said that he knew every tree and rock for miles around. 'I've fallen over most of them,' he explained.

For me the settlement at Mulberry Grove shows everything of life on this homely island. The school, with the sea at its door, the track leading to the petrol pump and the telephone box (the exchange closes after 5 p.m.), the collection of wooden houses, the post office, the store, the rusty taxi, and the people waiting either to use the telephone or for the arrival of the amphibian. There is no pub and no church, although social gatherings are held in the community hall, and church services in one of the houses. I think it is the only island of its size I have ever visited where there is no church. Perhaps they thought, like so many ventures, it would fail. The Mulberry Grove shop has a collection of paperbacked books so ancient they might be collectors' items, including, for some reason, the *Bi-Annual Report* (1968) *of the New Hebrides*, miles away in the South Pacific. The shop was said to be changing hands. Businesses, from shopkeeping to logging to gold-mining to whaling, do not seem to flourish on the Great Barrier. Perhaps the island will have to stay content with being beautiful, and with being amiable – some places are not meant to make a profit.

GREAT BARRIER ISLAND situated latitude 36°10′ S and longitude 175°20′ E; area 110 sq. m (285 sq. km); population approx. 570; New Zealand

THE INDIAN OCEAN, THE ORIENT AND THE PACIFIC OCEAN

Sampan women in the harbour at Lamma Island, Hong Kong.

The Seychelles
Round and About Paradise

> I think any requirement is fulfilled for deciding that the site of the
> district of Eden is near Seychelles.
>
> GENERAL GORDON, 1881

Islands throughout the world, because they are so often remote, unattain-
able, beautiful or mysterious, have been blessed with romantic names;
except, that is, where their discoverer happened to be Captain Cook who
called them after admirals, lords, or even learned bodies. His imagination
lagged far behind his navigation.

Cook did not explore the Seychelles. It was left to a poetic Frenchman,
Lazare Picault, and as a result the islands bear some of the most lyrical
names in the atlas. Silhouette, Félicité, Marianne, Cousin and Cousine,
Aride, Curieuse and Anonyme are as lovely as they sound. Once the main
island of Mahé was called Ile d'Abondance, but even as romantic an explorer
as Picault knew who paid his bills. He called it Mahé after the Governor
General of the Ile de France (Mauritius) whose name was Mahé de la
Bourdonnais – who was his patron.

There is plenty of room in the Indian Ocean and the Seychelles stretch
themselves across many miles of coloured water – from Bird Island a
thousand miles off Kenya to Aldabra and Farquhar only just clear of
Madagascar. To fly due north from Mauritius over the ocean during the
evening is to view a distant tranquillity; the islands appear far below, one by
one, solitary. The sky changes shades; small prim clouds loiter like
unemployed angels.

It is only in recent years that aircraft have opened up these isles to the rest
of the world. At one time the journey took five days from Mombasa in Africa.
The British found the islands a convenient place for banishing difficult
colonials, including an African king who kept slaughtering people, and the
Sultan of Perak, Malaya. On Cousin island today there lives a giant tortoise of
irreparable age who, it is said, once bit the exiled Archbishop Makarios of
Cyprus.

The pilot of the British Airways 747 had invited me to his flight deck to view the varied evening, to see the islands, apparently travelling south in the deepening shade. I took the fourth seat in the cabin, clamped on a pair of earphones and listened to the lady air traffic controller at Mahé airport providing instructions for our landing. Her voice came up to us, sounding precise and cool.

One of the curious sensations of sitting there through that landing was the unawareness of the huge length and bulk of the airliner at our backs. It was just as if four men were sitting in a saloon car, and three of them were driving it.

On the runway at Mahé was the Royal Swazi Airlines jet that had been used, shortly before, in an abortive attempt at a *coup d'état* in November 1981. It was wrapped in plastic sheeting to cover up the bullet marks. The attempt had been almost comic in its failure but the Seychellois were still anxious. At the Customs every sock in my bag was investigated with the intensity of someone looking for holes, and I was warned that there was a curfew in force and that I must be indoors by ten o'clock at night. Guns were poking out everywhere. So much for tranquillity.

In the times before the airport, Victoria town, Mahé, was one of the world's unmolested places. Ships arrived, unloaded and departed, all in good, slow time. The smallest statue of Queen Victoria in the Empire (hardly two feet in height, it was difficult to see whether or not she was amused) stood under the languid Union Jack and the palms at the crossroads of the wooden town. The newspaper contained little. It could be comfortably folded into a man's wallet. Rickshaws once rattled about the streets (there is one still on show at the Beau Vallon Bay Hotel) and perspiring Englishmen sought shade and drinks. The Seychellois, as their name suggests, nodded acknowledgment to their British lords and remained obstinately Indian Ocean French.

For in the mid-eighteenth century French colonists from Mauritius, a thousand miles south, had arrived in the Seychelles and began to build and trade. The British sailed in during the Napoleonic troubles and the French Governor, displaying admirable sense, unhesitatingly surrendered, quickly pulling down the tricolour and running up the Union Jack. The British sailed away contented. The Frenchman then, just as deftly, exchanged the flags again. When the British returned he surrendered once more and repeated this performance on a further *four* occasions. His seventh surrender, in 1810, was the final word. The British came back for good and – both sides accepting the principle that whomsoever you cannot beat you should join – retained the French governor as their administrator. Thus the French never lost their sway over the Seychelles and today many of the 64,000 inhabitants, Indian, Chinese, Arab, African, speak French as their second language after Creole.

There are a hundred isles and islets distributed across the local ocean, some inhabited by people, one – Aldabra – inhabited by a race of giant tortoises and others left to the birds and lizards. General 'Chinese' Gordon, who died his legendary death at Khartoum, was once sent to the Seychelles to advise on how the archipelago might best be defended – he failed – and travelled to the off-island of Praslin which he immediately, and in the face of much contrary evidence, pronounced as the original and authentic site of the Garden of Eden. This took the natives somewhat by surprise but they accepted it with a good grace, probably thinking of future commercial possibilities. The story has it that Gordon, tramping through the luxuriant Vallée de Mai, met a man who was the forebear of Boris Adam who still lives on Praslin. When asked his name, the man replied truthfully, 'Adam.' That finally convinced the General.

Boris Adam lives by the sea, renting boats and serving fish curry to anybody who happens by. Ronald Reagan happened by a couple of years before he became President of the United States. He wrote in Boris's visitors' book:

NAME: Ronald Reagan   PROFESSION: Politician
POINT OF EMBARKATION: Oblivion   DESTINATION: Unknown

It is not difficult to understand the wonder that Boris's ancestor noted in General Gordon's face as he tramped through the Vallée de Mai. Despite the geographical disparity it might easily be Eden. The coco-de-mer grows here, the most wonderful palm in the world, a soaring pillar, waving its crest at the sky 100 feet up and living to 800 years and more. Its coconut is probably the largest fruit in the world, weighing up to forty pounds. To buy one the visitor must go to an authorized dealer, pay 500 rupees (about £50) and have the prize stamped 'For Export'. In the thirteenth century Rudolf II, a Hapsburg king, paid 4,000 florins for one for the tree is said to be erotic; it is an aphrodisiac, the shape of the nut is anatomical and female and the catkins of the male tree are equally suggestive. The Seychellois say the trees get together at night and make love.

Even on Praslin, which boasts an airfield (the terminal building has a thatched roof) and a small stone shed hung with a Barclays Bank eagle, it is easy to be away from people among the thickly scented valleys, their birds and waterfalls, or on beaches like golden scimitars. I stayed in a lodge made entirely from the coconut palm, its fruit and its fine fanned leaves. There were only three other guests there. In the morning the dawn chorus was amazing. I went out expecting a thousand chortling, whistling, hooting birds. All I found was half a dozen minahs, performing all the impersonations. On the beach I met a Seychellois girl who was sorting through shells and seaweeds with her feet. 'I have found a pearl in a shell,' she explained sweetly. 'And I am looking for another for my second ear.'

Unlike most warm islands, the Seychelles are neither volcanic nor coraline. They are granite – like the English Channel Islands and the Scillies – with, sometimes, coral attachments. The huge, smooth brown rocks pile on each other's backs or lie in the water like bathing hippos.

They formed a comfortingly familiar horizon for John Phillips who lived on Cousin with his young wife, Vivienne, for he came from Cornwall. They were the only people on the island. The Phillipses met at Oxford University and successfully answered an advertisement for an ornithologist couple to care for the island's rare birds. They were island people too. They had been out to St Kilda, the loneliest outrider of Britain, and John's ambition was, one day, to be the birdman of Fair Isle.

On Cousin they lived in a bare house, eating mostly coconuts and fish, and getting to know the birds. Here are the dovelike fairy tern, which, uniquely for a seabird, lays its eggs in a tree – on the bare branch; the black sooty tern, and the noddy tern, and the rarest treasure, the brush warbler, which in all the world is known only on this island.

I walked up the gradient paths with John, through the sun-filtering trees and onto the hippopotamus rocks. We could look across to the twin island of Cousine, a green bonnet with a lace of surf about its rim, and a veil of green-blue sea. It was untroubled by human habitation. Lizards slid from under our feet, wagging across the warm rocks. John and Vivienne seemed to know every bird on the island, personally. He lifted stones and branches to reveal fluffy infants sitting as phlegmatically as maiden aunts. 'We have to guard them very closely,' he said. 'We get predators even here. The other night a barn owl, which had flown across from Praslin, crashed through the door and into the house. It gave us a hell of a shock.'

The young couple – Vivienne was from Yorkshire – were occupied and content. It did not seem odd to them that, because of the emergency curfew, they had to go indoors at ten every night even though they were alone on their island. 'We're usually indoors by that time, anyway,' shrugged John. 'And if that's the rule, it's the rule.'

On our trek we met up with Cousin's oldest inhabitant, George, the giant tortoise, the one that made his mark on history and on Archbishop Makarios. The size, colour and texture of one of those ancient leather armchairs, George pondered his way from one side of the island to the other, sometimes taking weeks for the journey. He had been doing that for more than a century.

If it were not for the palm trees and the sun, sailing into the miniature harbour of the island of La Digue would be much like arriving in some haven on the West of Ireland. The unofficial jetty, the limp water, the casual boats, and the suspicion that nothing much ever happens are the same. The island men were working on a lovely old schooner which was to become the La Digue boat, replacing an ancient and famous craft, the *Lady Esme*, which for generations was the island's transport to the rest of the world. The hammers sounded across the flat harbour, the water as clear as a window.

Three ox-carts were waiting to transport the arriving passengers from the jetty. There are only six motor vehicles on the island. There is a story that one day two of them collided head-on. I climbed into one of the carts, sat down and then stood up hurriedly – the left-hand horn of the ox next door was sticking through the slats of the cart and into my backside.

The road was dried mud, which an old woman was sweeping with little optimism and a broom made of palm fronds. The three ox-carts set off in a bunch and we had a dusty, bone-rattling 'Ben Hur' type of race for half a mile. The woman sweeping the road stood back with a sigh to let our party pass by.

Even at the uncomfortable pace and despite the dust clouds, it was easy to see how La Digue was. The shed-like shops, Oline's Boutique, J. E. P. Appassamy's Emporium and the Ocean Café, all sell Guinness and other commodities. On my second day I went into Oline's to purchase some toothpaste. The proprietor noticed my tape recorder. Being suspicious he dispatched his small son through a hole in the wall and a few moments later I was being conducted to the local police station to explain my presence on the island to the sergeant. The police thought I might be an anti-government spy. I suggested that a spy would hardly mumble openly into a tape recorder, but nevertheless they made me replay the tape, and seemed to think some of it might be in code.

'You should have seen the police in the British days,' shrugged Kersley St Ange, who keeps a lodge by the lagoon. 'They were pretty unpopular. One Christmas Eve the islanders kidnapped six of them and put them out on the coral reef. They were very wet when they were rescued. It was no way to spend Christmas.'

When the attempted coup took place Kersley St Ange had twenty-five German tourists on his hands. 'They had to stay here for three weeks,' he smiled elegantly. 'They got to like the local fish very much.'

The hills of Mahé are lofty and green in the sun. Beau Vallon Bay in the west of the island curves exquisitely with the shadow of Silhouette Island like a misty pyramid on the skyline. The trees come down thickly to the beach and its long blue rollers. Nearby at Bel Ombre a man called Reginald Cruise Wilkins spent twenty-five years of his life digging for a vast pirate treasure. You can see all his excavations, his walls and dykes, on both sides of the road. His pumps now stand rusting. For all his devotion and his gritty work he died without finding the treasure. Sometimes you can go through life never getting what you think you want. Even in Eden.

SEYCHELLES situated between latitudes 4–5° S and longitudes 55–56° E; area 171 sq. m (443 sq. km); population approx. 67,000; independent republic within the Commonwealth

Mauritius
Long Live the Dodo!

He seems to have been invented for the sole purpose of becoming extinct and that was all he was good for.
WILL CUPPY, *How to become Extinct*

Despite the obituaries, and no one has had more, I like to think that the Dodo is still with us. Alive, not too well (he never was), he plods myopically among his private hills on the island of Mauritius. I picture him, egged on by his wife, a sad survivor from the ancient days.

Mauritius was named after someone called Prince Maurice by the earliest Dutch sailors who made a landfall in the sixteenth century. They then set about butchering the Dodo, a trusting, cumbersome, harmless and inedible bird. The meek rarely inherit the earth.

The Dutchmen departed leaving piles of bones and feathers. Years later the skeleton of the Dodo was uncovered in a bog at Mare aux Songes, the place where the airport now stands. The bird that could not fly has a runway as a memorial.

Mauritius lies due east of Madagascar in the midriff of the Indian Ocean, the smaller offspring island of Rodriguez floating further out. Outside the two towns of Port Louis and Curepipe the countryside is green and echoing. There is much pastoral emptiness; in villages by brown rivers people sit and stare, roadmenders squat in the shade of perpetual tea-breaks, women carry loads on their heads, and men accompany them, hands in pockets and deep in thought. Fields of ruffled sugar-cane are broken by the explosion of the flame tree. Mountains are modest in height but eccentric in shape; sharp, ragged, like one of the opened pages of a childhood stand-up picture book.

The sugar plantations are punctuated everywhere by piles of rusty volcanic rocks, some as big as a house. Placed at intervals about the flat countryside they were built by slaves, the forebears of many Mauritians, to clear the land for growing. From the air they look, with their attendant shadows, like widespread trees, but at ground level they can be seen for what they are – the results of an amazing labour. Some remain bare, some are covered with runaway flowers, harsh grass or small trees. They are poignant and largely unnoticed memorials to a captive people.

The island is warm, and frequently wet. The rain is fierce and truncated, but often welcome and always useful. My Indian driver stopped his coughing car up in the hills during a ten-minute torrent. I thought he had stopped because he could not see to negotiate the hairpin bends. Not a bit of it. Cheerfully he took a handful of soap powder and threw it over the car then jumped back in. 'Always I keep vehicle clean, sir,' he assured. 'Most clean machine.'

One of the joys of travelling to Mauritius was leaving London. A foot of snow caked my car on a Siberian morning followed by a delay at Heathrow Airport because the planes could not be de-iced quickly enough and only one runway was fit for use.

As arctic men holding hoses sprayed the Boeing's wings with de-icing jets, the British Airways captain confided that he had never seen ice conditions like it – not even in Anchorage, Alaska. Eventually we squelched to the runway, roared off, soared through the blizzard, and into a sky full of sun. It had been up there all the time.

Seventeen hours later, far from the cold creaking of the English winter, we lost height over a glossy sea, crossed the white seam of coral reef, and dropped over the bright island. It appeared flat and verdant, with a deeply bitten coastline, a chocolate river cutting through its centre, and strange, imitation-looking mountains trapping a lake that stared up like a blind eye.

Elephant clouds drifted clumsily across the land, but the hills herded them and the sky was shining and clear over one of the world's more poetically named airports – Plaisance.

It is no exaggeration to say that the real landscape of Mauritius is in its people's faces. Outside the airport, around the many-legged banyans and haughty palms the people congregated, vividly clothed, busy, chattering: Indians, Chinese, Africans, some Europeans, all Mauritians. A woman in an aching pink sari, stood with great dignity, eating an ice-cream cone. An old man in pure white, his beard like a bib, stared at her with what appeared to be envy but may only have been admiration. Families fell on top of each other to greet someone arriving from the plane. Children danced, holding hands in circular excitement. Some people with no one to greet perhaps, stood, chattered and observed. A man dispensed evil yellow syrups from a container on his bicycle; another offered striped umbrellas, another sold fish. The airport has become the contemporary marketplace.

Mauritius, a British colony for 158 years, and still within the Commonwealth acknowledging Queen Elizabeth II, is entirely French. The languages spoken are French and Creole; children dutifully learn English at school, but many forget it as soon as they leave the playground.

Driving from Plaisance Airport through Beau Vallon, Plaine Magnien and Camp Diable, across the Riviera des Anguilles and past the Grand Bassin lake, it was hard to believe Britain counted this as hers. My destination was the hotel at a place on the west coast called Flic-en-Flac, a name supposedly derived from the noise made by drums and marching troops.

The journey, inevitably I was to discover, was down roads channelled through the green sugar-cane country. Mongooses, imported to kill the rats that ate the crop, scuttled across as though on some urgent business. Mountains popped up like stage scenery, small flags of cloud on their pinnacles. On the southeastern coastal corner is Morne Mountain, 1,800 feet high. The top can be reached if you are inclined – and inclined is the word

– by climbing up staples hammered into the rock. The mountain, they say, is haunted by the sad ghosts of slaves who escaped, clambered the sheer slopes, and made a fortress of the summit. Soldiers tried to climb after them but, pounded with rocks, were always repulsed. When slavery was abolished the soldiers went up again, to give the fugitives the good news. They were avalanched as usual but some sportingly managed to gain the top. The slaves, thinking they were about to be retaken, leaped from the bald height onto the rocks below, a classic case of jumping to conclusions.

It was raining in Port Louis, thick and warm, drumming on roofs and trees. Queen Victoria, prim on her plinth at the front of Government House, was soaking wet in no time. The inscription beneath speaks somewhat ambiguously of 'Our late and much regretted Queen'. She has enjoyed an appropriate and regal vista over the years, looking out along a lengthy colonial avenue of giant palms, upright, and ranged in two ranks like plumed guardsmen.

Empire administrators of the Victorian days would have, I fancy, only slight difficulty in recognizing Port Louis today. The mildly jaded elegance remains; wooden verandahs before the shops, small, flowered, open spaces; the aromatic harbour and the poise of Government House, pillared, palmed and passaged. Taciturn fans revolve in shaded rooms and restaurants along the streets. The curried scent of lunch drifts into the midday. The old British Queen shares a garden with Mahé de la Bourdonnais, the great French fighter and tradesman, whose influence as Governor General of Mauritius is still felt everywhere.

It was the French who built the Champs des Mars, the traditional wide avenue of their cities, constructed to allow the quick entry of an army into the centre of a city. Here the British improved matters by turning it into a racecourse, which it still is, usefully situated within the town. It was, unfortunately, or perhaps fortunately, off-season.

The rain had stopped for lunch and the population emerged to stroll about in the steam. The pavements were busy with interchanging faces: the Indian, the Oriental, the African, the European. Between themselves they spoke vividly in the language that bridges all the gaps, that, as Miss Chan Din Hin, a young Chinese put it, is easy to learn. 'Everyone makes it up as they go along,' she said.

Miss Chan works in a Government office. Her parents fled from China twenty-five years ago and her father now keeps a shop. She speaks English,

French, Hakki Chinese and, of course, Creole. She was planning her first trip to China. 'It will be a foreign place,' she agreed. 'I want to see it, but I do not think I will stay. The people must work too hard.'

At school in Mauritius she learned her French and English. At home her family speaks Chinese. In her everyday life the patois comes naturally. Everybody understands it. Written, it takes on an additional curiosity. There was a notice of a political rally (an election was coming up). 'Gran Miting,' announced the poster. 'On 20th Desam, 1981. Orators include Mr. E. Joomumbaccus.' At the Victorian Port Louis Opera House there was a season of *Joseph and the Amazing Technicolor Dreamcoat*. In Creole.

Although the Dutch first colonized and named Mauritius, it was the British and the French who squabbled longest over it. The island, up to the time of its independence in 1968, had been ruled by eighteen Dutch Governors, twenty-one French and thirty-one British. The French changed the name from Mauritius to the Ile de France and then the British, who might have easily called it something else, reverted to the Dutch name.

Pirates were here in great musters. They formed their own kingdom called Libertalia across the channel in Madagascar and there, flush with booty, made a touching attempt to settle down to everyday life. Understandably perhaps few would trade with them and they found themselves surfeited with stolen gold but with not enough food to eat. Most of them returned to piracy. At least they could steal food. The British and the French cottoned on to the importance of Mauritius as a base to protect their possessions in India. It was called the Star and Key of the Indian Ocean.

In the southeastern corner of the island today, in the village of Mahébourg, is a shaded plantation house, reached by a drive through trees. After a battle between the British and French in 1810, both commanders were carried here, severely wounded.

Suress, my Indian driver, President of the Mauritius taxi-men's union, met his verbal match here. It was Friday and the museum was shut because the curator was at the Mosque and there was no knowing when he might be done with his prayers. His wife, a staunch lady, stood firm and had a shouting match with Suress, from the door of her house behind the museum. The place was milling with chickens and ducks, and the louder the lady shouted, and the more Suress argued, the more frenetic the squawking of the livestock became. In the end, sweating and disgruntled, the taxi-drivers' champion returned. 'Tomorrow,' he announced, 'we come back. Maybe he get out of the Mosque by then.'

Dutifully we returned next day and it was worth it. In the airy house it was not difficult to imagine that day in August 1810, when the rival commanders in the battle of Grand Port, were brought bleeding up the steps. Sir Nesbitt Josiah Willoughby, a stern-looking sailor with a long jaw and a Nelsonian eye-patch was found on his ship, incompetently left for dead, under a Union Jack. He was taken to Mahébourg and treated in the same room as the French Commander, Duperre. There is no record of whether they were able to converse. They both recovered and lived not just to fight another day, but another thirty years and more.

In the museum is a remnant of another romantic story, far more famous than the fight at Grand Port. The battle is merely described in history books and recorded on the Arc de Triomphe in Paris, the second occurrence still lives as a great love story. A ship's bell, green and cracked, is all that remains of the *Saint Geran* which on a clear, moonful night in August 1744, was allowed to drift onto the rocks at l'Ile d'Ambre, off the Mauritius coast. She had suffered a stormy five months' passage from France and now, becalmed, and within sight of her harbour, she was allowed to fall among the rocks and reefs which tore into her hull. Among the awakened passengers were Mesdemoiselles de Mallet and Caillou, who were engaged to two officers, Messieurs de Payramon and de Longchamp. As the masts tumbled and the ship collapsed the two ladies were urged to take off their voluminous clothes, jump into the sea and swim for the shore. They stoutly refused on the grounds of delicacy and died for prudery, clasped in the arms of their gallant lovers. In another version of the tale we have Captain Delamare, who had permitted the disaster, refusing to take off his uniform because it was below his dignity as a sailor. It was probably the most competent decision he took all the long night.

The novelist, Bernardin de Saint Pierre, a friend of Rousseau, heard the story when he spent two years in the Ile de France, and from it he fashioned the romance of *Paul et Virginie*, one of the classic love stories of France, still read and enjoyed today. In this fictionalized version the heroine Virginie is returning to the island. Her faithful and patient lover, Paul, waits on the shore, only to see the *Saint Geran* wrecked within sight of the beach. His drowned beloved is washed up almost at his feet. He dies of a broken heart. A simple tale that has so far been published in five hundred editions.

The bell of the *Saint Geran* was found wedged in the wreckage by a diver in 1968. It stands in the museum, cracked but crudely reassembled. Soon after its finding it was stolen and smashed for scrap. Recovered and patched it now stands with a somewhat sorry appearance. So much for romance.

*

According to the tales the soil and rocks of Mauritius are congested with
buried pirate treasure. 'Only the Devil and I know where it is and the last
survivor will get the lot . . .' promised Captain Teach who rifled many a
passing ship in the island's waters. Tree-fellers uncovered an inscription,
'This is where I buried my wealth . . . he who finds it will sing for many a
day.' They found only some old pipes, some knives and bits of pottery.

'Walk up the cliff in an easterly direction as shown in my will,' instructed
Nageon de l'Estang who, in the eighteenth century, managed to combine the
professions of naval officer and pirate, a difficult task. 'After twenty to thirty
paces due east, in accordance with the documents, you will find the clues
used by corsairs to mark a circle, the river running only a few feet from its
centre. There lies the treasure . . .'

None of the many subsequent searchers found any treasure. Only Nageon
de l'Estang seems convinced that not one, but two, hoards were lying
waiting to be disinterred. According to his documents, a fabulous treasure
looted from India is to be gained for the asking in the south of Mauritius, near
a river's entrance to the sea. 'Three iron barrels and jars full of doubloons,
coins and ingots worth thirty million, as well as a copper casket full of
diamonds from the mines of Visapour and of Golconda.'

The words were enough to make yet another treasure hunter try his luck.
It was me. I went to seek it, accompanied by Suress, an amiable companion
rendered diabolically piratical by the absence of all his front teeth, leaving
two at the side projecting like fangs. A cutlass would have slotted in
perfectly.

We went off on a Saturday morning to the Baie du Jacotet on the southern
coast, where a river does run into the sea and where stories persisted of
half-buried pirate cannons, frequently used as pointers to hidden gold. It was
like the day in Madeira when I found the names of the English soldiers on the
old fountain. It was one of those adventures which only happen if you try.

Some labourers cutting through undergrowth with machetes directed us
to a tight bay where four villagers were fishing and boys were swimming
across the mouth of the Rivière des Galets, playing on rafts made of banana
and bamboo. Suress, not embarrassed, asked the men if they would mind
indicating the cannons pointing to the location of the pirate treasure. They
obligingly did so and went on fishing.

We had to cross the river and the swiftest way seemed to be by the banana
and bamboo rafts. The doughty Suress negotiated with the boys and we

found ourselves kneeling as if in waterborne prayer on these strung-together contraptions while the shouting boys towed us through the breaking water. My white trousers, last worn at a cricket match (The Duke of Edinburgh's XI versus Prince Charles's XI, none the less) the previous summer, were soaked and muddy before we reached the other side. 'Most people not come here,' mentioned Suress as we trudged through red mud and undergrowth like barbed wire. 'Next time I not come.' For some reason or other, when we were up to our knees in squelch and our necks in jungle, he mentioned casually that he had a cousin in England. In Tottenham.

Torn, wet and muddy, under the pointed sun we reached a further beach and there another fisherman pointed to the hinterland. The cannons were there, he indicated. We climbed a slope and looked down, searching the thick entangled undergrowth. My goodness! There it was! A cannon, twelve-foot long, almost choked by greenery. 'One more here,' called Suress. Sure enough, even more deeply buried in creepers was another cannon, the same size, pointing at right angles to the first. 'Somewhere there is a third,' I announced like Blind Pugh. 'Buried upright with its muzzle showing.' Suress returned to the fisherman. A few rupees fluttered. The man left his lines and led us along the empty beach. In a small enclave he scraped away the sand and revealed the round mouth of an upright cannon. My heart jumped.

I purloined a few rusty pieces from the cannon and they are here before me on my desk as I write this. Suress was disappointed because we did not find any treasure. But I think we did.

In the region of Mauritius called the Rivière Noire, lives a young Welshman named Carl Jones. His companions are giant fruit bats, delicate pink pigeons, a peregrine falcon from Wales called Sweetheart, and one of the rarest birds in the world – the Mauritius kestrel. He is trying to prevent what happened to the Dodo happening to this handsome hunter and is so engrossed in his work that he can be reached only with difficulty. Often he is halfway up a mountain, a cliff, or only a tree; when he is at home he is just as outlandish. To contact him you have to telephone the local police station.

He is a tall, wry young man, living among the birds and animals like a fellow creature, which is the way, he says, it should be done. 'You can't study animals or birds unless you live *with* them.' He had been up until three that morning feeding an infant fruit bat with cereal and milk.

We walked around the enclosure, his private kingdom. Adult bats as large as squirrels, folded their black silken wings around themselves like Sir

Gerald du Maurier folding his cloak. The pink pigeons, dainty as Delft, are oddly contrary. 'You just can't put them together and know that they will mate,' Carl confides. 'You have to try half a dozen different pairings before they click. You see, they have to fall in love. And once they do mate they make poor parents. I have to put the eggs under doves to hatch and then rear the baby until it is almost grown. Mother and father are just not interested.' Not surprisingly the pink pigeon was once thought to be extinct.

We considered the haughty Mauritius kestrel. It considered us. 'The world's rarest bird of prey,' sighed Carl. 'I know of two pairs in the wild and I have three birds which I hatched in incubators.'

'Will they breed, do you think?' I asked.

'With great difficulty,' he sighed. 'They're all males.'

On my last day in Mauritius I went back to see the Dodo, in Port Louis, and stood in the museum marvelling at the wondrous bird. It is only a model, a reconstruction (if the Dodo was ever constructed in the first place). Its twin is in the British Museum.

I could have stood admiring him all day. The size of three turkeys, with the doleful eyes and long face, he looked like my dog, my basset-hound.

Over the years this baggage of a bird was ridiculed by the name *Dodou*, Portuguese for a simpleton; the French called it *en sot*; it was also labelled *Didus Ineptus*. Unbelievably it is a member of the pigeon family; but it is a big pigeon.

There are stories of the poor, dopey creature being displayed in Europe, to great laughter which must have caused it embarrassment. An English sailor, writing to his brother in 1638 says, 'You shall receive . . . a strange fowle . . . which I had at the Iland Mauritius called by ye portugalls a Do Do, which by the rareness whereof I hope will be welcome to you . . . if it live.'

Perhaps it did for in the same year Sir Hamon l'Estrange, in his diary, records seeing a Dodo in London where its keeper demonstrated its ability to 'swallow large pebble stones . . . bigger than nutmegs.' Poor Dodo.

Looking at him, there safe at last in his case in Port Louis, I realized that this great ball of feathers with the hangdog look is (or was) the world's most wonderful bird. I thought that I, at least, would give him a proper name and immediately Maurice came to mind. I believe Mauritius was named for him not for some nebulous Dutch prince. Perhaps, and I hope, somewhere up in those green hills he still harmlessly potters about.

Long live Maurice the Dodo!

*

It was ten years before I returned to Mauritius. The dodo had still not reappeared. How strange that what is probably the world's most talked-about bird has never been seen by anyone.

On the British Airways flight I met Sir James Mancham, once deposed Prime Minister of the Seychelles and now in opposition in the restored island democracy. He told me that he had purloined part of the Seychelles chapter in the original edition of this book and used it in a volume of his own. He owed me a drink, he said. He left the plane at Mahé, dandily dressed and larger than life, inviting me to revisit the islands and see how much changed and happier they were. The Russians had gone.

Changes there may be; history moves irrevocably. But the Indian Ocean below the wings of the plane was still the same deep peaceful purple, decorated with small fluffy clouds moving slowly like homegoing sheep. There was still enough light when we reached Mauritius to discern the wide grin of the coral reef, the darkening deep sea held outside it, at arm's length from the land. The lagoons held within the reef were swirling and turquoise.

Those curiously peaked mountains, like some Disney cut-outs, cast their pointed shadows over the green land of the afternoon. Once again I was able to pick out clearly the piles of slave-stones scattered among the pale sugar-cane. Nobody had attempted to move them. We dipped and came into Plaisance Airport. This time I had my wife Diana with me. I was pleased to be back.

Proudly they told me that since my last visit Mauritius had gained its millionth inhabitant and no longer needed the population of Rodriguez, its satellite island, 370 miles away, to reach the grand total. Since I was last there it had also become a republic and we saw the President one day driving through the coastal villages in his car accompanied by only one motorcycle-borne policeman whose chief function seemed to be to scatter dogs and chickens. It is a peaceful place.

The 1,100,000 Mauritians seem to get along together. The Indians, the Creoles of African descent, and the small Chinese segment, active in business, the culinary arts, and games of chance live side by side in Port Louis, in Curepipe and in the small towns and villages scattered through the 720 square miles of the island.

'Nobody fights very much,' said Ravi Misra, a travel consultant who once managed Bombay Airport for Air India. He is a benign man with amused eyes who during our stay became quite proud of the sunburn on his dark, smooth forehead. 'I'm peeling,' he said pointing every day to the changing skin line. He looked like that advertisement for Ovaltine, a smiling globe, proclaiming 'The World's Best Nightcap'.

'Here in Mauritius races and religions knock along together pretty well,' he said. 'They live next to each other, not in separate communities, and they tolerate other people's ways of life and religious beliefs and festivals. Everybody pushes the boat out at Christmas.'

The island appears more settled, more sure of itself, and more prosperous than when I was last there. The hotels on the resort coasts would be hard to better anywhere in the world. They help to provide high employment. 'I was sorry to hear about Fergie and Andrew,' said the boatman taking us from Le Touessrok to the Ile aux Cerfs, a mile offshore. 'They were here, customers of mine. And George Best. He's been here too.' He patted the hull proudly. 'In this boat.'

Each of the island parishes – the romantically named Pamplemousses, Savanne and Rivière Noire, among them – has its own preserved characteristics and local rivalries. The Mauritians love football and important matches (the Fire Brigade versus the Cadets) are televised. Always the mountains push against the sky, but somehow they seem permanently just out of reach, misty, dreamlike in their stange shapes. Every village is busy with people going to and from the sugar-cane fields (forty per cent of the land is still taken up with these), carrying a few bamboos home for private use. The simplicity of a village house is enhanced by a cloud of bougainvillaea or the flamboyant flash of the flame tree. At weekends there seem to be weddings going on in every settlement, the cars decorated as extravagantly as the guests. Mauritians love their cars and, in a country where a new vehicle can cost many times more than a house, there are dazzling old Morris Minors and Austin Princesses. A visiting automobile enthusiast might think with pleasure that he had arrived in a time warp.

In Port Louis one evening we had a meal at a Chinese eating house and realised happily why *all* Mauritians, whatever their race, eat that way when they go out for a treat. We were then ushered into the Chinese gambling room next door, up some mysterious stairs, past a guard lolling on a chair, and onto a landing like an Eastern temple. It was like walking into an old movie starring Sydney Greenstreet wearing a creased suit. Walls and ceilings were decorated with shapes of red and gold, with symbols and lettering, and large tanks housing fish with dangerous expressions. There were notices on the walls, all in Chinese characters, except one which warned significantly in English, 'Obscene oaths not allowed.'

They would have been heard immediately, for in the gambling room, overlooked by a bronze bust of the establishment's founder, there was silence. People stood around the tables but it was so quiet you could hear the cards being dealt. There were five tables. Everything looked dusty and intriguing, not a bit like the glittering casino at the opulent San Geran Hotel, where once at roulette I had come up on the same number, nineteen, three times in succession. Nobody in the Chinese room was dressed up. They sat and stood around the tables, expressions orientally inscrutable. The game was pontoon.

One of the house rules is that if you are occupying a seat and not playing then you must give up the place to someone who wants to join in. As soon as I showed signs of interest a man at the far side of one table stood up, bowed graciously and indicated that I should take his place. A small lady dealt the cards. My first two hands were twenty-ones.

Eventually, well, not eventually, fairly quickly in fact, the house got its money back, and we set out for our hotel at San Geran on the far coast. Every journey in Mauritius takes at least an hour and you can drive on one route for two hours. That is a lot for an island only just over thirty miles from top to bottom and under thirty across the waist. But there are a lot of corners, some vertical.

I found that Carl Jones was still on the island, still intent on saving the wildlife. Almost ten years after I had seen him with his fruit bats and his pink pigeons, and he had told me of his efforts to save the Mauritian kestrel, he was still working, having done that particular job. Up in the foothills they have a colony of these small, fierce birds, and there are now 200 in the wild. 'The problem is,' said Alain O'Reilly who manages the reserve, 'that those reared here have no fear. They don't even keep a lookout when they are feeding. If you watch two mynah birds, one will feed and the other will watch for enemies. But not the kestrel. Sometimes the mongoose will get him.'

The mongoose, brought in to kill the rats at the time of the establishment of the sugar plantations, has proliferated and is now a major pest. 'We kill them and give them a post-mortem,' said Alain. 'We find toads, birds, lizards, but we've never found that they've eaten a rat.'

A quizzical Irishman with the party wondered about the plural of mongoose. We were eating venison curry. 'A chap in County Sligo,' he related, 'sent off for two mongooses, but he didn't know what the plural was, so he asked for one and added a p.s. "Please send another one as well."'

We saw a kestrel, no bigger than a small owl, dive from a tree to pick up a mouse. It returned to its nest to feed its young. Without the work of Carl Jones the bird would now be extinct. If Carl had lived a couple of hundred years earlier perhaps the dodo would still be with us.

MAURITIUS situated between latitudes 19°58′– 20° 32′ S and longitudes 57° 17′– 57° 46′ E; area 729 sq. m (1,888 sq. km); population approx. 1,100,000; independent state within the Commonwealth.

Lamma and Lantau Islands
China 'cross the Bay

The heart is an island
But the soul is the sky.
Old Chinese Proverb

Hong Kong, one of the world's most confined and congested places, is cast about by more than two hundred islands where it is possible to walk for many solitary hours among butterflies and birds.

On Lamma Island, sitting by, but not on, an armchair-shaped tomb on a sunny hill, I watched the distant harbour of Aberdeen on Hong Kong, looked across to the buildings piled like luggage on a wharf, and noted the aircraft shuttling towards Kai Tak Airport. I was so alone that, guided by only Chinese signposts, this intrepid explorer once more lost his way.

Even if I were still wandering there now, which by the way events turned out would not be all that unlikely, the adventure would have remained a satisfaction. In order to reach Lamma you go along the frenetic waterfront of Hong Kong Island and buy a ticket at the Outer Islands Ferry. Many of the population of the colony live on boats, or travel by them, and as the ferry pushed its way across the humid harbour, the spread of the remarkable city opened out like a frieze. It was mid-morning and the ferry was the least crowded place on that side of the water. I had a whole deck to myself, one man among rows of empty benches, like a lone, conscientious voter at an unpopular election meeting. At the centre of the vessel a cookshop blew out delicious noodly smells; from the rail I looked out onto the ominously thick water with its thousand boats; junks, tenuous sampans, often with a thin woman poling at the stern, fellow ferries, a hydrofoil, rushing, red and white striped like a footballer; a dense cargo ship, registered in Southampton, England, with railway carriages lining her deck giving her the appearance of a floating railway terminus. Our – or rather 'my' – ferry hooted, important hoots not much milder than a departing ocean liner, as we moved out into the streams of marine traffic. For all the varying sizes and speeds, for all the crossing courses, the frailty of some craft and the hugeness of others, there seemed little danger of collision.

Eventually the activity began to thin and, although we were still hemmed in by the city and its hills, the seaway opened out and I could see the outlying isles, approaching beyond the bow. Lamma is the third largest with an area of five square miles, much of which is green and open hillside, its population concentrated mainly in two settlements by the sea. There are no paved roads or vehicular traffic. My scheme was to arrive at the waterside village of Sok Kwu Wan, have a fish lunch, and walk across the rising land to Yung Shue Wan where I could conveniently board the return ferry. So much for the plan; in reality it was a little different.

We passed an islet with a coffee-pot lighthouse and a Union Jack, and then the ferry nosed into an opening in the side of the lofty island which grew ahead. The next hour was one of unexpected delight.

There was a festival taking place in Sok Kwu Wan. Its harbour was blowing with coloured flags and banners, the bom-bom of drums sounded from its random waterfront, and out in the open water were three immensely long canoes, ornamented with omens, each manned by fifty paddlers. Every boat had a dragon's head at its bow and at its centre a man pounding out time on painted drums. The three crews, each one in different colours, had just raced across the bay and there was overwhelming acclamation on shore, and on the boats, as the winners were announced. Drums rattled and boomed, and at the end of the jetty dragons were dancing. Chinese music clanged out from every alley and place. I saw it all, spellbound, while the ferry went between the jubilant flags to the quay.

For a while I watched the canoes, with their crews wearing fancy hats, race again across the olive water, urged on by drums, between the hundreds of houseboats, sampans and junks jammed against the harbour pontoons. Then the streets claimed my delighted attention; tight alleys, birds in cages, flowers tipping over, children shouting, people carrying great bundles on heads and shoulders, and – joy – the exquisite smell of Chinese cooking. All along the waterfront were outdoor cafés, crowded with families on this festive day – I counted twenty-three people around one table, great-grandmother down to the newest staring infant. I knew how he felt.

The lady at the place I had lunch (I kept to fish and rice in anticipation of my walk across the island) tried to explain the reason for the festivities. It was religious, she said, but not Christian. She was anxious to define the point. 'Lamma,' she said pointing to the ground, 'Lamma don't like Jesus. Hong Kong like Jesus.' I nodded that I understood there were other religions available. She told me the Chinese opera was making its once-a-year visit. That night would be one to remember.

I could have stayed in Sok Kwu Wan all day (or all month for that matter) but I had decided to explore the interior and I proceeded along the waterfront, past the exotic façade which was being erected for the opera performance, ducking under hanging banners and dangling laundry (the Chinese are never short of flags of one sort or another) and then out by a single path around the bay and up into the hills.

There was a softness up here, a humming quiet of bees and dragonflies, birds sounding drowsily, only for the music from the village to come to ear immediately I gained an exposed position. With no noise from vehicles it vibrated from far over the bay.

Once I was in the middle of the island, however, the noise ceased. I came upon a line of Chinese people, each with a black umbrella open, progressing in single file down the path, like a silent patrol. There was a school where children's chiming filtered out into the sunshine. I was reminded of the little school on Great Barrier Island, New Zealand. It might have been the same place. I suppose schools are much the same in such places everywhere. Two boys with satchels, almost as big as they were, approached grinning.

'How are you?' said one. I was not sure whether he was enquiring after my health or telling me his name. 'I am fine,' I ventured. 'How are you?'

'I am fine,' he replied.

'I am fine,' added his companion. They went on their way, apparently feeling a sort of triumph. I did too.

Down in the bay a figure in a wide straw hat paddled a raft scarcely the size of a suitcase. I descended the path to the beach and saw it was a woman. I waved but I realized she would be too occupied to respond. She could hardly have let go of that paddle without tumbling into the water. I came to a halt; a small group of houses with not a soul there except an old woman cleaning some fish. She politely waved a fish in greeting.

The interior of the island was empty. Not a living soul did I see as I walked the meandering path, through thickly smelling trees and hems of flowers, including the bougainvillaea which seems to grow everywhere that has a taste of warmth. There were patches of cultivated gardens, with beans and the sort of vegetables grown in England. Up in the silent parts, where the ground is pierced by rocks and the way climbs more than 1,000 feet into Mount Stenhouse, the central peak of the island, there were curious Chinese tombs, shaped like armchairs so that the dead can rest comfortably.

It was entirely pleasing wandering through that unusual country but it also seemed to be taking a long time. I kept catching a glimpse of the brow of a white chimney (true to modern form, a power station was being built on Lamma which only narrowly escaped the excesses of an oil refinery) and I attempted to navigate by that. The signs at the pathside, painted on rocks, were copious but were inconveniently in Chinese characters.

After two and a half hours on what should have been an amiable hour's stroll, I knew that once again this Doctor Livingstone had got himself lost. It was not so desperate as my experience on Dunk Island in Australia (there were no snakes for a start), but it was still hot and exhausting. Eventually the path unrolled to the seashore by a rubbishy little bay and I saw a man in a sampan shovelling a dreadful mess of food scraps into a container, presumably for his pigs or chickens. I went along the wooden jetty and asked him the way to Yung Shue Wan.

He appeared aghast and pointed vaguely far over the hills. A young woman arrived with a baby and she said, 'Long way, long way.' Once again I wondered if she were telling me her name.

'Sampan?' suggested the man pointing to his boat. 'Yung Shue Wan – sampan.' Now that boat was rotten; foul, slippery with oil and the debris of the pig food. But I couldn't walk over the hills again so we made a bargain and he decently placed a little stool on the fungicidal deck so that I would have somewhere to sit.

It took half an hour, around several capes and headlands, bouncing on the lively sea (I abandoned the stool because it kept slithering from beneath me) always with the thought that one extra bump would deposit me among the nameless muck in the hold of the boat. At last we reached the jetty at Yung Shue Wan and in my eagerness to disembark I all but ended up in the harbour.

Thankfully I got on the ferry and sat there trying to imagine what a gin and tonic was going to be like in the bar of the Hong Kong Hotel. Exploring islands is all very well, but there's nothing like a gin and tonic in comfort.

*

On the following day I found myself again on a small Chinese boat, but this time voyaging only across a creek barely fifty feet wide in the middle of a fishing village on the island of Lantau. The island is the largest of the congregation around Hong Kong at the foot of the Chinese mainland. It is green and serrated with roads climbing steep gradients enabling you almost to look down the chimney pots of the valley houses. It reminded me of the vales and vantage points of Madeira.

At the small town of Tai O, the sea comes right into the main street, making it necessary to cross by a ferry operated by a formidable Chinese lady who pulled it on a rope slung from one side of the creek to the other.

The weather was odd, the unsure combination of fog and wind in the mountains and along the coast. The fishing junks and sampans in the harbour at Tai O were webbed with mist. It came on to rain and the propelling lady on the ferry put an umbrella above her head and pulled the rope with one hand.

I was glad I visited Tai O because, again, the day was a special one. Not a festival, but the day when the registrar from the main island travelled across with his assistant and all the people who had married or had children over the past months gathered to complete the documents for him. They clamoured about a long trestle table in the council chamber in the town's slight street, sitting and standing three or four deep, like an overcrowded dinner party. The registrar, a young studious man who wanted to know how his profession worked in Britain, sat and dealt patiently with the customers. Many could not read or write and there was a nice moment when a married couple had to press their thumb prints onto a document which proved that their union was legal. Small babies hung on their mother's backs while their entry into both the register and the world was noted. It was an animated room and very hot. Every so often the registrar would decide to halt and his assistant brought him a dainty bowl of pale tea. Refreshed, he would then call on the next thumb to be pressed to paper.

The police station at Tai O has an altar to the god Kwan Tai who is the deity of policemen, and also of television people. Before a new television film is produced the whole company pray to Kwan Tai and hope for success.

Religion is an everyday matter in such places, however. I went up to Po Lin Monastery in the hills for lunch at the monks' rest house, where the food was vegetarian, and excellent, and eaten in the company of a solemn servant and a large television set, topped by a reclining Buddha. It was wonderful there, not for all the usual brass and bronze objects of such places, not for the ornate altars or temple bells, but for the weather. Fog fell in relays, thick around the curly roofs at one moment and then blown swiftly off by a following wind. Then it would abruptly return and the whole scene would be enclosed in mystery.

Back in Tai O there is another temple, a much more intimate place, just a door off the street by the post box and then into a decorated room with two altars to the Goddess of Fish, Tin Hau, and another to the policeman's god, Kwan Tai. What was pleasing about this shrine was that it was not only in constant use, as much as the stalls selling fruit and fish and vegetables, but that its custodian, a cheerful man in a vest whose name was simply Mr Chan, lived in the temple. He had a side-chapel all to himself with his table and chairs, his cuckoo clock, and his bed. He was pleased to have me take his photograph in this unique domesticity. The registrar poked his head into the temple and explained to me that Mr Chan was the happiest man for miles around. Who wouldn't be, living like that in the same room as the gods?

LAMMA situated latitude 22°9′ N and longitude 113°52′ E; area 5 sq.m (13 sq. km); population approx. 10,000. LANTAU situated latitude 22°37′ N and longitude 114°30′ E; area 55 sq. m (142 sq. km); population approx. 30,000. Both part of territory under lease agreement between Britain and China

Ōshima
Among the Seven Isles

In the hustle of the marketplace there is money to be made – but
under the Cherry Tree there is rest.
Japanese Proverb

The Seven Isles of Izu drop like a pendant below the city of Tokyo and the wide Bay of Sagami, the most distant some 160 miles out into the Pacific Ocean. On that furthermost island, Hachijo, there are touches of Polynesia; the people build outrigger canoes and grow bananas. They also enjoy a safe kind of bullfighting – the bulls contest each other, goaded on by men banging gongs and drums.

From there, going back towards the mainland of Japan, each one distant from its neighbour, are the isles of Mikura, Miyake, Kozu, Niijima, Toshima and Ōshima. They were once the summits of mountains in the range that has its roots in the snows of Mount Fuji, and is continued down the jewel of land known as the Izu Peninsula.

It was very strange for me to be flying from the old Tokyo airfield, Haneda, on a fresh spring morning in an aircraft of Nihon Kinkyori Airlines. In all my travels to the varied islands of the world, I had always found something familiar, people who spoke at least some of my language and whose lives I was able to understand. But – beyond Tokyo – this was a foreign place indeed.

Your intrepid explorer had made his first error the previous midnight when arriving from Taiwan. Like the seasoned traveller I must surely be by now, I marched from Narita Airport with my single suitcase (for once first off the plane) and tossed it wearily at a taxi driver who caught it and smiled when I said, 'New Otani Hotel.' It was only when this globetrotter had settled back that I remembered Tokyo had a *new* airport and saw a sign which said, 'Tokyo 75 Kilometres.' It was too late to go back for the bus, which all the unseasoned travellers take. It took an hour and cost a great many yen.

On this, the following morning, determined to regain my self-respect I got to the now secondary airport of Haneda by monorail, which made me feel a lot better. On the other hand I missed the plane. Three hours later I was on my way, over the springtime sea, down the leg of the Izu Peninsula, and looking out eagerly, as I always do, for my first sight of the island. The strangeness of it came home to me at once because I was the only non-Japanese on the plane. The stewardess, however, paid me the courtesy of repeating all announcements in English ('We shirtry be randing in Ōshima').

I could not see the island at all. This seemed odd because its active volcano is said to be visible for twenty-five miles, sending out puffs of vapour like an old lounger smoking a pipe. Sailors are reputed to use it as a mark, but here we were, *shirtry to be randing*, and there was not a sign of it.

It turned out to be there all the time, skulking under a great bundle of cloud, formless and grey as a bag of laundry. The vapour reached from the mountain top down to the skirts of the sea. We dropped across the approach; coves and fields and buildings began to appear and, judging by the exclamations, to everyone's relief, the runway of the airport. I remembered that this used to be a favoured excursion for people from Tokyo bent on suicide. More than a few one-way tickets were bought for Ōshima. So many visitors, in fact, went up the volcano and took a spectacular last leap from the world, that now anyone who goes to the top must apply at the police station if they want to walk the final fifty yards to the lip of the crater. Provided they seem to have a passable excuse they are given permission and an escort, who accompanies them to the edge, just in case. Ōshima was getting a bad name.

My arrival set off a small sensation. A relayed message, which had been understandably misinterpreted, had resulted in a whole posse of taxis and drivers waiting for me, waving banners and flags of various colours and shouting variations of my name. Since I had missed the earlier plane they were overwhelmingly glad to see me, a joy that was quickly drained when they realized that 'Resrie' Thomas was only one person and not some kind of club outing which they had patently been expecting. The banners and flags drooped sadly and the taxi drivers stood bowing gravely as, to my embarrassment, I had to choose one to take me to the hotel. I picked the oldest, but I was told later that although this was a nice recognition of age, he could not bow as low as the others. (This bowing business is wonderful. You find yourself catching the habit at once, the art being able to coordinate yourself with the other bowers in the group so that heads do not collide and spoil the effect. Everybody bows. Years ago in the mountains of Japan I was entranced to witness how the people on the wayside stations bowed the train on its way, and at Haneda that morning the mechanics who had been servicing the plane lined up and bowed beautifully as we taxied off, as if we were going on some important or perilous flight.)

By the time I left the sole room of Ōshima's airport the clouds had gone further up the slopes, the mountain pulling them up like a large woman hitching up a voluminous skirt.

Red camellias grow all the year in Ōshima and the early way to Mount Mihara was bright with hedgerows of many flowers. In springtime the cherry trees make the island glow. Some are very ancient; one is said to be 800 years old and is held in reverence. There was a formal grove of palm trees leading from the airport, an announcement that the climate is mild, as it undoubtedly is. It is also misty and wet.

As we progressed up the windy road so the vegetation became thicker and greener. It filled every space of the wayside and descended into choked jungles. Then, abruptly, as though we had reached the frontier to another place, we drove into the clouds. They devoured us at once, so that it was like flying, the sides of the way scarcely visible. The driver muttered something that sounded like a Japanese apology but found the many bends without difficulty. He was obviously used to it. I did not know we had reached the hotel until I saw a vaguely coloured patch of azaleas through the mist and realized we were in a garden. I stumbled towards the door, I could see a foggy figure bowing just ahead and he took my bag. England, he said, he liked and Scotland more because he enjoyed the sound of the bagpipes.

Looking around at the fog lolling across the mountain I had the thought that the bagpipes would not have sounded out of place.

The man who liked bagpipes was tall and anxious to help. He was porter, waiter, driver and translator at the hotel. Only he and the lady who was at reception had any smattering of English and my Japanese was confined to 'Sayonara', which (since it means 'goodbye') is a poor way to begin a conversation. They were excessively kind and courteous. Susumu, the man who drove me around in the hotel's van, conversed in an amazing sequence of words he had learned from American Country and Western songs.

The ingenuity of this language was astonishing. He had a line or lyric for almost any eventuality. When we were driving up the lanes towards the hotel he would repeat John Denver's words 'Country roads, take me home . . .' He judged any travelling time by how long it took to get to 'Phoenix', and the great waves that pushed against the rocks of his native island instantly recalled 'Galveston, Galveston, I can see your sea winds blowing . . .' He stretched even further back into the genre as we took the road to the volcano . . . 'She be coming round the mountain when she come.' He did not always get the pronunciation quite right, but it was original and entrancing.

At the hotel I had a Japanese room and ate Japanese food. The reception lady, Ōshima's other English speaker, said, 'This-o your Loom-o. Prease take-o shoes-o off-o. Breakfast-o eight-o-crock-o.'

The room had a coconut-matting floor, but was devoid of other furniture except for a cushion propped up on a stand in the centre, a television set, a refrigerator and an elegant dish containing the implements for Japanese tea-making. Outside the window the fog swirled and I felt suddenly homesick for a comfortable bed. I'm renowned for taking a nap on first arriving in a hotel anywhere. It helps you and the room get accustomed to each other. I felt quite helpless; there was nowhere to sit, nowhere to *be*. I kept wandering aimlessly. Then I found some neatly folded Japanese clothes, a black-and-white kimono, and a short, heavy, wide-sleeved coat. They were obviously meant for the guest so I put them on. Then I found a tin of mandarin oranges in the fridge and some processed cheese, plus several small bottles of whisky. I had not eaten since breakfast so I sat on the floor in my kimono and ate the oranges and the cheese. Outside the fog swirled ominously. I began to feel very sorry and solitary, like a Japanese marooned in the Shetlands. But (as he might well have discovered) the whisky was all right.

That evening I went down to dinner in my European clothes. Everyone else was clad in the hotel's kimonos and the waiter hinted heavily by bringing me a huge, comic, pelican-type bib, the sort that is hung around the necks of babies to catch the scraps. I bowed out and returned in my kimono which met with everyone's approval.

There was a group of about a dozen Japanese men, who, as far as I could tell, were all occupying the same room. I went along the corridor in my new clothes and one of them kindly tore himself away from the television (where, unless I am mistaken, a lady was singing the weather forecast) and took a photograph of me. Later that night the men got immensely drunk on Suntory whisky and at some stage I joined them and taught them to sing the English West Country folk song 'Widdecombe Fair'. Their rendition of the chorus 'Old Uncle Tom Cobbly and All' was both unique and endearing.

Mount Mihara not only dominates Ōshima, it *is* Ōshima. It reclines, 2,700 feet up, occasionally huffing and puffing, with the rest of the island merely its attendant foothills. Its crater, a baleful eye deep down, has been measured at 328 feet, although I doubt if anyone has been to the bottom to check. Throughout history it has abruptly lost its temper and given vent to mighty eruptions, lava rolling down through the houses, sending people hurrying out to the safety of the sea. Its last great fling was in 1942 when fiery debris was thrown up almost 1,000 feet. In Tokyo they thought it was the Americans getting their own back.

The top of the mountain is a desert of cinders and ash, giving way to the vegetation, thick and green, on the lower slopes. It is said that, for all the desolation up there on the cone, with the sulking winds and the barren dust, it is the home of many nightingales.

The clouds that clothed the top of the volcano prevented me getting there (like the Blue Grotto of Capri it is something that Nature denied me and will have to be visited on another day). Susumu drove me up the mountain road as far as the barrier, where you pay your entry fee of 800 yen (a strange business paying to get into a volcano) and move on to a twilight village which cowers below the business end. Susumu pointed out the path which leads to the top but no one was allowed to venture further today – even with the police escort. I had to content myself with a visit to the little cinema at the edge of the village where a film of the volcano and its various moods is shown. It was odd sitting there, alone, with the lamp burning on an altar at one end and the wind banging against the wooden sides of the building. The film showed men dressed as Martians lowering themselves into the crater (for what reason was unclear to me) and there was a shot, like something from a bloodthirsty Japanese drama, showing the distant, sprawled body of someone who had either fallen or jumped in.

Fortunately there was more to do than sit alone in a cinema on the side of a volcano. The lowlands were benevolent and sunny, the windy sea coming in, gathering its shoulders for its assault on the land. I walked into the small town of Motomachi where there is a wooden jetty along which the ocean rolled and licked. The place was clear with sunshine but rifled with the sharp wind and there were few people about. An old lady trotted delightfully through the gusts by the seashore, wearing the traditional Ōshima chequered headscarf adorned with a red camellia. Once all the women and girls of the island wore the distinctive draughtboard kimono, the white socks and this headdress, but now it is normally only seen on festive days. On the jetty were some men trying to fish and keep on their feet at the same time. Two jolly schoolboys came along, in their high-collared pageboy uniforms. They were delighted to pose for a photograph and, round faced, laughed and made Churchill-like V-signs. One of them, particularly, looked inordinately like Churchill in his early cadet days.

The town was nondescript, a few shops, clean and packed with sweets and gifts for the first of the expected summer visitors. I bought a bar of chocolate and by the fuss that was made I might well have been the initial customer of the season. Motomachi has a large anchor and chain at its centre, a memento of a shipwreck, and nearby a much more fascinating exhibit, a shrine to the legendary twelfth-century archer Tametomo, who was exiled to Ōshima.

An embarrassment to the Japanese emperors, this Oriental Robin Hood was shipped to Ōshima but eventually escaped to the Ryukyu Islands, the long tail of Japan that runs southwest towards Hong Kong. There he married a princess and attained power and respectability.

The shrine was a surprise. It was in a room which also accommodated a table-tennis table. Tametomo stood at one end, behind a sort of shop window, wearing his fearsome armour and with his powerful bow at hand. Two ladies stood demurely at his side. It was tempting to think that when things were quiet at night they climbed down for a game of table tennis.

A nice bony old lady showed me the hero and then staggered ahead up some steep steps to a lookout place which she indicated Tametomo had used to spot the approach of enemies. There was also a stone, impressed with his fingerprints, which he had once hurled at someone he did not like.

The Japanese like making models. Along the roads of Ōshima, and there is really only one main road which circumnavigates the island, are placed, at intervals, short, replica policemen, to remind motorists of the speed limit through habitations. The road curls with the carved coastline. At several points, where it has been cut through the rock, there are patterns of strata, curved like rainbows. The sea was blue and wild, advancing hungrily on the cliffs only to meet its eternal rebuff. It is the same everywhere; the attacking sea can only win by stealth. Inland the greenery filled every valley, with odd handkerchief farms and smallholdings carved out of the jungle. In the south was a splendidly deep harbour, a place called Habu, where a volcanic crater toppled, at some unknown and ancient time, into the ocean causing, one would imagine, a good deal of steam. The result is a beautiful place, three sides of the old crater hemming in the wharves and blue-roofed houses and the many boats, and the fourth opening out into the ocean. By accident it became the perfect port.

On the thoughtful water, dozens of fishing boats lay reflectively, with one or two larger vessels loading at the wharves. The brown and black rocks rose in a scenic horseshoe, with flowers and shrubs tumbling over the crevices. The sun shone benignly and there was no wind here and few people.

Okachi, on the upper coast, across the mountainside from Motomachi, is reached through silent valleys, full of tangled greenery. Occasionally there are hamlets by the roadside, one with another pair of friendly imitation policemen, red- and blue-roofed houses, vegetable gardens and fishing coves. But it was all quiet and sunlit, the mountain sheltering it from the wind.

I stayed three days in Ōshima and never once did the summit of the mountain reveal iself (nor the ends of the hotel, for that matter) but although I missed the volcano it was, for me, another unique island, and the visit was worth it. At the end the tall and solemn Susumu, the County and Western enthusiast, took me to the airport where we shook hands and bowed with great care and ceremony. Then he recited, straight and serious, 'You leaving on a jet plane. Don't know when you be back again . . .'

ŌSHIMA situated latitude 34°8′ N and longitude 133°5′ E; area 35 sq. m (91 sq. km); population approx. 10,500; Japan

Kauai
High in the Rainy Mountain

As we were extremely unwilling, notwithstanding the suspicious
circumstances of the preceding day, to believe that these people were
cannibals, we now made some further enquiries on the subject.
CAPTAIN COOK, killed by cannibals in Hawaii 1779

The wettest place in the whole world is Mount Waialeale on Kauai in the
Hawaiian Islands. It averages 500 inches of rain a year but 686 inches were
measured in 1981. Sometimes the rain is so powerful that meteorologists
cannot reach the crater at the summit to read their own gauges. It is the only
mountain on earth with a swamp on the top and is one of the most amazing
and beautiful places I have ever seen.

There is only one way to the top of Waialeale and that is by helicopter.
Even then the cone is only rarely accessible, perhaps once every two
months when the air briefly clears. I happened to choose one of those days.

The helicopter was like a cheerful yellow butterfly (the company which
flies it is called Papillon) and the pilot was a young Texan, Robert Bloom,
quietly flamboyant, if that's possible; he was drafted during the Vietnam
war, he learned to fly, and then never went outside Texas. 'I was real glad
about that,' he said with laconic honesty.

Before we took off from Princeville, an airport with a garden and flower
pots like a country railway station, Robert looked at the mountain 5,000 feet
high, parcelled by its foothills, and announced that we were really lucky.
Today we were going to make it to the crater, and that did not often happen.
'And I've got a great music programme for you,' he added. He noticed my
grimace. Surely, I argued, to fly up to one of the world's most alluring and
inaccessible places was enough without orchestral accompaniment. No, he
wanted me to hear the music as well. 'Okay,' I said, 'I'll hear the music.'

So after getting into the glass bubble, the rotors limbering up, I put on the
earphones. Robert climbed aboard and I was in the co-pilot's seat. I began to
feel like James Bond. The pilot muttered to the control tower. We were clear
to go. Over us the blades swung and sounded. The aircraft rose gingerly,
tentative for the first few feet and then, as if feeling free, banked away and

snorted for the hills. It was wonderful right from the start. He drove that machine like a motorbike, up the flanks of foothills, over the crests, down into crevices and valleys, roaring across jungled trees and pounding rivers, high then drifting deliberately into the most solemn canyons I have ever seen, ten waterfalls at a time whispering over their edges; then, quickly again, along bouldered slopes making goats gallop for cover, over more ridges, zipping over the last few feet so that yet another stunning vista yawned before us; over the crashing sea and a spouting school of whales, back again; banking, turning, holding, hovering . . . And all to the resounding music of *Star Wars*. What an adventure!

It was like finding yourself accidentally caught up in the middle of a Cinerama spectacular; like being aboard a rollercoaster and riding through a dream. We scooped up a valley, merely feet – inches it seemed at times – clear of rocks and trees, and, braking, nosed into a dangling cloud. We emerged into green sunshine and an awesome crater bitten into the top of the earth. It was unbelievable; the most astonishing place. We sidled into the crater itself, walls on all sides, rivers of white water, and right before our noses a single majestic waterfall plunging nonchalantly from the topmost ridge.

I did not need the music, but I had to admit it enhanced the thrill. The pilot pointed down. We were going to land in the crater of Waialeale, once sacred to the ancient people of Kauai, and a place where only a few have stepped before.

As far as I could judge the floor of the huge hole was a riot of rocks and rivers tumbling from the waterfall pool. But in the middle of it all was a brief grass island, barely the size of the helicopter itself, and that is where we landed. Robert edged the machine in alongside the thunderous arm of the waterfall and set it down with the ease of a handshake on the wet grass. We climbed out.

This was the secret place, the Sanctuary of the Gods. I stood and regarded the waterfall, and there are few more quieting sights than 100,000 tons of water toppling above your head.

'We're sure lucky today,' shouted Robert looking at the blue sky beyond the spray. 'Already we've had over 400 inches of rain this year and it's still only May. Waialeale looks like she's going to break last year's record – 686 inches and that's a lot of water.'

Six months previously three honeymoon couples had been landed at this place. A mishap prevented the helicopter taking off again and radio communication broke down too. Night came on. 'Nobody knew what had happened,' related Robert. 'The Navy sent a helicopter to search but the Navy had never been up here so I had to come with them. That was hair-raising. It was dark and getting through these canyons in daylight is difficult enough. One of the Navy guys was leaning through the hatch with a big light picking out the walls of rock. I had to tell them which turn to make and when. It was all very, very quiet in there, believe me.'

It was hopeless. They had to go back and return at first light. They found the machine. 'The newly-weds were okay,' said Robert. 'They'd all slept together in the helicopter.'

'How about the pilot?' I asked. Robert grinned and said, 'He slept underneath.'

Four-fifths of Kauai is inaccessible to anything but helicopter. Boats can land on the great copper-rocked Na Pali Coast, but there are few landfalls that are not hazardous. (Oddly enough there is a government hut on one of those cut-off beaches – where we landed in the helicopter – which has an official notice saying 'No Admittance!' Bureaucracy travels far.) Within the island are the hidden places left to rivers, clouds and rainbows. Two cows and one man live inland from the unapproachable coast. The animals are the remnants of an attempt at ranching in one of the more communicative valleys. The man wanders wild in the interior, seen only occasionally by the forest rangers.

Hemming the coastline of the almost circular island is a road which omits the thirty-mile chunk of the Na Pali. By some whimsy of wind and weather the seaside regions have only a fraction of the rainfall of the big mountain, between fifteen and twenty inches a year, and it is here that the tourists go.

But even along the holiday fringe there are some curiously neglected places. Hanapepe is a wry little town at the mouth of an ancient tribal valley. Its name means 'make-baby' but there appears to be little activity of any sort there today. It has the silence and demeanour of somewhere that has been running down for a long time; it possesses a decrepit charm; rusty buildings, leaning walls and weeds in the vacant streets. There are some tired, but picturesque, shops and a few lurking bars. At the centre of the muddy street is the Dance and Voice Training Establishment.

Older things are in far better order. The origins of the extraordinary Menehune Fish Pond, 900 feet long, enclosed in green banks, is legendary. The Menehune were a miniature people, two feet in height, who accomplished prodigious feats of building and engineering overnight, always working under cover of darkness. (Perhaps they were the origin of the Seven Dwarfs?) The great fishpond was commissioned by a Prince and Princess who broke the rules by spying on the fairy people at work. They were, predictably, turned into rock for their pains and stand noticeably overlooking the magic valley.

Kauai needs tourists, since its other main industry, sugar-cane, is at the mercy of hazardous world markets. But fortunately it will be some time, perhaps never, before the influx of tourists reaches anything like the proportions of Honolulu, ninety miles away. There 'Aloha' has become a slogan rather than a greeting, a farewell, or an endearment; not something that should happen to a poetic word. On Waikiki are multitudes of visitors hung with sweat and flowers. And there are few more daunting things than having a *lei* placed around your neck at two o'clock in the morning at Honolulu Airport.

Kauai has its hotels and condominiums, a word even more hatefully abbreviated to condos; it has all the trappings and the tours. At the Coco Palms Hotel you can have ukulele and hula lessons and be wed in a church built for the film *Sadie Thompson* starring Rita Hayworth. (Extras offered at the service include two singers who sing 'Hawaiian Wedding Song' made famous by Andy Williams – $25 and a conch-shell blower – $7.50). The officiating clergy is likely to be just as exotic. A beautiful Hawaiian girl, auditioning as a singer and hula dancer at the hotel, has also performed wedding ceremonies at the chapel. She produced a business card for me giving her hula name, Elethe Aguiae, and on the other side, the Reverend Elithe Hoylea. The latter did not look right in lights, she said.

But Grace Guslander, the remarkable lady who ran the resort, started with no more than a boarding house, and she had properly preserved something of the old Hawaii among the packaged hours and days that so many people demand and for which they return expectantly each year. In the grounds of Coco Palms, which stands on the site of an ancient tribal palace, is a modest museum, overseen by a courtly Hawaiian lady called Mrs Sarah Kelekonia Sheldon whose great-great-grandfather was a retainer in the household of the last Hawaiian King.

She sits surrounded by pictures, books, flags and furniture which her ancestor would have known and touched. There is a huge four-poster from Kentucky, with a native Queen's picture above it, for it was her bed. The canopy is a Hawaiian flag, that curious banner with eight red, white and blue stripes and in one corner a Union Jack.

This amalgam was the brainchild of King Kamehameha, the first ruler of *all* the Hawaiian Islands (Kauai was the last to come under his throne and did so then only by the persuasion of a fleet of European mercenaries with gunboats). His Majesty had been presented with a red ensign by Captain George Vancouver, the British navigator, in 1793. He persuaded himself that he was a link between his royal line and that of Great Britain, and flew the flag, a Union Jack on a red ground, at his palace. In retaliation Kaumualii, the subdued ruler of Kauai, still with local powers, conferred upon himself the title of King George.

The comic-opera element is strongly in evidence. The Russians appeared upon the scene in the person of Georg Anton Scheffer, a German doctor working for the American-Russian Alaska Company, a consortium with fingers spread far. He privately persuaded Kaumualii that, with the help of the Tsar, he could reverse the roles with Kamehameha and become king of all Hawaii.

Together they raised a fortress on Kauai, the ruins of which are still to be seen today. It was called Fort Elizabeth, after the queen of Russia, and was built in the form of a six-pointed star. Scheffer and King Kaumaulii, the odd couple, built this fort in 1817, but afterwards the adventure came inevitably to grief (the Tsar in distant Moscow said he preferred not to become involved) and the fort was left to tumble quietly down. Half a century after the episode thirty-eight cannons, clogged with rust, earth, weeds and flowers, were prised from the battlements. Today's joke about the fort is that little is to be seen except the footings of overgrown walls, but a short distance away is a public convenience of distinct blockhouse characteristics. Tourists, seeking the Russian fort, take photographs of that.

The Hawaiian alphabet is only twelve letters long, but these repeated, over and over, like a gargle, add up to some of the world's longest words. In the same tradition its most elongated word *Umuhumunukunukuopuopaa* (or thereabouts) is given to a fish so small you could not write its name on its back. By contast, high in the mountains is still to be found the O-o bird, although few in number, for the breed was all but exterminated by the natives to collect the bright yellow feathers for the sumptuous cloaks of the Hawaiian kings. Eight thousand birds made one cloak.

When Captain Cook discovered the Hawaiian Islands (which he, being a prosaic man, dubbed the Sandwich Islands after the Earl of Sandwich) he came first to Kauai in the *Resolution*, landing at Waimea Bay in January 1778. This solid but extraordinary adventurer, who the following year was to die at the hands of capricious and cannibalistic natives on a neighbouring island, was greeted by the King of Kauai as an expected God called Lono. The soothsayers had predicted a visit by fair-skinned deities, breathing fire, and journeying on floating tree-clad islands.

Over the blue horizon came the tall-masted ships, their men puffing away at their pipes, the officers wearing tricorn hats. The first Kauai natives to greet the newcomers reported that in addition to breathing fire the gods had three-cornered heads.

When standing at the spot of Cook's landing, the beach piled with the rubbish of a recent storm, I looked across to the shadow of Niihau, the only island in the group that Captain Cook might recognize today. Niihau is isolated, kept apart from the rest of the world and Hawaii by the decree of the Robinson family which has owned it for generations. It had one strange moment of limelight on the day of the Pearl Harbor attack in 1941, for one of the Japanese planes, hit by gunfire, crashed on the island. Since nobody on Niihau ever heard any news (they still don't) the armed pilot was able to take over the island single-handed. Eventually he shot at the only policeman, who, despite having three bullets in his chest, killed the Japanese by throwing him furiously against a wall.

Today Niihau has about 200 inhabitants, all of pure Hawaiian blood, and the archaic Hawaiian language is still taught in the school there. Supplies (and that means water too, for, within sight of Kauai's great drenched mountain, Niihau has only five inches of rain a year) are carried across on a World War II landing barge. There are no paved roads and no electricity (and thus no television) on the island and visitors are actively discouraged. 'For anyone but an inhabitant to go there is very difficult indeed,' a Kauai islander told me. 'If you took a boat across yourself you would probably be met by a Robinson employee on horseback – and holding a gun.'

A few years ago a party of educationalists from Honolulu was permitted to land on the island to inspect the school. When they returned, as from another world, and told their stories on Hawaii television some were in tears for they had witnessed the islands as they once were; they had seen both beauty and simplicity. Back in the ruins of highrise buildings, cars, jet airliners, dust and commercialism, they realized that the killing of 8,000 birds for a royal cloak for the earliest Hawaiian rulers had only been the beginning. They knew what they, as a people, had lost forever.

KAUAI situated latitude 21°40′ N and longitude 160°35′ W; area 551 sq. m (1,427 sq. km); population approx. 138,856; Hawaiian Group, USA.

Tahiti
Slightly This Side of Heaven

Oh, Heaven's Heaven! – but we'll be missing
The palms, and sunlight, and the south.
RUPERT BROOKE, *Tiara Tahiti*

In the old days there was a bar on the waterfront at Papeete called Quinn's, legendary throughout the South Pacific and beyond; a place of women, shadows, heat and booze, and justly popular. Now the site is occupied by a French insurance company, housed in a sanitized office block, which advertises protection against *divers risques, accidentes, maladies*, all things that were nightly occurrences at Quinn's.

Tahiti, like everywhere, has changed. No one could change the green of the hills nor diminish the extravagance of a sunset, but now the island has an autoroute (albeit one of the world's shortest), luminous hotels and restaurants and a ferry made from an assembly-kit that replaces the old ragged schooner that once sailed south to the Austral Islands. The site of Paul Gauguin's last house is a used car lot; the leper colony is down to its last forty-two lepers. Who can argue but that it is a better place?

Gauguin might be flattered to know that there is a drive-in cinema bearing his name, but I think not. As the tourists have advanced on Tahiti, together with the French H-Bomb squads, and international airlines, so a little of the romance has seeped away. And yet, of all the words and places in the world, Tahiti always meant romance – to a point. Rupert Brooke went to the island and prosaically fell in love with his landlady's daughter, Herman Melville was in jail there for mutiny, Zane Grey holds the big-fish record, Somerset Maugham walked off with Gauguin's painted doors, and Robert Louis Stevenson would rather have lived in Tahiti than Samoa, but the postal service was better to Samoa so, a businesslike Scot, he went there to live (and die) instead.

In the initial days of World War I the German cruisers *Scharnhorst* and *Gneisenau*, prowling the Pacific, shelled Papeete, causing much damage to the simple town and blowing up part of the wall of the yacht club, resulting in an aperture that was for years sportingly retained as a door. Even that's gone now and the yacht club has moved to new premises. Some worthwhile things have fortunately been preserved, the tomb of King Pomare V being one.

Pomare V was the final Tahitian king. At the end of 1880 he was enthusiastically pensioned off by the French colonists and devoted the remaining few years of his life to drinking – crowning his mausoleum (on the touchline of a soccer pitch) is a huge, unmistakable Benedictine botttle. Purists or historians will say it represents a burial urn, but if you have ever seen a Benedictine bottle, that's a Benedictine bottle.

In the rural areas, even today, times alter only reluctantly. The policemen still occupy their spare time delivering mail or turning a blind eye to the weekly cock-fighting jamborees that survive under the subterfuge of chicken fighting. *Le Truck* – half-lorry, half-bus – one of the world's more exciting public transport systems, still carries the population, its chattels and animals, to anywhere the people wish to travel, bumping along rough roads, through floods and flowers, nowadays to the sound of raucous rock-'n'-roll.

After Louis Antoine de Bougainville, one of the early Europeans in the South Pacific, had returned to France with his stories of Tahiti in the eighteenth century, the naturalist Commerson wrote:

Tahiti is perhaps the only country in the world where men live without vices, without prejudices, without necessities, without disputes. Born under a most beautiful sky, nourished on the fruits of an earth which is fertile without tillage, ruled by patriarchs rather than kings, they know no other god but Love.

Life was never quite as good as that again.

For a change James Cook was not the first to arrive in Tahiti – he was third. He anchored in the *Endeavour* in April 1769, carrying instruments and astronomers to observe the Transit of Venus, the planet passing across the sun (something they never properly achieved – at the earth's best vantage point – due to the shortcomings of their instruments). But Samuel Wallis, with the young Furneaux, and Bougainville had been there before him, seeking, as were all explorers in those days, the unknown continent at the foot of the world – *Terra Australis Incognita*. It was reasoned that there had to be something down there to counterbalance the great land mass at the top of the earth. Wallis was one of that rare breed, an easily satisfied explorer, and having discovered Tahiti and prised his sailors loose from the women there, he returned shamefacedly home. Furneaux, however, was to voyage again and leave his name forever on the islands to the south of that legendary land of Australia they had been seeking.

Point Venus, where Cook made his landfall, is a flat, disappointing sort of place, with a municipal-looking lighthouse – a memorial in the form of Venus (the star not the goddess) and a column surmounted by a ball representing the earth. There are notices saying 'Keep Off The Grass' which Cook would have ignored but not Wallis. Another marker commemorates those two men and also Bougainville. Other names, more recently chalked or scratched on the memorial, include Lavinia, Lou Lou and Kasonova. A nice touch.

The first thing Cook did on arrival was to get the name of the island wrong. He reported it as *Otaheite* not appreciating that the native informing him was saying 'O Taheite' or 'It is Taheite'. Then, however, he performed one of his everyday miracles, the strengths that compensated for his occasional lack of imagination, and with the botanist Sir Joseph Banks and eight sailors he set out to row and walk around the uncharted island.

It took only a week for Cook on his tour to circumnavigate the ninety-five miles. He produced an astonishing map which, even today, has only been changed in detail, for there is still only one basic route around the fringe of the island with a few brief indentations into the hills. The interior, like that of Kauai in Hawaii, remains isolated and unknown. In the 1950s it took a year and a half to clear a track through the vegetation around Mount Orohena (7,353 feet) so that a climbing party could get to the summit, the first to reach there since remembered time. On the top the climbers found a lonely human skull.

Today if you make the same trek as Cook you follow a road that varies between a new autoroute to a winding way curling around headlands and staggering across rivers on temporary bridges. The coastal route was likened to the shape of a dumb-bell by Cook, and also a lady's hand looking-glass by someone with more romance. Today it might be described as a table-tennis bat. Much, but not all, of the coast is protected by a beautiful coral reef.

At one point, however, where mountain streams divulge into the sea, the water temperature is minimally colder and the sensitive coral cannot survive. A rent shows in the reef and the ocean takes advantage of the gap running to the land with fierce glee as if to make up for its taming elsewhere. The weather and the landscape vary together. Hot sunshine becomes, in the course of turning a corner, hard, grey rain. Clouds gather like mountains along a coastline that is mild and smooth, changing to fierce rocks and battered out-islands.

In their camps along the Tahitian coast are France's marines, occupied in guarding their country's H-Bomb tests among the blameless atolls of the South Pacific. Native Tahitians, when summoned for National Service, can serve their time on the island or in France. Predictably there is an overwhelming enthusiasm for France.

The tradition of overseas service is long. In the Mitchell Library in Sydney I read a letter from Mary Hassall of Paramatta, Australia, written to her brother Thomas at 411 Oxford Street, London, on 8 September 1818, describing the arrival there of 'John Henry Martin, a religious Tahitian' who had lost his right arm fighting (for the British) at Waterloo. He was going home with a pension of twenty pounds a year.

Papeete has a magnificently deep and protected harbour. I remember, years ago, sitting over a drink on the jetty and watching a full-blown ocean liner curve into the entrance, come to the quay and stop as nonchalantly as a motor car being parked alongside a kerb. She then took ten days to sail out again, seawater having somehow seeped into her oil tanks. An extraordinary airlift of oil from California, carried in a fleet of hurriedly hired aircraft from Britain, had to be mounted before she could leave. It must have been an expensive cruise for somebody.

The harbour, severely damaged in the gross German bombardment of 1914 – and how strange that the Great War should have one of its first conflagrations so far from the main belligerents – was rebuilt in a tropical, haphazard fashion, in keeping with its past. Photographs taken in Paul Gauguin's day and on display at the museum dedicated to the artist, reveal the nineteenth-century Papeete waterfront crammed with commerce, masts sprouting everywhere, barrels on the wharves. Today it is less romantic, more businesslike, with people leaving their offices for lunch; banks and buffets, tourist agencies, airlines and the insurance companies declaring their *divers risques*, a phrase in itself, perhaps, sounding to have dangerous maritime connections.

In these days the Chinese run most of the businesses. They were brought in as sweated labour to grow cotton during the American Civil War, the reasoning being that the crop in the Southern States would fail or be destroyed or uncollected. The supposition proved wrong and the venture foundered, but the Chinese, as is their custom, triumphed. When a Tahitian wife goes shopping today she says simply, 'I am going to the Chinaman.'

Tahiti has another connection with the war between the States. In the village of Papara the church has a tombstone carrying the inscription, 'Dorence Atwater, at the age of 16 entered the Union Army as a volunteer with Kilpatrick's Cavalry in the war of 1861–65. He was captured by Confederate Scouts disguised as Union soldiers in July 1863, while carrying despatches and taken to Bell Isle prison.'

Atwater's journey from the dreaded Bell Isle to Tahiti was diffuse and included a year in the death camp at Andersonville. It was twelve years later, in Tahiti, that he married a native princess called Moetia, and lived there for all his remaining life.

I spent an evening on the waterfront of Papeete, where the canoes are still pulled up clear of the water. The ferry, a metallic, square vessel, was leaving for the outer islands. In the warm darkness it backed out into the harbour, its lights reflecting romantically. For looks it hardly replaces the old schooner (or the Bermuda flying-boat, full of matronly grace, that used to ply between the South Pacific harbours) but it looked well enough on the limp water, people silhouetted on the deck, others waving from the shore.

I ate at one of the little mobile stalls on the quay, the *brochettes*, where people have a cheap dinner, much as they did in the open-air carparks in Singapore – a stool against the counter and a plate of spiced fish. The market people were settling for the night, arranging themselves and their children on the pavements of the port. Before midnight they are all in place, on rugs, boxes, benches, or spread-eagled on the market stalls themselves, lying out of doors so that they will be there at dawn to claim their pitch. When it rains they pull sheets of plastic over themselves and their families and go back to sleep. It is strange to think that Tahitians used to dream of going to 'Tahiti' when they died.

It is a long time now since 'Paradise'. Gauguin, in 1891, and the other dreamers went to Tahiti to find it. The painter arrived just at the end of the age of innocence, although there was some still left. In his story, *Noa Noa*, he wrote of how he found his wife, Tehura, who was thirteen years of age.

The lonely, weary artist had travelled on despondent horseback through the island villages. At one place a woman asked him where he was going.

'To find a wife,' he replied.

'This is a village of pretty women. Do you want one?'

'Yes.'

'If she pleases you, I will give her to you. She is my daughter.'

The lithe young girl was brought to him. 'Do you want to live in my hut?' he asked.

'Yes.'

The mother said, 'She will come if you will make her happy. In eight days she will return here. If she is not happy she will leave you.'

They lived together for two years, an idyllic, island love story of the fiery man and the little native girl. Their bamboo hut at Mataiea has gone without trace, as has Gauguin's later home at Punaauia, which is now the site of a secondhand car-yard. Somerset Maugham went away from Mataiea with the three painted glass doors from Gauguin's hut. He wrote *The Moon and Sixpence* about the stormy genius who fell in love with an island, and a girl, only to end his life in pathetic poverty. The Tahitians always believed that Maugham would return the doors to them one day, or at least leave them to the island in his will. But they were sold in a Sotheby's auction to an American banker. The Gauguin Museum in Tahiti has to console itself with a lump of granite from the artist's native Brittany (the most tenuous exhibit, I think I have ever seen in a museum) plus his sewing machine and sad little harmonium from his last home. He did not even die in Tahiti, but at Atu Ona in the remote Marquesas Islands. He was predictably alone and penniless. In the museum there is a copy of his death certificate and a photograph of his grave surrounded by posed and patently disinterested island ladies.

There is a strange story told that in 1914 the poet Rupert Brooke, forsaking England and honey still for tea, arrived at the village of Mataiea, with the intention of searching out 'lost Gauguins'. His quest was hardly begun because he fell in love with his landlady's lovely daughter, Mamua, whom he remembered in his poem 'Tiara Tahiti'. The three Gauguin painted doors were a stone's throw away from the village where he was living but he was so bemused by Mamua that he never found them. Maugham did not arrive until two years later, by which time Brooke was dead and buried on another island – Skyros in the Aegean. Mamua died just after Maugham's visit in 1916 – of influenza.

There are, fortunately, happier stories. Along the beach from the Gauguin Museum lived – in a house once owned by another writer, Robert Keable – an optimistic Englishman called Roger Cowen, who in 1958 set sail from Ramsgate to see the world. 'There were five of us,' he remembered. 'And we managed to get right down here in the Pacific before we were wrecked on a small island about 300 miles south of Tahiti. I'd like to say it was a hair-raising adventure, but it wasn't. We weren't even on the boat at the time! We were ashore getting to know the natives.' Eventually a trading schooner picked them up and brought them to Tahiti, where Roger had been since. 'At first I became a vegetable grower and then I had a rabbit farm with

800 rabbits,' he laughed. 'Now I've got a restaurant, a Chinese wife and two kids. It all seems a long way from Ramsgate.'

Robert Louis Stevenson was already famous and wealthy when he arrived with his entire family in Tahiti in 1888, searching for a climate that he hoped might ease his tuberculosis. He loved the island and its brown people and walked around the village of Tautira in striped pyjamas. The family lived royally in the chief's house where, contrary to his voluptuous surroundings, Stevenson worked hard on his grim Scottish novel *The Master of Ballantrae*. His publishers, however, suggested that Samoa rather than Tahiti might be a better place for their prize author since the mail ships from Australia to England called there regularly. So Stevenson went to Samoa. They called him Tusitala, 'The Teller of Tales', and he is buried there, like Rupert Brooke, beneath the epitaph he composed for himself. Today the church at Tautira, in Tahiti, has a lasting gift from the writer's mother – a silver communion service that is still used each Sunday.

The coastal road from Papeete climbs One Tree Hill, which before the siting of the lighthouse at Point Venus was the seamark that guided mariners to the safe anchorage, among them the *Bounty* mutineers in 1789. At sea they had cast off the autocratic Captain Bligh, who had loaded breadfruit on his ship at Matavai Bay, Tahiti, and returned hurriedly to the arms of the local ladies whose charms had so ensnared them during their six months' stay. Later, some had second thoughts and, under Fletcher Christian, sailed to the secret island of Pitcairn, taking with them a dozen Tahitian women. It was eighteen years before the crew of a Nantucket whaler called at Pitcairn. By that time only one man was left, John Adams, who lived with a large and varied harem. He had, however, chosen religion and lived a proper Christian life.

The authors of *Mutiny on the Bounty*, James Norman Hall and Charles Nordhoff, both lived in Tahiti – Hall at Matavai Bay (where the *Bounty* had anchored). Two famous films have been made of the saga. When the Charles Laughton version was being produced it was found that the twentieth-century Tahitian girls, used as extras, were frequently lacking teeth (an endemic omission – and extraordinary considering their reputation for great beauty). Each had to be fitted with a false set and, in some cases, wigs were necessary as well.

On the road around the forehead of the island is the sad tomb of the last King Pomare, with its warning bottle, and not far away the site of the folly of one of his forebears, King Pomare II, who listened too long to the missionaries and tried to build a temple longer than Westminster Abbey in London or St Peter's in Rome.

Local timber, however, had few advantages over the masonry of Europe and because of its limitations, and those of the Tahitian builders, the temple's length of 712 feet was sobered by a maximum width of 54 feet and a height of 18 feet; not a structure to take the viewer's breath away.

There were also acoustic shortcomings. When a full congregation of 6,000 was present, no one at the back or even in the middle could hear a word of what was going on at the front. So three pulpits were installed along the nave, and three different sermons were preached.

Everywhere in the South Pacific, the missionaries had much to answer for. Tahiti's road was partially built by natives as a punishment for failing to attend matins or evensong. Certainly some missionaries, and some missionary societies, became rich on the proceeds of the evangelism, but others merely tried to do their best. Their descendants are still to be seen today, young Americans aboard bicycles, each wearing a proper collar and tie even in the steaming heat – Mormons on a missionary crash course of six weeks.

I watched them cycling by from the roadside where, as it happened, I had paused at an appropriate spot. There was a river in which shouting Tahitian children were swimming naked. Gracefully a man cast a net into the current further upstream and beyond that the green mountains lay against the fetid grey sky. I had stopped to look at a grave in the unkempt grass of a field beside the river. It was the burial place of a missionary's wife. The tablet said simply, 'Mariah, wife of J. W. Clark. Died 11.5.1863 aged twenty-three years.' There was a design of a little flower cut into the stone. Who knows what story lies there?

Nearby was a neat red-roofed house with a Tahitian cutting his front lawn as phlegmatically as a suburban husband anywhere. The shouts of the children echoed from the thick river, the fisherman hauled in his net, and I thought there was thunder growling in the hills but it was only a youth on a motorcycle. Tahiti was as near, and as far from, Heaven as ever.

TAHITI situated latitude 17°30′ S and longitude 149° W; area 386 sq. m (1,000 sq. km); population approx. 115,000; France

Index

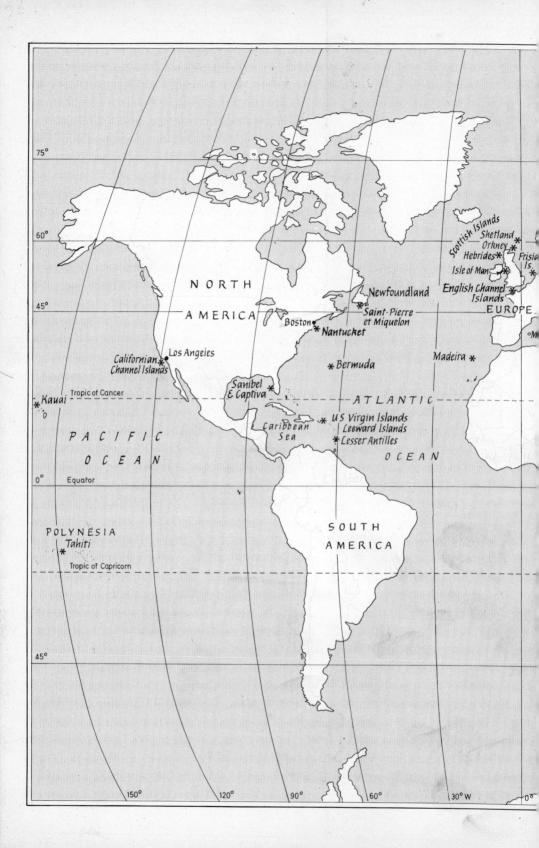

75°

60°

45°

NORTH
AMERICA

Scottish Islands
Shetland
Orkney
Hebrides
Isle of Man
Frisia
Is.

English Channel
Islands

EUROPE

Newfoundland

Saint-Pierre
et Miquelon

Boston

Nantucket

Californian
Channel Islands

Los Angeles

Bermuda

Madeira

M

Tropic of Cancer

Kauai

Sanibel
& Captiva

ATLANTIC

PACIFIC

OCEAN

Caribbean
Sea

US Virgin Islands
Leeward Islands
Lesser Antilles

OCEAN

0°

Equator

POLYNESIA
Tahiti

SOUTH
AMERICA

Tropic of Capricorn

45°

150°

120°

90°

60°

30° W

0°